'This is a book which is absolutely essential to anyone interested in people living with dementia and their care. It is rare to find a text that addresses the complexity of culture and ethnicity in such a person centred way, and unravels for us the implications for how we provide services and make care available to people of all backgrounds.'

– Charlotte L. Clarke, Professor of Health in Social Science, University of Edinburgh

'This book is extremely timely and is a welcome contribution to our understanding and thinking about how to support people with dementia and their families from an increasingly diverse background. Within the different chapters it skilfully combines a range of important issues and useful information as well as including powerful stories and perspectives of families affected by dementia. Definitely one for the bookshelf for both those supporting families affected by dementia as well as policy decision makers.'

– Rachel Thompson, Professional & Practice Development Lead for Admiral Nursing, Dementia UK

of related interest

Personalisation and Dementia
A Guide for Person-centred Practice
Helen Sanderson and Gill Bailey
Foreword by Jeremy Hughes
ISBN 978 1 849053 792
eISBN 978 0 857007 346

Creating Culturally Appropriate Outside Spaces and Experiences for People with Dementia
Using Nature and the Outdoors in Person-centred Care
Mary Marshall and Jane Gilliard
ISBN 978 1 849055 147
eISBN 978 0 857009 272

Dementia and Social Inclusion
Marginalised Groups and Marginalised Areas of Dementia Research, Care and Practice
Edited by Anthea Innes, Carole Archibald and Charlie Murphy
ISBN 978 1 843101 741
eISBN 978 1 846420 252

DEMENTIA, CULTURE AND ETHNICITY

ISSUES FOR ALL

Edited by Julia Botsford and Karen Harrison Dening

Foreword by Alistair Burns

Jessica Kingsley *Publishers*
London and Philadelphia

First published in 2015
by Jessica Kingsley Publishers
73 Collier Street
London N1 9BE, UK
and
400 Market Street, Suite 400
Philadelphia, PA 19106, USA

www.jkp.com

Library of Congress Cataloging in Publication Data
Dementia, culture and ethnicity: issues for all/edited by
Julia Botsford and Karen Harrison Dening.
p. ; cm.
Includes bibliographical references and index.
ISBN 978-1-84905-486-7 (alk. paper)
I. Botsford, Julia, editor. II. Harrison Dening, Karen, 1957- , editor.
[DNLM: 1. Dementia--ethnology--Great Britain.
2. Attitude to Health--ethnology--Great Britain. 3.
Cultural Characteristics--Great Britain. 4. Cultural Competency-
-Great Britain. 5. Ethnic Groups--Great
Britain. WM 220]
RC521
362.1968'300941--dc23
2014040509

British Library Cataloguing in Publication Data
A CIP catalogue record for this book is available from the British Library

ISBN 978 1 849054 867
eISBN 978 0 857008 817

Printed and bound in Great Britain

CONTENTS

FOREWORD

It is a pleasure to write a foreword for this important contribution to the field of dementia. Most people would agree that the profile and awareness of dementia has never been higher. In February 2015 the Prime Minster announced a follow up to his 2012 Dementia Challenge outlining the significant changes that had occurred in dementia over the preceding three years, building on the previous three years since the birth of the landmark National Dementia Strategy. While the themes are similar in terms of living well with dementia, risk reduction, public awareness, diagnosis, post diagnostic support, end-of-life care and research (to name but a few) the conversations about dementia are maturing to encompass the whole range of experience of people affected by dementia and their carers.

It is in that space that this book strikes a particular chord in that it deals with culture and ethnicity to further our understanding of the individual experience of dementia and how that impacts on the person, their carers and their families. It is so rewarding and illuminating to drill down to tap the huge resource of personal experience and how extraneous factors can influence the expression and experience of dementia.

Each chapter is a standalone treatise on important aspects of dementia. Understanding the effects of our culture, ethnic background but most importantly the combination of these will further our depth of understanding and empathy that we all know is the cornerstone of good person-centred care. In this way we can strive to improve the lived experience of dementia.

The editors and contributors are to be congratulated on bringing to life this hitherto relatively neglected but incredibly important aspect of dementia.

Alistair Burns CBE
Professor of Old Age Psychiatry
University of Manchester

1

INTRODUCTION

Julia Botsford

This book is about the relationship between culture, ethnicity and dementia. It explores the ways in which ethnic and cultural identities impact on people with dementia, their families and friends, as well as those who seek to diagnose, treat, care for and provide services for them. It is aimed at anyone who works in the field of dementia care or who is interested in this area. It is, as far as we know, the first book of its kind to be published in the UK.

Dementia, culture and ethnicity in context

Dementia is a growing global concern. Around 800,000 people in the UK and 44 million worldwide are currently estimated to have Alzheimer's disease or another form of dementia (Alzheimer's Research UK 2014), and these numbers are set to increase exponentially in the coming decades.

Wherever you are in the world, the likelihood of being affected by dementia is already huge. To illustrate, in 2010 the Alzheimer's Research Trust estimated that as many as 25 million people (42% of the UK population) were affected through knowing a close friend or family member with the condition (Alzheimer's Research Trust 2010). And yet, how we perceive the many and varied impacts of dementia, as well as the ways in which we react, is not the same for everyone. There is growing evidence that ethnicity and cultural backgrounds are significant in relation to how both individuals and communities deal with the onset of the cognitive changes associated with dementia.

In addition, ethnicity and culture appear to have an impact on how people are supported, or not, by family, communities and statutory and non-statutory services, through the experience of living and dying with dementia.

Much of the research about dementia and ethnicity has, until recently, been conducted in the US. However, whilst evidence from the US tells us about the significance of ethnicity and culture in relation to the ethnic groups that are found in the US, we must be cautious about making assumptions about its relevance to the UK experience and to the specific ethnic communities living in the UK. For the time being, the evidence base in the UK remains relatively small. However, it is increasing, as it must if we are to fully understand the complexities surrounding the experiences of dementia in different groups. This is a point made more than once in the pages that follow.

Nevertheless, it is only recently that the importance of understanding and responding to cultural needs in dementia has gathered any significant momentum in the UK. Policy-makers and service providers alike are now finally recognising that an increasing cultural diversity among the UK older population will mean a need to re-examine how services operate (APPG on Dementia 2013) as well as a need to address the specific information and awareness needs of minority ethnic groups, who often present later than other groups, or only in crisis (Mukadam, Cooper and Livingston 2011).

Dementia, culture and ethnicity: issues for us all

Whilst many of the chapters in this book focus on minority ethnic groups, it is important to recognise that culture and ethnicity are not only the preserves of minorities. They embrace everyone, even if unnoticed or taken for granted, in our everyday lives. We may not focus on such issues, except when ticking a box on a form, but nevertheless, we all have an ethnicity, however we might define it. Our culture and ethnicity affect who we are, how we see the world and how we behave. They also influence how we are perceived by others, and therefore impact on the way we develop and maintain relationships – be they personal or professional.

My own interest in the issues covered in this book arose many years ago. For over a decade my clinical practice has been as an Admiral Nurse in a culturally diverse borough of North London. Admiral Nurses work with other professional colleagues to improve the quality of life for people with dementia and their families, using two main approaches – clinical casework with carers and people with dementia, and through a teaching and advisory role to other professionals.

In common with many parts of the capital city, there are areas where I work where 'White British' could be considered a minority ethnic community. As a White British Admiral Nurse I often found myself working with people from different cultural backgrounds to my own, and over the years became increasingly interested in the links between culture, ethnicity and the experience of living with dementia. This led me to undertake doctoral research with issues of ethnicity at its core, exploring couple relationships through the experiences of Greek Cypriot and African Caribbean partners of people with dementia (Botsford 2010; Botsford, Clarke and Gibb 2012). This study is briefly referred to later, in Chapter 8.

The initial idea for this book came out of a symposium session titled 'Dementia, Culture and Ethnicity: Issues for Us All', which took place at the 2012 National Dementia Congress in Brighton, which I organised and presented along with my Dementia UK[1] colleagues Joy Watkins, Vincent Goodorally, Christine Gillham and Manjit Kaur Nijjar – the latter a member of the Uniting Carers network[2], whose personal story, along with those of several others, can be found in Chapter 12.

1 Dementia UK is a national charity committed to improving the quality of life for all people affected by dementia. It works with host organisations to provide Admiral Nurses – specialist dementia nurses. More information can be found at www.dementiauk.org.

2 Uniting Carers is run by Dementia UK. It is a network for carers and relatives of people with dementia who wish to be involved in research and fundraising.

The symposium session touched on many of the core themes that have found their way into this book. As part of this symposium we presented a video in which people from different cultural and ethnic backgrounds responded to the question, 'What do my culture and ethnicity mean to me?' The range of responses highlighted the fact that they are, indeed, issues for everyone, and that people's own perspectives on their own culture and ethnicity are unique. Although the issues may seem most pertinent to minority ethnic communities, it is a fallacy to assume that they are not relevant, or indeed, highly important, to everybody, whoever they are.

Use of terms

In writing and talking about culture and ethnicity there are sensitivities and ambiguities that need to be acknowledged. The English language is constantly evolving, with terms that might have been considered acceptable in the past now considered at best naive or at worst racist. These changes derive from broader shifts in attitudes, as well as from increasing awareness and appreciation of difference within a multicultural society. However, whilst these changes are positive in themselves, it is worth acknowledging the risk that the imperative to employ only 'politically correct' language, if coupled with uncertainty about what this actually means, could get in the way of the genuine and open debate needed in this area.

The expressions 'black and minority ethnic' (BME) and 'black, Asian and minority ethnic' (BAME) are both terms commonly found in the literature. In this book we have made an editorial decision to use the term 'black and minority ethnic' (BME) as the principle term for any individual group who, by virtue of numbers and in relation to ethnicity, is in a minority. This term includes both white and non-white (including Asian) groups and individuals. Adoption of one term is intended to reduce any confusion. We have also tended to use the term 'minority ethnic' in preference to 'ethnic minority' – again these are both terms in common use in the literature and common parlance. The term 'minority ethnic' is preferred here because it stresses the fact that everyone belongs to an ethnic group, and the one under consideration is in a minority. The alternative, 'ethnic minority', suggests that the group in question is in a minority because of its ethnic nature. These may seem subtle distinctions, but again, to avoid confusion, we have decided to use this term throughout.

Structure and content of the book

This book collects together writings by some of the key experts in the developing field of dementia, culture and ethnicity. Contributors include researchers, practitioners and importantly, family carers. These contributions from family carers give a powerful and often moving window into what it is like for families living with dementia. We were unable to include any accounts from people with dementia from a minority ethnic background, but it is hoped that as awareness increases and stigma reduces, more people will be willing to come forward to share their experiences.

In Chapter 2, Omar Khan from the Runnymede Trust[3] gives a detailed and comprehensive analysis of the implications of two major social trends – the increase in the relative number of older people, coupled with the increasing ethnic diversity within the older age group.

Chapter 3 is about meanings. It highlights the complexity and nuances in how the everyday terms of 'race', 'culture' and 'ethnicity' are used, and teases out their explicit and implicit meanings before going on to look at how culture and ethnicity impinge on our attitudes towards health and disease, and on people's understandings of dementia.

Chapter 4, by Ajit Shah and Sofia Zarate Escudero, examines the issues from a medical perspective. This chapter pieces together what is known about the prevalence of dementia in specific ethnic groups, through a detailed review of available evidence.

3 The Runnymede Trust is the UK's leading race equality think tank. More information is available at www.runnymedetrust.org.

This evidence seems to suggest that some groups may be more at risk than others, although people from minority ethnic groups tend to be less well represented in terms of service uptake. Shah and Zarate Escudero consider some of the obstacles that people from minority ethnic groups may face in accessing an accurate diagnosis, and they make a plea for greater attention to address these issues at a local and national level.

The next chapter, by Jo Moriarty, picks up many of the same issues, but from a social perspective, exploring culture and ethnicity in relation to attitudes towards dementia, diagnosis and service uptake. She not only explores why uptake may be lower in BME groups but also why, having accessed them, their experiences may be less positive. She emphasises that the resultant health inequalities need to be better understood through research, as well as better addressed by service providers.

In Chapter 6 Karan Jutlla, who researched dementia within the Wolverhampton Sikh community, vividly illustrates many of the points made in the two preceding chapters. She examines in depth the experiences of dementia and caregiving within South Asian communities in the UK. The importance of cultural norms associated with attitudes to caregiving and family roles, as well as the very real stigma attached to mental ill health and dementia, have major implications for awareness-raising and service provision in these groups.

In Chapter 7 Vincent Goodorally explores some of the challenges service providers need to consider in order to engage effectively in their work with people from minority ethnic groups. He stresses the importance of a meaningful assessment process, and introduces a specific tool that offers a framework to help practitioners to assess cultural needs.

The next chapter discusses some of the issues of working within and across ethnic groups, in particular focusing on communication. It pays particular attention to the challenges of working with people who speak a different language, who may see the world from different reference points to the practitioner's own. The so-called 'insider–outsider' debate is considered, and the chapter offers some guidance on working with interpreters.

Chapter 9 presents a number of short case studies where culture and ethnicity are the focus of practice. Here, contributors describe how they have placed culture and ethnicity at the heart of their work, and have developed projects that address key aspects of need. Each in their different ways highlights practical ways of promoting access and engagement within communities who may be less well represented in terms of service uptake, and illustrates why it is important and worthwhile working with ethnic community groups. Specific projects presented here include a Singing for the Brain group tailored to South Asian people, a Somali dementia cafe, a connecting communities project aimed at promoting awareness in minority ethnic communities in London, a Carer Information and Support Programme adapted for South Asian people, a wide-reaching project aimed at promoting awareness and good practice in the Irish community, a social group for South American older people, and a project to develop dementia-friendly Sikh Temples (Gurudwaras). Each of these projects is different, and approaches need in its own way, but all of them show that a targeted intervention can make a big difference.

Chapter 10 addresses culture and ethnicity issues within care homes. Alisoun Milne and Jan Smith point out the urgent need to develop culturally competent care and enhance good practice with minority groups across the care home sector. They present an overview of the issues faced by the growing number of care home residents who are from minority ethnic backgrounds, and also discuss workforce issues including recruitment and retention, the pros and cons of matching staff to residents, and training issues. Once again, they highlight an urgent need for more research.

In Chapter 11, end-of-life care issues are examined. Karen Harrison Dening considers what is known about palliative and end-of-life care for people with dementia from minority ethnic groups. There is currently a limited evidence base, but some of that which is already known in respect of older populations with dementia generally is also applicable to people from minority ethnic groups. Much that has been discussed thus far in preceding chapters, such as access to services, language and communication, has an equal bearing on what is considered a 'good death' for this group of people. This chapter mirrors the conclusion made frequently throughout this text in that there is a need for more research.

Chapter 12 is perhaps the most important chapter. It is really the heart of the book, and the stories told here illustrate many of the points discussed in other chapters, but from a real life perspective. In this chapter, Joy Watkins and Shemain Wahab have brought together 11 very different accounts of how culture and ethnicity have impacted on the lives of families affected by dementia. Told in their own words, the accounts come from a variety of subjective perspectives and ethnic backgrounds including Irish, white British, Sikh, Trinidadian and Chinese. Others cannot be defined in one simple label, such as that of Daphne, who describes the rich interweaving of South African and Jewish heritage, and how it affected her husband when he developed dementia and needed residential care. Then there is Gillian, who titles her piece 'Danish, Polish, Mexican, British, Dementia, Ugandan and Indian?' The stories also illustrate the individuality behind ethnicity labels, and the real isolation and stigma that dementia can bring for some people.

The carers in these accounts are aware of whether the service providers they encounter are the same or different to themselves, but this matters more to some than others. What makes the most impact seems to be the human connection that is (or isn't) established. Cultural experiences and values are important to families, but service providers need to look beyond simplistic or surface assumptions about groups, and get to know the people they work with as unique individuals.

In the final chapter Jill Manthorpe identifies the importance of having policies and strategies, both at a national and local level, that support and drive forward practice that respects culture and diversity in relation to dementia care. She provides a critical review of the evolution of UK policy to date, not only examining dementia-specific policy, but also that which is relevant to age and equality. She reminds us of the key role of practitioners as instigators, implementers and recipients of policy.

This book presents a range of different perspectives on the significance of culture, ethnicity and dementia. It represents the first UK collection of writings on these issues. We hope that it will both inform and inspire you.

References

Alzheimer's Research Trust (2010) 'Dementia statistics.' Available at www.alzheimersresearchuk.org/dementia-statistics/, accessed on 12 February 2010.

Alzheimer's Research UK (2014) *Defeat Dementia: The Evidence and a Vision for Action*. Cambridge: Alzheimer's Research UK.

APPG (All-Party Parliamentary Group) on Dementia (2013) *Dementia Does Not Discriminate: The Experiences of Black, Asian and Minority Ethnic Communities*. July. London: Alzheimer's Society. Available at www.alzheimers.org.uk/site/scripts/download_info.php?downloadID=1186, accessed on 11 December 2014.

Botsford, J. (2010) 'Dementia and Relationships: Experiences of Greek Cypriot and African Caribbean Partners.' Unpublished Thesis.

Botsford, J., Clarke, C.L. and Gibb, C.E. (2012) 'Dementia and relationships: experiences of partners in minority ethnic communities.' *Journal of Advanced Nursing 68*, 2207–2217.

Mukadam, N., Cooper, C. and Livingston, G. (2011) 'A systematic review of ethnicity and pathways to care in dementia.' *International Journal of Geriatric Psychiatry 26*, 12–20.

Section One

EXPLORING THE ISSUES

2

DEMENTIA AND ETHNIC DIVERSITY

NUMBERS AND TRENDS

Omar Khan

Two major societal trends are its progressive ageing and increasing diversity. These changes are not limited to the UK, but extend across the developed world, and increasingly in the developing world too. This is the context for this important volume on dementia and ethnicity, and in this chapter I outline and explain the meaning of these trends in more detail. In so doing, I also suggest some possible implications for service delivery, or for ensuring that black and minority ethnic (BME) people and families experiencing dementia are treated with fairness and dignity.

Increasing diversity

According to the 2011 Census, 14 per cent of the UK's population is BME (ONS 2012). This total of nearly 8 million people is roughly the same as Scotland and Wales combined. Compared to 2001, there are over 3.3 million more BME people living in the UK, with significant growth among most populations. And in 1991, the first year ethnicity was collected in the Census, the total population of BME people in the UK was only 3.1 million, or less than the decennial growth between 2001 and 2011, and less than the current BME population in London.

In 2010, the Runnymede Trust estimated that there would be as many as 20 million BME people living in the UK by 2051, or around 30 per cent of the total population (Lievesley 2010).

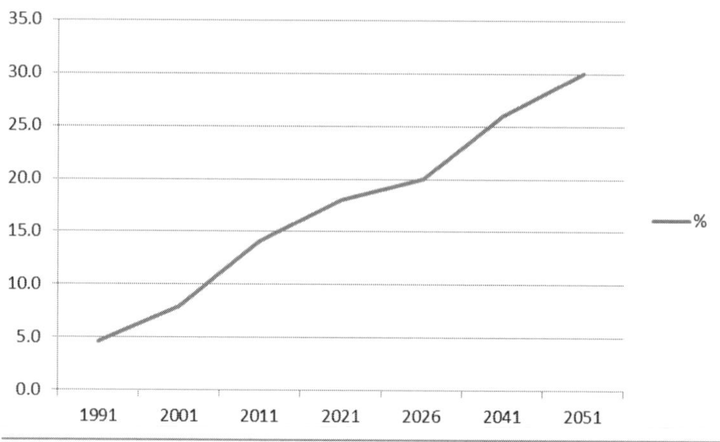

FIGURE 2.1: BLACK AND MINORITY ETHNIC POPULATION IN THE UK, 1991–2051 SOURCE: LIEVESLEY 2010

Note: Data from 2021 and beyond is based on projections and increasingly subject to error. The estimate above is based on projections for 2026 and 2051 only.

The BME population is not only growing, but is more diverse than in the past. Until the 1990s migration was predominantly from the 'Old' or 'New' Commonwealth, in the latter case primarily the Caribbean and South Asia. These sources of migration had a British colonial past and other links including the English language. In the past few decades, and particularly in the 2000s, there has been much more growth, both from Europe and from elsewhere in the world, with the 'Other Asian' (including perhaps Sri Lankans, Iranians, Filipinos, Thai and Kurdish) being the largest single rate of growth between 2001 and 2011. At the same time there has been a notable growth in the 'Mixed' population.

As a result, there is significant diversity *within* the BME population. Figure 2.2 does not include the diverse 'White Other' group that now accounts for nearly 5 per cent of the UK population, and includes not only Polish people, but also possibly

Americans, Australians, Jewish people, French, Germans, Turkish and South Africans.

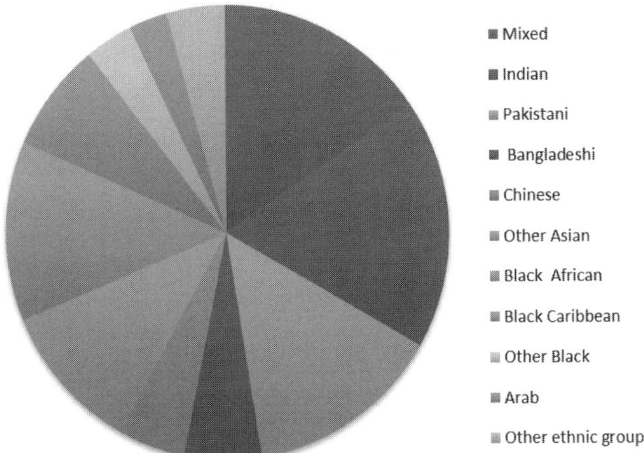

FIGURE 2.2: UK BLACK AND MINORITY ETHNIC POPULATION, BY ETHNIC GROUP (2011) SOURCE: CENSUS 2011

Progressive ageing of the minority ethnic population

The rise in the number of minority ethnic people in the UK has been driven by population growth and immigration. This obviously indicates the relatively younger profile of BME people. In the 2001 Census, there were 230,000 BME people over the age of 65, but this is expected to increase significantly in coming decades, to around 2.7 million by 2051.

Table 2.1 shows the younger age profiles among minority ethnic populations as reported in the 2011 Census. While nearly 1 in 5 white British people are over 65, only 1 in 27 Bangladeshi people are. The median age for white British people is 42, but it is only 24 for Bangladeshi, 28 for Black African, 31 for 'White Other' and 32 for Indian people. Research projections illustrate how this is likely to change. A report on Birmingham estimates that by 2026 the number of Bangladeshis over 65 will almost triple, 'the number of Africans over 65 will rise fivefold and the number of white people over 65 will decline' (Barnard and Turner 2011, p. 9).

TABLE 2.1: AGE DISTRIBUTION OF MINORITY ETHNIC GROUPS

Group	Median age	% under 16	% over 65	Under 16 to over 65 ratio
White British	42	18	19	0.9
White Irish	53	6	31	0.2
White Gypsy or Irish Traveller	26	32	6	5.4
White Other	31	15	6	2.5
Mixed	18	45	3	15.6
Indian	32	19	8	2.4
Pakistani	25	33	4	7.5
Bangladeshi	24	35	4	9.4
Chinese	28	13	5	2.6
Black Caribbean	40	17	14	1.3
Black African	28	30	2	12.4
Black Other	23	38	3	12.2
Arab	27	29	3	8.4

SOURCE: BASED ON CENSUS 2011

Even among the over-50s, there are currently relatively few minority ethnic groups, especially compared to the 39 per cent of White British people over 50. Only 10 per cent of Bangladeshi, 11 per cent of Black African, 17 per cent of 'White Other' and 23 per cent of Indian people in the UK are over 50. Conversely, the White Irish population has a significantly older population, with over half over 50, and nearly a third over 65, with implications for dementia prevalence explained further below.

Conversely, minority ethnic groups generally have large populations under the age of 16. While 18 per cent of White British people are under 16, this rises to 45 per cent for 'Mixed' people. The relatively low proportion of 'White Other' (and, to a lesser extent, Chinese and Indian) people under 16 is partly explained by the high number of recent migrants in this group. Recent migrants are usually in their 20s and 30s, so have low proportions over 50 as well as under 16.

The age distribution of various ethnic groups will also affect the ability of families to care for those experiencing dementia, an issue we take up further below. I have constructed a ratio based on the 2011 Census that compares the proportion of under-16s and over-65s to give a very rough sense of how dementia will affect communities and families somewhat differently.

For the white British population this ratio is almost 1:1 there are roughly the same numbers of people over 65 and under 16 and more than twice as many people over 50 as under 16, indicating the relative availability of the 'sandwich' generation to provide care, and all the pressures that implies (Ben-Galim and Silim 2013). For some minority ethnic groups, this ratio is over 10:1 there are 12 times as many Black African people under 16 as there are over 65, indicating the potential for young people to help support older relatives, although children cannot and should obviously not be primary carers.

For all these groups, then, there appear to be relatively more people under 65 to care for people experiencing dementia. However, we must be somewhat cautious in interpreting these data. White Irish groups, for instance, have a much lower proportion of under-65s, and so appear to have fewer family carers. While there is some truth in this finding, it also raises an important point: ethnic identification can change over time, and across generations.

For example, many people who currently identify as 'White British' may have had Spanish or Irish or Canadian parents. The rise in the 'Black Other' and relative stagnation of the 'Black Caribbean' population is at least partly explained by the fact that British-born children with Black Caribbean parents may not feel the 'Caribbean' category captures something meaningful or genuine for them. The effect of these generational changes in ethnic identification is most obvious for White Irish and 'Mixed' older people: they may have children and grandchildren to help care for them, but these younger relatives may identify with a different ethnic group.

Dementia projections among BME people

Having outlined the future growth and ageing of the BME population, we can now turn to the issue of dementia prevalence within this population. In estimating this prevalence, it is important to understand that rates of prevalence increase as people age, from around 1 in 1400 from age 40–64, to 1 in 100 at age 65–69, to around 1 in 6 at age 80+ (Alzheimer's UK figures used by Lievesley 2012; APPG on Dementia 2013).

This is relevant because even as minority ethnic populations age, in the coming decades much of this older population will be in the 65–69 range, with comparatively few aged 85 or older. So essentially it will take a few decades for the increase in the older BME population to have the full effect in terms of dementia prevalence.

By 2051, the total numbers of people living with dementia will likely rise by 2.5 times compared to today. While the rise in the number of white British cases is notable, the roughly eightfold rise among BME people is even more striking, from fewer than 20,000 in 2011, to over 160,000 in 2051. So while the current numbers of minority ethnic people living with dementia may seem relatively few, this number will increase rapidly in the coming decades, an issue that raises important questions regarding the provision of care.

Figures 2.3 and 2.4, produced by Nat Lievesley of the Centre for Policy on Ageing, comparing the 'White Other' and Indian populations, show how a longer 'lag' in the ageing of the former population means that dementia cases increase somewhat slowly to 2031, but then increase sharply thereafter. For Indian groups, ageing has already begun to impact the number of dementia cases, though it, too, rises more after 2031.

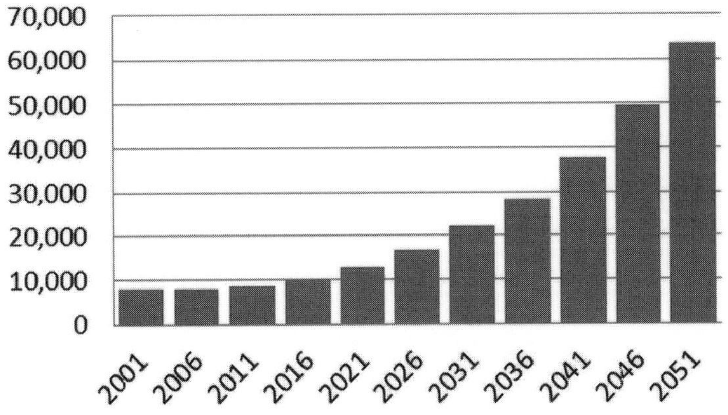

FIGURE 2.3: DEMENTIA CASES IN THE 'WHITE OTHER' POPULATION OF ENGLAND AND WALES

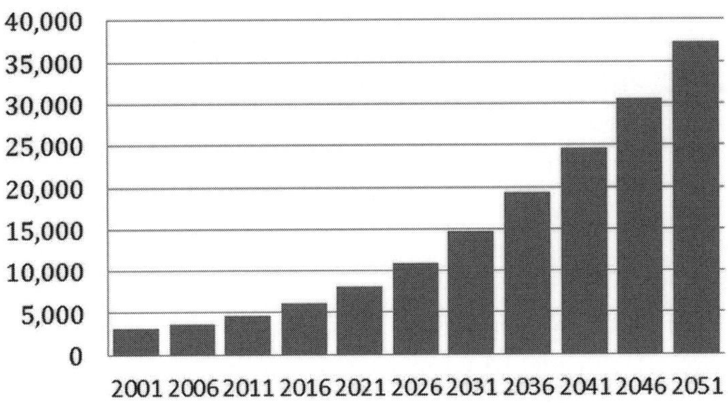

FIGURE 2.4: DEMENTIA CASES IN THE INDIAN MINORITY ETHNIC POPULATION OF ENGLAND AND WALES

Figure 2.5 further indicates the nature of this growth, and how it affects different groups differently. In reading this chart, it is important to understand that it compares the *rate of change* of dementia cases between 2001 and 2051. This shows that while the white British population will still have the most dementia cases overall, the number in 2051 will be roughly similar to the number in 2001. By 2051, however, there will be six times as many Black Caribbean cases, 12 times as many Indian cases, 22 times as many Bangladeshi cases and 45 times as many Black African cases of dementia compared to 2001.

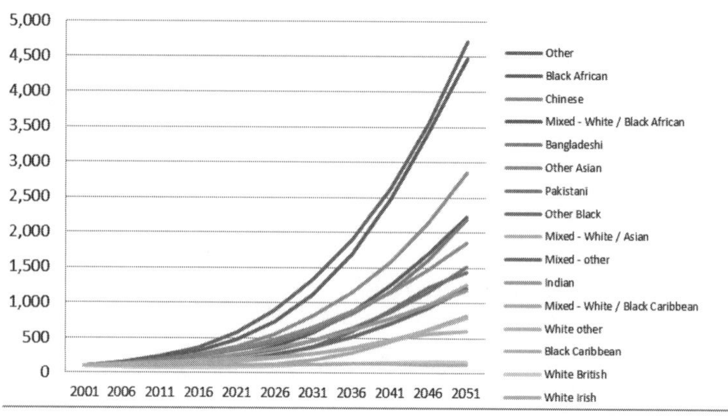

FIGURE 2.5: THE IMPACT OF DEMENTIA ON INDIVIDUAL ETHNIC GROUPS

Needs, preferences and experiences of BME people living with dementia

Having set out the numbers, it is important to indicate, albeit briefly, some of the particular needs and issues that arise from these figures. That is, it is important to say something about why these figures matter, and what they suggest for the future of dementia.

First of all, many minority ethnic people may have different or particular needs. Most obvious is the case of language. For those who already cannot speak English fluently enough to interact with health professionals and carers, dementia poses obvious challenges, from proper diagnosis to adequate care. Evidence further suggests that even those who speak fluent English as a second language can gradually lose their facility in English, or even in both their first and second languages as their dementia progresses.

The issue of language raises an important point: almost all minority ethnic people over 65 living in the UK in 2014 were born overseas. Large-scale migration to the UK is often dated to the 1948 arrival of the *Empire Windrush* ship, and a person born in 1948 turns 66 in 2014. For a few decades, therefore, minority ethnic people living with dementia in the UK will still have been born overseas. Table 2.2 indicates the proportion of people in each ethnic group born in the UK, showing also the continued effect of migration as well as ageing among minority ethnic groups.

TABLE 2.2: ETHNIC GROUP BY PLACE OF BIRTH (%) (2011 CENSUS)

Ethnic group	Born in UK (%)
White British	97.9
White Irish	33.4
White Other	14.5
Mixed	80.5
Indian	42.9
Pakistani	56.1
Bangladeshi	51.9
Chinese	23.7
Black Caribbean	60.1
Black African	32.7
Black Other	68.4
Arab	27.6

SOURCE: BASED ON CENSUS 2011

In addition to language needs, minority ethnic people may have other needs and concerns. People who may have had a particular self-identity and experience of living in the UK, for example, as Black British, may not feel as comfortable in a care environment where there are no or few other black people, or where there is no Caribbean food or where the pictures on the wall mainly depict the English countryside. Reminiscence activities may also remind older BME people of a time when they experienced racism or hardship, and so may need to be tailored to adapt to those experiencing the early stages of dementia.

As people's dementia progresses, they may also be confused about why a particular carer is in their home, and this is, of course, also an issue for white British people whose carers may appear unfamiliar. These are difficult issues to navigate, and in other chapters in this volume authors explain the value and challenges of providing culturally competent care.

Another significant demographic change is that BME people are increasingly living in more diverse areas, meaning that more and more services around the UK will need to adapt to many different needs and preferences among minority ethnic people. Recent research from the University of Leeds (Wohland *et al.* 2010) offers some fascinating data on the geographic distribution of the future minority ethnic population. This research suggests a potential doubling in the proportion of the number of BME people living in rural areas, from around 10 per cent to around 20 per cent between 2001 and 2051, during which time the overall number of BME people is expected to triple.

The researchers divided the country into five areas: 'Urban UK' (not London), 'Rural UK', 'Prosperous', 'Urban London' and 'Celtic Fringe'. In 2001, BME groups were much more likely to live in London than white people, and much less likely to live in rural areas (and less likely to live in prosperous areas). The Leeds team found that BME people will increasingly live in more diverse areas of the UK, and in less deprived areas; the minority ethnic population is becoming increasingly less clustered (or 'segregated') every year.

Table 2.3 shows that, whereas nearly one-third (32 per cent) of white people lived in what the researchers termed the 'Rural UK', only 8 per cent of black people and 17 per cent of Chinese or 'Other' people did so. Conversely, only 7 per cent of white people lived in 'Urban London', compared to 33 per cent of Asian people, and fully 63 per cent of black people.

TABLE 2.3: GEOGRAPHIC DISTRIBUTION OF ETHNIC GROUPS IN THE UK, 2001 AND 2051

	White		Asian		Black		Chinese/ Other	
	2001	2051	2001	2051	2001	2051	2001	2051
Urban UK (not London)	27	26	41	40	19	21	23	25
Rural UK	32	34	12	20	8	20	17	21
Prosperous	16	16	11	11	9	10	18	14
Urban London	7	8	33	27	63	48	34	33
Celtic Fringe	17	17	4	2	1	1	9	7

SOURCE: ADAPTED FROM WOHLAND *ET AL.* (2010)

By 2051, however, these differences will have narrowed considerably, with the white population's distribution changing by only 1–2 percentage points in each category. However, BME people will have shifted considerably, such that 1 in 5 people within every group will be living in the 'Rural UK'. While other population movements are to be expected, the majority of the movement to the 'Rural UK' will be because of a decrease in the proportion of minority ethnic groups living in London, especially among Asian and black people. The findings suggest that the number of BME people living in rural areas will rise, from under 500,000 to over 3 million by 2051, fundamentally shifting our notion of the rural, but also of minority ethnicities and indeed, of ageing and dementia.

Wider social experiences not only related to dementia or health also affect BME people experiencing dementia. In particular, BME groups have higher rates of poverty (rising to 60 per cent among Bangladeshi households), higher rates of unemployment, and lower rates of savings and pensions (see Khan 2009, 2010; Mawhinney 2010). Of course, not all minority ethnic people experience poverty, but those who do, not only cannot access paid-for services, but may also find the costs of travel too expensive.

Another potentially relevant issue is the size of household among some minority ethnic groups. Among the Pakistani and Bangladeshi population, for instance, as many as 1 in 10 households are 'multigenerational', with grandparents, their children and grandchildren living in the same home. This could mean that people experiencing dementia have more support, though conversely, it may also mean that they are more concerned about how their dementia affects their children as well as their grandchildren.

This raises another issue, namely, that some ethnic groups sometimes find that their community is *not* particularly supportive of their experience of dementia. This issue is addressed in other chapters in this volume, but there is no word for dementia in many languages, and ageing is sometimes viewed in a more negative light. This affects not only people living with dementia, but also their carers. Where a community deems older people 'crazy' or even 'possessed', they may feel particularly isolated from a social group or setting that previously was deeply important to them, as they fear judgmental attitudes from their ethnic group.

This sort of experience may also mean that it will often be inappropriate to try to 'match' the ethnic background of carers and those living with dementia. One consequence is that there is likely to be a need to train more carers across all ethnic groups in various languages, including Mandarin, Punjabi and Hindi. This could also have the effect of giving these carers skills and experiences that will serve them well in the wider labour market, particularly given the future change of the global economy.

Conclusion

Explaining the numbers and trends of the BME population and their current and future experience of dementia is a necessary first step in developing responses to that experience. In the coming decades, there are particular needs and preferences arising from the minority ethnic groups' place of birth, language, relative poverty and cultural needs.

Responding to these needs will be necessary to ensure that older people from minority ethnic groups living with dementia are treated with dignity and respect. Yet it is also important to be flexible about how best to respond to these needs. Furthermore, these needs are likely to change over the generations. As a rising share of the older minority ethnic population is British-born, this will give rise to different experiences and needs than their migrant-born parents, some of which we may not yet know.

At present, the number of minority ethnic people living with dementia may appear small, but as this chapter shows, it will rise significantly with each passing decade. This will, of course, mean that the extent of any particular changes to service provision will increase in the future, but the key question is how we best ensure that those living with dementia and their carers receive appropriate care and support, which, in the case of minority ethnic groups, and indeed, other groups, may also mean tailored personalised interventions.

References

APPG (All-Party Parliamentary Group) on Dementia (2013) *Dementia Does Not Discriminate: The Experiences of Black, Asian and Minority Ethnic Communities.* July. London: Alzheimer's Society. Available at www.alzheimers.org.uk/site/scripts/download_info.php?downloadID=1186, accessed on 11 December 2014.

Barnard, H. and Turner, C. (2011) *Poverty and Ethnicity: A Review of the Evidence.* York: Joseph Rowntree Foundation.

Ben-Galim, D. and Silim, A. (2013) *The Sandwich Generation. Older Women Balancing Work and Care.* London: Institute for Public Policy Research.

Khan, O. (2009) *Why Do Assets Matter?* London: Equality and Human Rights Commission.

Khan, O. (2010) *Saving Beyond the High Street.* London: Runnymede Trust.

Lievesley, N. (2010) *The Future Ageing of the Ethnic Minority Population of England and Wales.* London: Runnymede and Centre for Policy on Ageing.

Lievesley, N. (2012) 'Dementia Estimates among the Ethnic Minority Population of England and Wales.' Presentation to a joint Runnymede–Age UK conference on ageing and ethnicity, London, December 2012.

Mawhinney, P. (2010) *Ready for Retirement? Pensions and Bangladeshi Self-employment.* London: Runnymede Trust.

3

MEANINGS, IDENTITIES AND HEALTH

Julia Botsford

Introduction

The UK is often described as 'multicultural' or 'racially diverse'. In Chapter 2, the changing demographic landscape of the UK was highlighted in terms of the increasing ethnic variation among the older population, and its consequences for dementia care over the coming decades. But what exactly do we mean when we talk about race, culture and ethnicity in this way?

This chapter examines and considers the concepts of race, culture and ethnicity, and discusses their meaning and significance in relation to identity, health in general and dementia in particular.

Race, culture and ethnicity: defining the terms

The terms 'race', 'culture' and 'ethnicity' are related to each other and are often used in everyday language as if they were identical or interchangeable. While each of these terms refers to aspects of individual or group identity, they are by no means identical in their meanings. Precise definitions are hard to pin down, and even in the academic literature there is some confusion, so it is worth spending some time considering them in turn.

'Race' is a controversial concept in that it derives from a Darwinistic notion that biological differences exist between certain groups of human beings, and that these have been passed down genetically through generations, resulting in distinctive physical differences which are evident in skin colour, hair, shape of head, and facial and body features. Classically, five distinct major racial groups have been identified, each broadly derived from a unique continental ancestry. These are African, Caucasian, Pacific Islander, Asian, and Native American (Risch *et al.* 2002).

Although these racial archetypes are recognisable, racial groups are not pure. Nor have they ever been. This is illustrated by the fact that significant genetic variations have been found between members of the same racial group (Witherspoon *et al.* 2007), and that these variations have been found may even be greater than those found when comparing individuals from different groups.

The validity of using classifications based on race has been challenged over the past 50 years or so, and is now more or less out of favour when used in these terms. Some have even gone so far as to state that 'race does not exist in scientific terms' (Bradby 1995, p.407). And yet the concept remains, and in everyday language it persists within terms such as 'race relations', 'mixed race' and 'racism'. The latter is important in terms of the attention it draws to the negative social consequences of a belief in race, where individuals within specific groups are discriminated against on the grounds that they are perceived as all the same as each other but different (and inferior) to other groups, often those who hold the power within society. The negative impact of racism cannot be over-emphasised. Perhaps for this reason, the term 'race' is still sometimes used by researchers, implying a broader biosocial construct, which not only refers to biological factors but also incorporates the significance of power and exploitation in the lives of many people from minority groups.

So the concept of race is problematic. It over-emphasises nature over nurture, and increasingly there is recognition that not only is a hard and fast taxonomy based on biological difference a gross over-simplification, but that group-level differences may be associated with both biological and non-biological factors, namely, cultural and social issues, such as experiences of migration.

Historically, in the UK the terms 'white', 'black' and 'Asian' have tended to be used in preference to Caucasian and African, for example. When describing minority populations we tend to refer to groups as either 'black and minority ethnic' (BME), 'black, Asian and minority ethnic' (BAME) or even 'black, Asian, minority ethnic and refugee' (BAMER). These terms appear to take implicit account of the cultural elements of the group experience.

Essentially, the term 'culture' relates to behaviours, values, beliefs and attitudes that bind individuals together into communities. Most simply it is defined as 'how we view and do things in our group' (Henley and Schott 2001, p. 2).

Another definition of culture is:

> a system of meanings and symbols. This system shapes every area of life, defines a world view that gives meaning to personal and collective experience, and frames the way people locate themselves within the world, and believe in it. Every aspect of reality is seen as embedded within webs of meaning, that define a certain world view that cannot be studied or understood apart from this collective frame. (Corin 1995, p.273).

The concept of ethnicity or ethnic group adds a further dimension, in that it emphasises membership of a specific group and may be seen as the active expression of culture (Valle 1998). People identify with particular social groups in respect of cultural factors that are based on a tradition of common descent and a shared history. In other words, the term 'ethnicity' refers to a common heritage shared by a particular group, where heritage includes history, language, rituals, and preference for music and foods (Zenner 1996). Bradby, drawing on Brah (1996), defines it as:

> The real or probable, or in some cases mythical, common origins of a people who may also have visions of a shared destiny which are manifested in terms of the ideal or actual

> language, religion, work, diet, or family patterns of those people. (Bradby 1995, p.406)

Ethnicity or ethnic group therefore implies a shared culture, but more than this, a shared heritage. Nevertheless, in using the term there can still be confusion. Sometimes it may be applied to language-based or nationality-based groupings, for example, 'German', 'Australian', or 'Greek'. Sometimes it is confused with racial concepts, for example, in references to 'blacks', 'whites', or 'Asians'.

Glazer and Moynihan (1976) suggest that the term 'ethnicity' is a relatively new one, having first been used during the 1930s, but not making its first appearance in a dictionary (the *Oxford English Dictionary*) until as late as 1972. The word 'ethnic', however, is much older, and is derived from the Greek word *ethnos*, meaning 'people'.

O'Hagan (1999) considers the term 'ethnicity' as inherently pejorative, citing its even earlier etymological roots in the Latin word *ethnikus*, meaning those who were not Christians or Jewish, such as heathens or pagans. He notes that this emphasis on what he describes as 'otherness' is highly significant, and this seems to be borne out by the fact that around the Second World War, the term 'ethnics' was a term used in the US to refer to Jewish, Italian, Irish and other people considered 'inferior' to the dominant group of primarily British descent. More recently, Eriksen (2002) considered that in everyday language, the word 'ethnicity' still had a ring of 'minority issues' and 'race relations', but notes that in social anthropology it simply relates to aspects of relationships between groups that consider themselves, and are regarded by others, as being culturally distinctive. In other words, the term 'ethnic' is applicable to all groups, whether in the so-called minority or majority within a given society, and should therefore not be seen as having any inherently political aspect.

However, whilst there remains a tendency to focus on minorities when making reference to ethnicity, it is a fact that everyone has an ethnic identity. Nevertheless, it is not uncommon to find studies which explore the experiences of minority ethnic groups using comparisons with, for example, 'indigenous whites' (Parker and Philp 2004), or 'the white majority' (Turner, Christie and Haworth 2005), as if these terms represented a homogeneous group, which is far from the case.

The term 'indigenous' itself is a questionable one in this context, given Britain's history of continuous immigration and invasion going back millennia, to the Angles, Saxons, Romans, Vikings and Normans. Not only that, but the concept of a white majority is dubious too. The relative invisibility of certain distinct and often disadvantaged white ethnic groups including Irish, Kurdish and Turkish Cypriot people and Gypsies and Travellers has been pointed out by a number of authors (Chance 1996; Enneli, Modood and Bradley 2005; Jesper, Griffiths and Smith 2008; Tilki *et al.* 2010).

Culture and ethnicity: beyond the labels

Culture and ethnicity are useful concepts that can assist in our understanding of how an individual relates to the world around them, and what their wants and needs may be. They help to explain attitudes and behaviours at a group level, but are only part of the story when it comes to individuals. As people we all acquire cultural beliefs during childhood and beyond, through many influences including our family, religion, school, local community and society. What and who we become as individuals is strongly affected by these influences, but also by our own unique personalities. This is the case for all of us, irrespective of which ethnic group we may consider ourselves part of. Whilst in reality we all have an ethnic identity, this may not be an aspect of ourselves that we are conscious of on a day-to-day basis, except, perhaps, when filling in forms!

Ethnicity is a socially constructed phenomenon (Johnson 2008). How we identify as individuals depends at least in part on the current societal views. That these are fluid rather than fixed is illustrated by tracking the development of UK Census surveys. The first national population survey was completed in England in 1841, and has been taken in every subsequent decade thereafter.

However, although there has been a history of immigration for many years, it was not until 1991 that a question about ethnicity appeared in the survey, with an 'ethnicity question' having been controversially dropped just prior to the 1981 England and Wales Census (Bhrolcháin 1990). Instead, people were required to give their country of birth, but otherwise no other data relevant to ethnic identity was collected because, although there was significant population diversity, it was considered too sensitive to ask people about their ethnic identity, and no acceptable format had been identified.

As a consequence of lobbying from groups interested in race/ethnicity relations, a question was included in the next Census. By the 2001 Census the ethnicity codes included five primary distinctions (White, Mixed, Asian or Asian British, Black or Black British, and Chinese or Other), along with further subdivisions within each of these. Thus, a person ticking 'White' could be either 'British', 'Irish' or 'White Other', with a free text box to name this; and a person ticking 'Black or Black British' could choose between 'African', 'Caribbean' or 'Other' (with a free text box for writing this). By the 2011 England and Wales Census (there are slightly different categories available for the Scottish Census and the Northern Ireland Census), the five main categories remained, but had been further refined. Thus, under 'White' the options now included 'English/Cornish/Welsh/Scottish/Northern Irish/British', 'Irish' and 'Gypsy or Irish Traveller', and under 'other ethnicity' 'Arab' was now also included for the first time (ONS 2010).

In reality, the census classifications are broad, and contain multiple subgroups. Indeed, Aspinall (2002) calls for clearer precision in defining minority ethnic populations, and suggests that terms such as 'Asian' or 'mixed race', or 'black' and 'white' are so broad as to be almost meaningless and practically useless. This raises the question of who defines the labels, and are they imposed or adopted?

Whilst ethnicity should be subjective and self-determined (NHS Connecting for Health 2009), even this underplays a complexity. Not only may individuals classify themselves differently to the way others, including health professionals or researchers would (Hillier and Kelleher 1996), but these self-perceived labels may also vary according to time and circumstances. For example, Jayaweera (1993) talks of multiple ethnic identities co-existing for an African Caribbean woman. She may be black in the context of her experiences of racism, but also both Jamaican and West Indian in relation to her ethnicity and family bonds.

Thus, whatever terminology is used needs to take account of factors such as acceptability, alongside usefulness. Ethnicity labels are inherently problematic and inconsistently applied, and this brings with it the potential both for individuals to have problems in relating to them, and for organisations to collect data that is useful and meaningful.

The temptation to view each identified ethnic group as having a single culture that can be known and defined should be resisted. The reality is much more interesting. In the everyday world, culture may seem a rather abstract and theoretical notion. People can be seen behaving and interacting in certain ways, for example, preparing certain foods, enjoying characteristic music, or engaging in particular religious or cultural festivals, but the more subtle and invisible assumptions behind these 'products' of culture may go unrecognised (Brownlee 1978).

It is hard to describe specific ethnic cultures without falling back on these outward signs and what are sometimes unhelpful and even damaging stereotypes. Take, for example, the challenges of defining traditional 'White English' culture. One might cite a preference for fish and chips, a liking for tea, an obsession with the weather, refer to the so-called 'stiff upper lip' or emotional reserve, or even a willingness to stand patiently in queues. Alternatively, one might refer to the English 'binge-drinking' culture or describe the English as willing to put old people into homes rather than care for them at home. Clearly these characteristics may or may not have some grain of truth in them, but they do not hold true for everyone, and it would be insulting and dangerous to treat individuals as if this were the case. The same applies across all cultures.

Nor is culture in itself static or inflexible. Although to outsiders it might appear as if the culture of a particular ethnic group is traditional and fixed, especially if it is very different from one's own, such as in the case of migrant groups, this is not the case. Over the years, societal values and norms change, hence generational differences arise.

For migrant groups, cultural values are prone to change as aspects of the 'host culture' are adopted, to a greater or lesser extent, by members over time. For example, words and expressions from the host (in this case, English) language will start to creep in, and customs will be adopted and become internalised by the ethnic group (Valle 1998).

Often these changes are gradual and almost imperceptible, even to the individuals themselves, although they may be starkly evident for those who return to their country of origin at a later date to find they talk differently or act differently to those who never left. One Greek Cypriot woman referred to her sense that she and her family considered themselves Greek Cypriot when in London, but on returning to the island, are gently mocked for their 'English' ways, and referred to as 'Charlies'. However, the rate of this process varies, and a counter phenomenon may be the tendency within cultures to hold on to the traditions the early settlers brought with them more strongly than those who have remained at home. Indeed, there may also be an impulse for second or third generation migrants to re-adopt traditions that had been abandoned in order to reconnect with and celebrate their cultural heritage.

This process, which has been termed 'acculturation', or cultural exchange, whereby ethnic group members will be influenced, consciously or unconsciously, directly or indirectly, by living within a host society (Kottak 2005), occurs at different rates for different groups, and for different families or individuals within these groups. This means that there will be a variation in the degree of expression of cultural values to be found, even within specific ethnic groups.

Furthermore, subdivisions and micro-cultures exist, even within ethnic groupings. Alongside membership of a group based on shared ethnicity, an individual is simultaneously a member of any number of additional subcultural groups, each exerting its own overlapping and in some cases conflicting normative influences on beliefs and behaviours. Thus, whilst individuals may have shared cultural reference points through their ethnicity, their presentations will vary as a consequence of the interplay between these multiple factors. The notion of a single culture within an ethnic group is clearly a gross over-simplification. Intersecting aspects of cultural identity may be equally or indeed of far greater personal significance to the individual than their ethnic identity. For example, being deaf, or gay, or a Northerner, or a biker, may be more significant. As individuals, our ethnic identity is an important part of who we are, but it is not in itself enough to define us. As Jutlla put it, 'Whilst cultural norms are important to know, the extent to which they are followed are individual decisions' (Jutlla 2013, p.35).

Culture, ethnicity and health and illness

Professional and lay representations or explanatory models of health and illness are culturally determined, and can be seen to change over time and place. They are influenced by both individual and collective knowledge, beliefs and attitudes. How we make sense of changes in how we feel, and how we perceive alterations in our state of wellbeing, is influenced by our understanding of what is happening to us, and this will, in turn, affect what action, if any, we take. The ways in which individuals adjust to changes in their own health status will be influenced by the cultural values they are exposed to (Kleinman, Eisenberg and Good 1978).

Schweder *et al.* (1997) described seven general systems of understanding health and illness, that they termed 'causal ontologies of suffering'. These, in turn, are linked to ways of responding in order to alleviate suffering. They divided them into biomedical, interpersonal, socio-political, psychological, astrophysical, ecological and moral frameworks. Murdock (1980) conducted a survey of 139 societies, and found differing explanations around illness. For example, in sub-Saharan Africa explanations tended to be based on moral transgressions, whereas in East Asia the tendency was more for interpersonal explanations, and in the circum-Mediterranean area there was greater emphasis on witchcraft explanations for illness and death.

It has been suggested that another significant factor in the development of distinct cultural health belief frameworks is that of individualism versus collectivism (Hofstede 1980). Within this dimension the predominantly Western culture of individualism, where the focus is on the separateness, uniqueness and autonomy of members, is contrasted with that of societies where community and divinity discourses are emphasised, such as within Hindu society (Marks *et al.* 2005). In individualist societies the cultural value emphasises personal responsibility for health (Brownell 1991). For example, the traditional Greek Cypriot culture is predominantly collectivist (Papadopoulos, Leavey and Vincent 2002), as are South Asian cultures (Lawrence *et al.* 2008), while the African Caribbean and white British cultures are more individualist in nature (Patel and Stein 2007).

Explanatory models of health and illness within contemporary Western societies, including the UK, are largely framed within a medical model that can be seen to stem directly from Cartesian dualism, and beliefs about the mind–body split. Within the medical model the causes of ill health are sought in altered functioning in the biology of an organism, and therefore responses are largely based on physical or pharmacological approaches (Crossley 2000). In this approach the sick person would seek advice from a medical doctor or other health professional, and expect physical treatments such as pills or surgery.

Although the purely medical model has faced increasing competition in recent decades, it nonetheless remains a dominant approach, with its main challenger being the biopsychosocial model (Engel 1977). This model allows for an integration of the psychological and social aspects of illness alongside the purely biological, summed up as the 'three Ps' (people, prevention, psychology) as opposed to the 'three Ds' (diagnosis, disease, drugs) of the medical model (Marks *et al.* 2005). In this model, the role of psychological and social determinants of health and recovery are recognised alongside the purely physical ones. Here there is recognition that emotional and other factors need to be addressed in order to address general health and wellbeing.

Understandings of dementia

Within the medical model the term 'dementia' refers to a collection of symptoms that include a decline in memory, concentration, reasoning and communication skills, and a gradual loss of the skills required to complete the tasks of everyday living. The ICD-10 definition describes dementia as:

> A syndrome due to disease of the brain, usually of a chronic or progressive nature, in which there is disturbance of multiple higher cortical functions, including memory, thinking, orientation, comprehension, calculation, learning, capability, language, and judgement. Consciousness is not impaired. Impairments of cognitive function are commonly accompanied, occasionally preceded, by deterioration in emotional control, social behaviour, or motivation. The syndrome occurs in Alzheimer's disease, in cerebrovascular disease, and in other conditions primarily or secondarily affecting the brain. (WHO 1993)

From a medical perspective, dementia is caused by underlying diseases. There are estimated to be more than one hundred separate medical conditions that may produce these symptoms, and each has its own specific pathological disease profile. The most common among these are Alzheimer's disease, multi-infarct dementia and dementia with Lewy bodies (Knapp, Prince and Albanese 2007). In addition, the existence of mixed pathologies is now increasingly being acknowledged. Whilst having much in common with each other, there are some clinical features specific to each of these underlying conditions.

Alzheimer's disease tends to begin insidiously, often with mild memory loss. As the condition develops there is likely to be a decline in the person's ability to carry out daily living activities independently, and the person may need additional support. Changes in behaviour frequently occur, and these may be challenging or distressing to both the person with dementia and/or their family. Multi-infarct dementia is more likely to follow a step-wise progression, being associated with small strokes. The presence of behavioural changes such as depression and apathy is a common feature. Dementia with Lewy bodies is characterised by the presence of visual hallucinations, a fluctuating pattern of cognitive functioning and some of the motor features of Parkinsonism (McKeith *et al.* 2005).

At present the diagnosis can only be confirmed with certainty post mortem, since the technology has not yet become available which would enable accurate imaging of brain pathologies during a person's lifetime. Diagnosis is therefore made on the basis of presumed aetiology, extrapolated from the person's history, psychometric test scores, and their physical and neurological presentation. Screening tests to rule out other conditions are carried out, and in some, but not all, cases, neuroimaging tests will be done.

During the 1980s there was a shift towards what was then called the 'new culture of dementia care' (Kitwood and Benson 1993). Kitwood (1987) outlined an alternative to the medical way of understanding the presentation of dementia. He argued that the idea of linear causality between organic brain change and behaviour was far too simplistic, and pointed out that pathology on its own was not enough to explain the extent to which a person was affected. Instead, he proposed that a combination of psychological, sociological and biological conditions underlay the development of dementia, and that recognition and understanding of the interplay between these factors was essential to an appropriate response.

Kitwood formulated the presentation of dementia as having five key factors. Alongside neurological impairment, which is, of course, the single most significant factor within the medical approach, he emphasised even more strongly the person's personality, biography, general health and the social psychology surrounding them. He proposed that a person with dementia remains a person, but that aspects of the environment within which they find themselves may conspire to either maintain or destroy that personhood. He coined the term 'malignant social psychology' by which he meant that interactions with others could have the effect of disempowering, invalidating or devaluing the person with dementia (Maciejewski 2001).

This view reinforces the need for people with dementia to be treated as individuals, with respect and dignity. It also requires that they be understood in the context of their social circumstances and backgrounds. Instead of seeing behaviours as manifestations of pathology, or symptoms of disease, this approach sees behaviours as attempts to communicate. A person's ethnic background is one aspect of their identity, and is therefore extremely relevant when we are seeking to engage that person or are actively communicating with them. Awareness of a person's ways of being will be crucial to making sense of what they are saying through their behaviours, especially where their ability to express themselves verbally is compromised.

Dementia has the potential to lead to profound changes for both the person who is directly affected and for those around them. How these changes are understood and recognised may be seen to hinge on a number of factors including the cultural perspective from which they are being viewed. In some African cultures dementia symptoms are perceived as a sign of possession.

For example, in Nigeria they are thought by some to be caused by possession by devils (Uwakwe 2000).

In some non-Western cultures, cognitive decline in old age is considered natural and simply part of the ageing process rather than as a symptom of disease (Dein and Huline-Dickens 1997). The view of dementia symptoms as normal is also quite prevalent in Western cultures, and where this is the case, it might be explained by the fact that it concurs with a dominant, and ageist societal view of older people as 'forgetful, peculiar and dependent' (Mackenzie, Bartlett and Downs 2006, p.43).

It is therefore likely that the symptoms of dementia will be interpreted very differently, according to whether they are perceived as being within the spectrum of 'normal', or as a manifestation of an abnormality or disease. Where they are considered normal, this could lead to acceptance rather than a search for explanation and help. However, other factors may also influence when and whether people seek help.

It is widely accepted that there is no specific term for dementia within the South Asian languages (Seabrooke and Milne 2004), and that dementia is seen as shameful, and therefore to be hidden away (Patel *et al.* 1998). It is therefore not surprising that South Asian people may tend to present late or in crisis to dementia services, or not at all. A study which explored perceptions of ageing, dementia and age-related mental health difficulties amongst British people of Punjabi Indian origin (La Fontaine *et al.* 2007) found that people aged between 17 and 61 described old age as a time of social withdrawal and isolation. They found that symptoms of dementia were felt to be due to a lack of effort from the person, or maybe a lack of family care. This study reinforced the sense of stigma attached to dementia and mental health problems in old age, as well as a lack of knowledge and engagement with services.

Adamson (2001) identified a relative lack of dementia knowledge among the UK Caribbean population. A more recent study of the experiences of Asian, Black Caribbean and white British people with dementia (Lawrence *et al.* 2011) identified that appraisals of the impact of the condition were culturally informed, with Black Caribbean people showing particular concerns about maintaining autonomy and fearing the possibility that they might be regarded as 'crazy' or 'mad'.

Another study, which looked at the experiences of African Caribbean and Greek Cypriot partners of people with dementia (Botsford, Clarke and Gibb 2012), identified a general tendency within both groups to rationalise early signs of dementia as either part of normal ageing ('when a person reach 60 he's supposed to start losing his memory' – African Caribbean woman) or the result of exaggerated personality traits. In this study both groups reported delayed contact with services, although there appeared to be a cultural difference between approaches, in that the Greek Cypriots actively sought medical help whereas the African Caribbean people were more likely to present to service in crisis or as a result of another condition. The same study also noted a tendency for Cypriots to view dementia as a medical condition rather than a mental condition, and for the African Caribbeans to associate it with stress and having experienced hardship earlier on in life, and to be a form of mental illness or even 'madness', in line with Lawrence *et al.*'s findings.

Ethnicity and health variations

There is wide acknowledgement that ethnicity is a significant variable in relation to both health outcomes and service uptake in the UK. There tend to be poorer health outcomes for BME populations as well as lower than expected service uptake by minority groups in general (Smedley, Stith and Nelson 2003; Szczepura 2005). In relation to dementia, people from minority ethnic communities often tend to present late or in crisis (Mukadam, Cooper and Livingston 2011).

Chinese people are noted to have one of the lowest service uptake rates of all (Chau 2008). The reasons are unclear but are likely to be multifactorial. A possibility is that there are lower disease prevalence rates. One study showed long-term conditions had a 40 per cent prevalence rate among the older population in general, compared to a 20 per cent prevalence rate in the older Chinese population (NHS Health and Social Care Information Centre 2005). On the other hand, another study (Yu 2000) suggests higher rates of certain conditions, and raises the possibility that Chinese people experience challenges relating to lack of English language skills and other access problems. Furthermore, some Chinese women have found it difficult relating to mainstream health services in the UK because of differing understandings of the nature of their condition, for example, a view that a sore throat is due to an excess of internal 'heat', which would be alien to a typical Western health professional (Chau 2008).

Problems with accessing health care have also been highlighted in relation to other ethnic communities. Gypsies and Travellers have been found to experience worse overall health than the rest of the population, or indeed when compared to other non-Travellers in socio-economically deprived areas or other minority ethnic groups (Parry *et al.* 2007; Peters *et al.* 2009), but have difficulties using mainstream health services. Perhaps this may be due to lifestyle and attitudinal factors including a low expectation of health and a suspicion towards mainstream services (van Cleemput *et al.* 2007).

In relation to dementia it has been proposed that there is greater prevalence in some ethnic groups. It is not yet clear what the reasons for this are, but it has been proposed that it may be due to a difference in known risk factors – for example, higher rates of hypertension and strokes have been found in the African Caribbean population and of diabetes in the South Asian population (Adelman *et al.* 2011).

In a cross-sectional study of migrant elders in Islington, where a total of 1085 people over the age of 65 were assessed for psychiatric diagnoses, significantly higher rates of dementia than in general population studies were found in the Caribbean sample (Livingston *et al.* 2001). The researchers did not find that migration per se accounted for this increased risk, since it was not common to all migrant groups in the study, and indeed, they found that Greek Cypriots did not have higher dementia rates but were more at risk for depression.

Although the Islington study corrected for both socio-economic factors and years of education, many commentators have drawn attention to the existence of poorer socio-economic status within minority ethnic groups as compounding factors that make it difficult to attribute prevalence differences to ethnicity alone (Iliffe and Manthorpe 2004). Difficulties in screening and diagnosing because of a lack of culturally sensitive psychometric testing tools (Parker and Philp 2004) have further clouded the situation.

Within UK health care there is an urgency to understand and address health inequalities (DH 2007). Johnson (2008) suggests that in the past the dominant view in the NHS was that everyone should be treated the same, and therefore that to record or even to inquire about a person's ethnicity might be regarded as potentially discriminatory. More recently, however, the balance has swung dramatically in the opposite direction, and an understanding of the ethnic make-up of service users is now regarded as essential – NHS service providers are required to collect data on the ethnicity of people using their services (CRE 2002; DH 2007).

But do cultural and ethnicity factors alone account for differences in health experiences and outcomes? In fact, as discussed earlier, there is growing recognition that it may be socio-economic differences, and factors such as discrimination that might account for variance, as opposed to cultural aspects per se. For example, for people with dementia and their carers, there is often a so-called 'quadruple jeopardy' of age, dementia and minority ethnic membership, coupled with poorer socio-economic status (Bowes and Wilkinson 2002). This illustrates the complexity of isolating the impact of ethnicity from other complex factors. Interpreting variations in health is highly complex, as aspects other than ethnicity come into play. For example, it may be that for people growing up outside the UK, the length of time in education is shorter than that of people born in the UK (Richards *et al.* 2000). This, in turn, will influence performance in cognitive testing (Parker and Philp 2004). Indeed, it has been found that longer periods of schooling carries a reduced risk of dementia (Powell 2002); thus, lifestyle factors rather than ethnicity itself may be the issue, both in relation to incidence of dementia and diagnosis of dementia.

That ethnic variation in health outcomes exists leads to the need to consider how these might be addressed. The *National Service Framework for Older People* called for all services to be 'culturally appropriate, reflecting the diversity of the population that they serve' (DH 2001, p.4). And yet, this document also acknowledged the importance of an individual approach. Some documents, however, appear to have been based on an assumption that cultural appropriateness is based largely on the availability of targeted services. This is implicit, for example, in the *Forget Me Not 2002* update (Audit Commission 2002), where it was reported that only a small minority of areas (6 per cent) had culturally appropriate services for older people with mental health needs, although a further 49 per cent had them 'to some degree' (p.39).

That this is a somewhat simplistic view is borne out elsewhere. For example, one survey within the London Borough of Haringey indicated that there was variation in how members of three minority ethnic groups wanted specific services to be provided, with only one group, Gujarati people, calling for separate services, and even here this was not a universal wish. For Irish and African Caribbean study participants the emphasis was on the quality of service rather than cultural exclusivity (Brownfoot 1998). Iliffe and Manthorpe (2004) called for recognition of the diversity of all service users, with an emphasis on enabling access to mainstream services which address individual needs rather than the development of what they see as 'segregated' or 'specialist' services for people from minority backgrounds. This has long been a controversial and contested area for local service providers, with no clear evidence on the best models of service provision (Daker-White *et al.* 2002).

Conclusion

In this chapter we have considered the terms 'race', 'culture' and 'ethnicity', and discussed what they mean in relation to individual and group identities and conceptions of health and disease. Whilst the concept of race is particularly poorly defined and remains controversial, there is a recognition that who we are is bound up with our ethnic background and the cultures we live in. These influence, but do not determine, how we view our own identity and health, and as a consequence how we will interact with health and social care services. The recognition that services must take account of this, and adapt in order to address the growing diversity that exists within the UK older population, must be a key driver for all statutory and non-statutory dementia care services.

References

Adamson, J. (2001) 'Awareness and understanding of dementia in African/Caribbean and South Asian families.' *Health and Social Care in the Community 9*, 391–396.

Adelman, S., Blanchard, M., Rait, G., Leavey, G. and Livingston, G. (2011) 'Prevalence of dementia in African-Caribbean compared with UK-born White older people: two-stage cross-sectional study.' *British Journal of Psychiatry: Journal of Mental Science 199*, 119–125.

Aspinall, P.J. (2002) 'Collective terminology to describe the minority ethnic population.' *Sociology 36*, 4, 803–816.

Audit Commission (2002) *Forget Me Not 2002 – Developing Mental Health Services for Older People in England.*

Bhrolcháin, M.N. (1990) 'The ethnicity question for the 1991 Census: background and issues.' *Ethnic and Racial Studies 13*, 4, 542–567.

Botsford, J., Clarke, C.L. and Gibb, C.E. (2012) 'Dementia and relationships: experiences of partners in minority ethnic communities.' *Journal of Advanced Nursing 68*, 10, 2207–2217.

Bowes, A. and Wilkinson, H. (2002) 'South Asian people with dementia: research issues.' In H. Wilkinson (ed.) *The Perspectives of People with Dementia.* London: Jessica Kingsley Publishers.

Bradby, H. (1995) 'Ethnicity: not a black and white issue. A research note.' *Sociology of Health & Illness 17*, 3, 405–417.

Bradby, H. (2003) 'Describing ethnicity in health research.' *Ethnicity & Health 8*, 5–13.

Brah, A. (1996) 'Re-framing Europe: en-gendered racisms, ethnicities and nationalisms in contemporary Western Europe.' *Feminist Review 45*, 9–25.

Brownell, K. (1991) 'Personal responsibility and control over our bodies: when expectation exceeds reality.' Health Psychology 10, 303–310.

Brownfoot, J. (1998) *The Needs of People with Dementia and their Carers within Three Ethnic Minority Groups in Haringey*. London: London Borough of Haringey.

Brownlee, A.T. (1978) *Community, Culture and Care: A Cross-Cultural Guide for Health Workers*. St Louis, MO: C.V. Mosby.

Chance, J. (1996) 'The Irish: invisible settlers.' In C. Peach (ed.) *Ethnicity in the 1991 Census (Vol. 2): The Ethnic Minority Populations of Great Britain*. London: HMSO.

Chau, R.C.M. (2008) *Better Health Briefing 10: Health Experiences of Chinese People in the UK*. London: Race Equality Commission.

Corin, E. (1995) 'The Cultural Frame: Context and Meaning in the Construction of Health. In D. Chapman Walsh, B. Amick, S. Levine and R. Tarlov (eds) *Society and Health*. New York: Oxford University Press.

CRE (Commission for Racial Equality) (2002) *Ethnic Monitoring: A Guide for Public Authorities*. London: CRE.

Crossley, M. (2000) *Rethinking Health Psychology*. Buckingham: Open University Press.

Daker-White, G., Beattie, A.M., Gilliard, J. and Means, R. (2002) 'Minority ethnic groups in dementia care: a review of service needs, service provision and models of good practice.' *Aging & Mental Health 6*, 101–108.

Dein, S. and Huline-Dickens, S. (1997) 'Cultural aspects of aging and psychopathology.' *Aging & Mental Health 1*, 112–120.

DH (Department of Health) (2001) *National Service Framework for Older People*. London: DH.

DH (2007) *A Practical Guide to Ethnic Monitoring in the NHS and Social Care*. London: DH.

Engel, G.L. (1977) 'The need for a new medical model: a challenge for biomedicine.' *Science 196*, 129–136.

Enneli, P., Modood, T. and Bradley, H. (2005) *Young Turks and Kurds: A Set of 'Invisible' Disadvantaged Groups*. York: Joseph Rowntree Foundation.

Eriksen, T.H. (2002) *Ethnicity and Nationalism: Anthropological Perspectives (Anthropology, Culture and Society)*. 2nd edition. London: Pluto Press.

Glazer, N. and Moynihan, D.P. (1976) 'Introduction.' In N. Glazer and D.P. Moynihan (eds) *Ethnicity: Theory and Experience*. Cambridge, MA: Harvard University Press.

Henley, A. and Schott, J. (2001) *Culture, Religion and Patient Care in a Multi-ethnic Society: A Handbook for Professionals*. London: Age Concern England.

Hillier, S. and Kelleher, D. (1996) 'Considering culture, ethnicity and the politics of health.' In S. Hillier and D. Kelleher (eds) *Researching Cultural Differences in Health*. London: Routledge.

Hofstede, G. (1980) *Culture's Consequences: International Differences in Work-Related Values*. Beverly Hills, CA: Sage.

Iliffe, S. and Manthorpe, J. (2004) 'The debate on ethnicity and dementia: from category fallacy to person-centred care?' *Aging & Mental Health 8*, 283–292.

Jayaweera, H. (1993) 'Racial disadvantage and ethnic identity: the experiences of Afro-Caribbean women in a British city.' *New Community 19*, 383–406.

Jesper, E., Griffiths, F. and Smith, L. (2008) 'A qualitative study of the health experiences of Gypsy Travellers in the UK with a focus on terminal illness.' *Primary Healthcare Research and Development 9*, 157–165.

Johnson, M.R.D. (2008) 'Making difference count: ethnic monitoring in health (and social care).' *Radical Statistics 98, 36–45.*

Jutlla, K. (2013) 'Ethnicity and cultural diversity in dementia care: A review of the research.' *Journal of Dementia Care 21*, 2, 33–39.

Kitwood, T. (1987) *Dementia Reconsidered: The Person Comes First*. Buckingham: Open University Press.

Kitwood, T. and Benson, S. (1993) *The New Culture of Dementia Care*. London: Hawker.

Kleinman, A., Eisenberg, L. and Good, B. (1978) 'Culture, illness, and care: clinical lessons from anthropologic and cross-cultural research.' *Annals of Internal Medicine 88*, 251–258.

Knapp, M., Prince, M. and Albanese, E. (2007) *Dementia UK: The Full Report*. London: Alzheimer's Society.

Kottak, C.P. (2005) *Windows on Humanity*. New York: McGraw Hill.

La Fontaine, J., Ahuja, J., Bradbury N. M., Phillips, S. and Oyebode, J. (2007) 'Understanding dementia amongst people in minority ethnic and cultural groups.' *Journal of Advanced Nursing 60*, 605–614.

Lawrence, V., Murray, J., Samsi, K. and Banerjee, S. (2008) 'Attitudes and support needs of Black Caribbean, South Asian and White British carers of people with dementia in the UK.' *The British Journal of Psychiatry: The Journal of Mental Science 193*, 240–246.

Lawrence, V., Samsi, K., Banerjee, S., Morgan, C. and Murray, J (2011) 'Threat to valued elements of life: The experience of dementia across three ethnic groups.' *Gerontologist 51*, 1, 39–50.

Livingston, G., Leavey, G., Kitchen, G., Manela, M., Sembhi, S. and Katona, C. (2001) 'Mental health of migrant elders – the Islington Study.' *British Journal of Psychiatry: Journal of Mental Science 179*, 361–366.

Maciejewski, C. (2001) 'Psychological perspectives.' In C. Cantley (ed.) *A Handbook of Dementia Care*. Buckingham: Open University Press.

Mackenzie, J., Bartlett, R. and Downs, M. (2006) 'Moving towards culturally competent dementia care: have we been barking up the wrong tree?' *Reviews in Clinical Gerontology 15*, 39–46.

Marks, D., Murray, M.P., Evans, B. and Estacio, E.V. (2005) *Health Psychology Theory, Research and Practice*. 2nd edition. London: Sage.

McKeith, I.G., Dickson, D.W., Lowe, J., Emre, M. *et al.* (2005) 'Diagnosis and management of dementia with Lewy bodies: third report of the DLB Consortium.' *Neurology 65*, 1863–1872.

Mukadam, N., Cooper, C. and Livingston, G. (2011) 'A systematic review of ethnicity and pathways to care in dementia.' *International Journal of Geriatric Psychiatry 26*, 12–20.

Murdock, G. (1980) *Theories of Illness: A World Survey*. Pittsburgh, PA: University of Pittsburgh Press.

NHS Connecting for Health (2009) NHS Data Model and Dictionary (online). Available at: www.datadictionary.nhs.uk/data_dictionary/attributes/e/end/ethnic_category_code_de.asp?query=ethnicity&rank=70&shownav=1, accessed on 31 March 2008.

NHS Health and Social Care Information Centre (2005) *Health Survey for England 2004: The Health of Minority Ethnic Groups – Headline Tables*. Public Health Statistics.

ONS (Office for National Statistics) (2010) 'Estimated population resident in the United Kingdom, by foreign country of birth. April 2009–March 2910 (Table 1.3).' Available at www.statistics.gov.uk/StatBase/Product.asp?vink=15147&Pos=&ColRank-1&Rank=272, accessed on 22 November 2010.

O'Hagan, K. (1999) 'Culture, cultural identity, and cultural sensitivity in child and family social work.' *Family Social Work 4*, 269–281.

Papadopoulos, C., Leavey, G. and Vincent, C. (2002) 'Factors influencing stigma: a comparison of Greek-Cypriot and English attitudes towards mental illness in North London.' *Social Psychiatry and Psychiatric Epidemiology 37*, 430–434.

Parker, C. and Philp, I. (2004) 'Screening for cognitive impairment among older people in black and minority ethnic groups.' *Age and Ageing 33*, 447–452.

Parry, G., van Cleemput, P., Peters, J., Walters, S., Thomas, K. and Cooper, C. (2007) 'Health status of Gypsies and Travellers in England.' *Journal of Epidemiology and Community Health 61*, 198–204.

Patel, N., Mirza, N., Linbald, P., Armstrup, K. and Sinaoli, O. (1998) *Dementia and Minority Ethnic Older People: Managing Care in the UK, Denmark and France*. London: Russell House.

Patel, V. and Stein, G. (2007) 'Culture and international psychiatry.' In *Seminars in General Adult Psychiatry*. Trowbridge: Cromwell Press.

Peters, J., Parry, G., van Cleepmut, P., Cooper, C. and Walters, S. (2009) 'Health and use of health services: a comparison between Gypsies and Travellers and other ethnic groups.' *Ethnicity & Health 14*, 359–377.

Powell, A. (2002) 'On issues pertinent to Alzheimer disease and cultural diversity.' *Alzheimer Disease and Associated Disorders 16*, Supplement 2, 43–45.

Richards, M., Brayne, C., Dening, T. and Abas, M. (2000) 'Cognitive function in UK community-dwelling African Caribbean and White Elders: a pilot study.' *International Journal of Geriatric Psychiatry 15*, 621–630.

Risch, N., Burchard, E., Ziv, E. and Tang, H. (2002) 'Categorization of humans in biomedical research: genes, race and disease.' *Genome Biology 3*, 7, *Comment 2007*.

Schweder, R.A.N., Much, C., Mahapatra, N. and Park, L. (1997) 'The "big three" of morality (autonomy, community, divinity) and the "big three" explanations of suffering.' In A.M. Brandt and P. Rozin (eds) *Morality and Health*. London: Routledge.

Seabrooke, V. and Milne, A. (2004) 'What will people think?' *Mental Health Today 10*, 4, 27–30.

Smedley, B.D., Stith, A.Y. and Nelson, A.R. (eds) (2003) *Unequal Treatment: Confronting Racial and Ethnic Disparities in Health Care*. Washington, DC: National Academics Press.

Szczepura, A. (2005) 'Access to health care for ethnic minority populations.' *Postgraduate Medical Journal 81*, 141–147.

Tilki, M., Mulligan, E., Pratt, E., Halley, E. *et al.* (2010) 'Older Irish people with dementia in England.' *Advances in Mental Health 9*, 3, 219–230.

Turner, S., Christie, A. and Haworth, E. (2005) 'South Asian and white older people and dementia: a qualitative study of knowledge and attitudes.' *Diversity in Health & Social Care 2*, 197–209.

Uwakwe, R. (2000) 'Knowledge of religious organisations about dementia and their role in care.' *International Journal of Geriatric Psychiatry 15*, 1152–1153.

Valle, R. (1998) *Caregiving across Cultures: Working with Dementing Illness and Ethnically Diverse Populations*. London: Taylor & Francis.

van Cleemput, P., Thomas, K., Parry, G., Peters, J. and Cooper, C. (2007) 'Health-related beliefs and experiences of Gypsies and Travellers: a qualitative study.' *Journal of Epidemiology and Community Health 61*, 205–210.

WHO (World Health Organization) (1993) *International Classification of Diseases*, 10th edn. Geneva: WHO.

Witherspoon, D.J., Wooding, S., Rogers, A.R. and Marchani, E.E. (2007) 'Genetic similarities within and between human populations.' *Genetics 176*, 1, 351–359.

Yu, W.K. (2000) *Chinese Older People: A Need for Social Inclusion in Two Communities*. Bristol: The Policy Press.

Zenner, W. (1996) 'Ethnicity.' In D. Levinson and M. Ember (eds) *Encyclopaedia of Cultural Anthropology*. New York: Holt.

4

DEMENTIA AND ETHNICITY

IMPLICATIONS FOR DIAGNOSIS AND MEDICAL CARE

Ajit Shah and Sofia Zarate Escudero

Introduction

This chapter systematically examines various aspects of dementia in the context of different cultures and ethnic backgrounds, including definitions of culture and ethnicity, population demography, epidemiology, pathways into mental health care, available services, and relevant government guidance and legislation. It brings together a range of diverse aspects of dementia, culture and ethnicity in the British context.

Definitions of race, culture and ethnicity

Race, culture and ethnicity are often, but erroneously, used interchangeably. 'Race' is a phenomenological description based purely on physical characteristics (Bhopal 1997), such as colour or appearance. 'Culture' describes the various characteristics that individuals share and those that bind them into a community. Thus, it is possible to be culturally similar, but racially different. 'Ethnicity' is more difficult to define and identify because components of race and culture, along with various other characteristics including language, religion, upbringing, nationality and ancestral place of origin, are incorporated (Pringle and Rothera 1996; Rait and Burns 1997). Moreover, it can also be a personal expression of identity affected by life experiences and place of habitation, and it is a dynamic concept that evolves over time (Senior and Bhopal 1994).

A controversial definition of minority ethnic individuals is that they are those with a cultural heritage distinct from the majority population (Manthorpe and Hettiaratchy 1993). The use of this definition may be appropriate in the UK, where the indigenous white population forms the majority, but this definition poses serious difficulties in other countries, such as Australia, where the indigenous population is in a minority. Using the latter definition, individuals from the Indian subcontinent, African Caribbean, African, Irish, Other European, South African and many other origins can be described as minority ethnic individuals in the UK. They are, currently, collectively referred to as black and minority ethnic (BME) individuals. The definition of BME groups used in the UK government document *Delivering Race Equality in Mental Health Care* (DH 2005a) was 'all people of minority ethnic status in England. It does not only refer to skin colour but to people of all groups who may experience discrimination and disadvantage, such as those of Irish origin, those of Mediterranean origin and East European migrants'(DH 2005a, p.11). This definition has also introduced the concept of disadvantage, which may not always be present. Moreover, BME older people comprise a heterogeneous group of unique individuals and collective experiences (Manthorpe and Hettiaratchy 1993; Rait and Burns 1997). Thus, these groups should not be amalgamated and consideration should be given to individual BME groups.

Some studies have used country of birth as a proxy for ethnicity (Livingston *et al.* 2001; Shah, Dennis and Lindesay 2009a). There is a close match, with concordance rates ranging from 85 to 96 per cent, between the country of birth and ethnicity in those aged 65+ in England and Wales (OPCS 1993a; Wild *et al.* 2007), although this is less likely to be accurate over time when second generation migrants begin to enter old age.

Demography

The size of the older population is increasing worldwide because of increased life expectancy and falling birth rates (Shah and MacKenzie 2007). The proportion of BME individuals over the age of 65 in England and Wales has progressively increased, from 1 per cent in 1981 to 3 per cent in 1991 to 8.2 per cent in 2001 (OPCS 1983, 1993b; Shah 2007b; Shah, Oommen and Wuntakal 2005b); these figures were based on country of birth. The corresponding figure from the 2011 Census preliminary data is 6.7 per cent (ONS 2013). The total number of older people from all BME groups combined was estimated as 738,092 in 2011.

The prevalence of dementia doubles for every 5.1 years increase in age after the age of 60 (Hofman *et al.* 1991; Jorm, Korten and Henderson 1987). Thus, the absolute number of cases of dementia in the BME population will also increase as these populations grow older.

Epidemiology

There is a paucity of prevalence studies of dementia in BME populations, and the existing studies have concentrated on the African Caribbean and Indian subcontinent origin BME populations. They have, in general, reported prevalence for all types of dementias amalgamated rather than for specific types of dementia.

A pilot study of people over the age of 65 reported the prevalence of dementia as 34 per cent in the African Caribbean group and 4 per cent in the White British group in London (Richards *et al.* 2000). This study, although old, was a pioneering study, which laid the methodological foundations for this type of research. The high prevalence figure, which is inconsistent with other studies described below, may be due to problems with methodology, and should thus be treated with caution.

A population-based study from Bradford, using a Hindi version of a dementia diagnostic interview, reported a prevalence rate of 7 per cent compared to 4 per cent using a clinician's diagnosis for dementia in Indian subcontinent elders (Bhatnagar and Frank 1997).

A population-based study in Leicester, administering various dementia diagnostic interviews with the help of a Gujarati-speaking psychiatrist, reported prevalence rates of 0 and 20 per cent in the 65–74 and 75+ age groups respectively (Lindesay *et al.* 1997b). This prevalence was higher, but not statistically significant, than in the comparison group of indigenous white British elders. The stability of the diagnosis of dementia was confirmed at 27-month follow-up by another Gujarati-speaking psychiatrist using similar diagnostic techniques (Shah, Lindesay and Jagger 1998).

A population-based study in Liverpool, using a dementia diagnostic instrument in English or an 'ad hoc' translation during the interview, reported prevalence rates of dementia in English-speakers as follows: Black African, 8 per cent; Black Caribbean, 8 per cent; Black Other, 2 per cent; Chinese, 5 per cent; and Asian, 9 per cent (McCracken *et al.* 1997). These figures were similar to the 3 per cent reported among indigenous white British elders. Prevalence in Black African and Chinese people who did not speak English was 27 and 21 per cent respectively, and these figures are higher than those for indigenous elders. The comparison group was derived from another study with a different method of sampling. It is possible that the higher prevalence among non-English speakers was an artefact of communication and translation difficulties, and this issue is unresolved.

A population-based study from Islington in London, using country of birth as a proxy for ethnicity, reported the following prevalence for dementia: African and Caribbean-born, 17 per cent; Cyprus-born, 11.3 per cent; Ireland-born, 3.6 per cent; and UK-born, 10 per cent.

Another population-based study in Islington reported the prevalence of dementia as 9.6 per cent in African Caribbean older people compared to 6.9 per cent in white indigenous older people after controlling for a range of confounding variables (Adelman *et al.* 2011). Although the most prevalent type of dementia in both groups was Alzheimer's disease, this study raised concerns over cardiovascular risk factors and the possibility that vascular dementia may be more prevalent in this BME group.

The limited literature suggests that the prevalence of dementia among BME elders is either similar to or higher than in indigenous white British elders. Moreover, vascular dementia has been reported to be over-represented in those born in Africa or the Caribbean when compared with those born in the UK (Adelman *et al.* 2011; Stevens, Leavey and Livingston 2004). The possibility that vascular dementia may be more common amongst those of Indian subcontinent origin has also been raised (Seabrooke and Milne 2004), but this is yet to be substantiated in prevalence studies. Possible reasons for the prominence of vascular dementia in these two BME groups are linked to higher prevalence of diabetes and cardiovascular diseases in these groups (discussed below).

Early onset dementia (that is, before the age of 65) is thought to be more common in BME groups, with a prevalence of 6 per cent compared to a prevalence of 2 per cent in the equivalent white British group (LSE, King's College London and Alzheimer's Society 2007).

Risk and protective factors

In the dementia literature many factors that increase the risk of developing dementia have been identified and are referred to as 'risk factors'. Similarly, factors that protect against the development of dementia are referred to as 'protective factors'. Most existing studies have examined risk and protective factors in cross-sectional studies designed to estimate the prevalence of dementia. There is a clear paucity of longitudinal case control or cohort studies and studies using incidence rates (Adelman *et al.* 2011; Shah, Adelman and Ong 2009b). Risk and protective factors have been examined for dementia, cross-sectional cognitive impairment independent of the diagnosis of dementia, and cognitive decline over time.

Risk factors identified in cross-sectional prevalence studies include increasing age, years of education, inability to speak English, living in residential care, being born in Africa or the Caribbean, history of hypertension and current untreated hypertension (McCracken *et al.* 1997; Livingston *et al.* 2001; Stevens *et al.* 2004). The association with inability to speak English, found in the Chinese and African Caribbean group, is controversial, and may be an artefact of poorly validated measurement instruments (Shah, Lindesay and Nnatu 2005a).

Among African Caribbean older people with low levels of education, cross-sectional cognitive impairment (as opposed to a diagnosis of dementia) was associated with hypertension, diabetes and raised triglyceride levels (Stewart *et al.* 2001a). However, dementia in the same ethnic group was not associated with diabetes, past or present smoking and alcohol consumption (Stevens *et al.* 2004). Among African Caribbean older people with normal or higher levels of education, cross-sectional cognitive impairment was associated with high cholesterol levels and manual occupation (Stewart *et al.* 2001a). It is difficult to interpret these mixed findings and to reach any robust conclusions about the potential effect of cardiovascular risk factors and their interaction with levels of education. One possibility is that those with lower levels of education either do not seek treatment or do not adhere to the treatment of potential risk factors. Physical exercise appeared to offer protection against cognitive impairment in the older African Caribbean population (Stewart *et al.* 2001a).

In a sample of Europeans, African Caribbeans and South Asians, low and high diastolic blood pressure, higher evening diastolic blood pressure on ambulatory monitoring, antihypertensive medication use and mean arterial pressure were associated with cognitive impairment some 20 years later and independent of a range of covariates (Taylor *et al.* 2013); the association with mean arterial pressure was strongest after the age of 50. However, there were no substantial differences between the different ethnic groups.

Longitudinal cognitive decline, over a three-year period, in the older African Caribbean population, was associated with ageing, and this decline was stronger in those with diabetes mellitus, but weaker in those reporting vigorous physical exercise at baseline (Stewart, Prince and Mann 2003). Shorter leg length (a marker for early life environment and childhood nutritional status), independent of age, gender and education, was associated with cross-sectional cognitive impairment but not cognitive decline in the older African Caribbean population (Mak, Kim and Stewart 2006).

Traditionally, the presence of a gene called APOE (apolipoprotein) allele e2 is known to have a protective effect for developing Alzheimer's disease, and the presence of a gene called APOE allele e4 increases the risk of developing Alzheimer's disease; findings to support both these observations in the African Caribbean group have been reported (Stewart *et al.* 2001c). Cross-sectional cognitive impairment was negatively associated with APOE allele e2 and positively, but more weakly, with the APOE allele e4 (Stewart *et al.* 2001c). The effect of both alleles was greater after the age of 70, and in those with hypertension, diabetes mellitus and lower levels of educational attainment. There was no direct association between angiotensin I converting enzyme genotype and cognitive decline, although the DD ACE genotype strengthened the association between cognitive decline over three years and age (Stewart *et al.* 2004).

Raised levels of an inflammatory marker, IL-6, were associated with cognitive decline over three years among African Caribbean older people (Jordanova *et al.* 2007); however, no association was found with C-reactive protein or serum amyloid A. Raised levels of homocysteine levels were associated with cross-sectional cognitive impairment in older African Caribbeans with low educational attainment (Stewart *et al.* 2002).

The findings for APOE alleles and for homocysteine levels are consistent with the existing world literature. The other findings are less robust in the context of the world literature, and their relevance in the BME context is unclear. The genetic studies referred to above were from one research group and are over a decade old; there are, unfortunately, no recent studies. There are no published studies yet of genetic and other biological markers in other BME groups, although such studies are currently in progress. Risk and protective factors have not been systematically studied across the more prevalent BME groups in the UK, and the vast majority of studies are over a decade old. Moreover, the interaction between the different risk and protective factors (for example, levels of education and diabetes and hypertension) has not been examined adequately.

Scale of the issue

The absolute number of cases of dementia in the entire BME population has been estimated to be 11,860 in the UK in 2004 (LSE *et al.* 2007), and between 7270 and 10,786 based on the 2001 Census (Shah 2008). The National Dementia Strategy document (DH 2009) reported an estimated 15,000 people with dementia were from BME groups. A more recent estimate by the House of Commons All-Party Parliamentary Group on Dementia (APPG 2013) reported that 25,000 people with dementia were from BME groups in England and Wales. These figures are likely to significantly increase with the anticipated demographic changes.

Access to Old Age Psychiatry Dementia Services

General practitioners (GPs) act as gatekeepers to accessing other primary care services and secondary care services. Older people from several different BME groups are well aware of services provided by GPs (Barker 1984; Bhalia and Blakemore 1981; McCallum 1990), and have high general practice consultation rates (Adamson *et al.* 2003; Balarajan, Yuen and Raleigh 1989; Donaldson 1986; Gillam *et al.* 1989; Lindesay *et al.* 1997a; Livingston *et al.* 2002). However, despite the prevalence of dementia in different BME groups being comparable to or higher than in the indigenous white British group, the prevalence of BME older people in contact with Old Age Psychiatry Dementia Services (OAPDS) is generally low (Beattie *et al.* 2005; Blakemore and Boneham 1994; Bowes and Wilkinson 2003; Daker-White *et al.* 2002; Jagger 1998; Lindesay *et al.* 1997a; Rait and Burns 1997; Seabrooke and Milne 2003; Shah and Dighe Deo 1998). Moreover, BME people with dementia present to services at a more severe stage of dementia than their white British counterparts (Mukadam *et al.* 2011a, 2011b).

Potential explanations for low service uptake

The pathway to reach secondary care OAPDS encompasses several sequential stages: recognition of a problem by the patient or the family; consultation with the GP; recognition of the illness by the GP; referral to secondary care specialist services by the GP; and recognition of the illness in secondary care (Goldberg and Huxley 1991). Potential difficulties in this pathway may be due to factors related to patients and their families, general practice and secondary care (Shah *et al.* 2005a).

PATIENT AND FAMILY FACTORS

Older people and their family members may be unfamiliar with symptoms of dementia, not recognise the symptoms and dismiss them as a function of old age (Adamson 2001; Bowes and Wilkinson 2003; Marwaha and Livingston 2002; Purandare *et al.* 2007; Shah *et al.* 2005a). These reasons may be amplified if the older person is unable to communicate potential symptoms to family members and/or the GP either due to lack of appropriate vocabulary or fluency in English (Shah 1997a; Thomas, Thornton and Shah 2009; Thornton, Shah and Thomas 2009). Family members may not be able to communicate their concerns to the GP for the same reasons. Older people and their family members may believe that nothing can be done, lack awareness of available services, or of access procedures for available services, believe that available services are inadequate, inaccessible and culturally insensitive, have had previous poor experience of services, and may fear stigma attached to dementia (Age Concern and Help the Aged Housing Trust 1984; Barker 1984; Bhalia and Blakemore 1981; Bowes and Wilkinson 2003; Hopkins and Bahl 1993; Manthorpe and Hettiaratchy 1993; McCallum 1990; Lawrence *et al.* 2006; Lindesay *et al.* 1997a; Livingston *et al.* 2002; Mukadam *et al.* 2011a, 2011b). Some patients may choose to consult traditional healers rather than GPs (Bhatnagar 1997). Some BME older people may feel that they are a burden on their families (Lawrence *et al.* 2011). Family members may also feel that it is their duty to continue to look after older people, fear that others may criticise them for seeking help, delay seeking help until they cannot cope or others comment on the problems, and believe that diagnosis alone may be purposeless (Adamson 1999; Lawrence *et al.* 2008; Mukadam *et al.* 2011a, 2011b).

GENERAL PRACTICE FACTORS

High awareness of general practice services, high general practice registration and consultation rates, the statutory offer of an annual physical and mental state examination for those over 75 (Secretaries of State for Health, Northern Ireland and Scotland 1989), emphasis on a single assessment process and shared care protocols for dementia, and the National Dementia Strategy (DH 2009) should theoretically enable easier diagnosis and access to OAPDS. However, relatively few BME older people receive the annual physical and mental state examination (Lindesay *et al.* 1997a), the number of BME individuals over the age of 75 is small (Shah 2007a), and the impact of the National Dementia Strategy remains to be evaluated.

Several factors may lead to failure in identifying dementia during GP consultations (Shah *et al.* 2005a). First, the prevalence of dementia may be low in those consulting their GP (some potential reasons for this were described above). Second, the severity of the dementia in those consulting GPs may be lower. Third, symptoms of dementia, including behavioural and psychological signs and symptoms of dementia, which often lead to clinical presentation, may be less frequent, less severe or different in BME older people consulting GPs than in indigenous older people (Shah 2007b). The behavioural and psychological symptoms of dementia were different in older people originating from the Indian subcontinent compared to their indigenous white British counterparts (Haider and Shah 2004). Fourth, data on the clinical presentation, diagnostic features and the natural history for dementia in BME older people are sparse (Haider and Shah 2004; Patel 2000; Patel *et al.* 1998; Shah 2007b). Individual GPs are likely to see relatively few BME older people with dementia from individual BME groups; hence, they are likely to lack the clinical experience, expertise and diagnostic skills needed for the diagnosis of dementia in BME older people, and even psychiatrists experience this difficulty (Lindesay 1998; Shah 1999). Fifth, these difficulties may be exaggerated by language and communication difficulties, age and gender of the assessor, the context and setting of the assessment, and the attitudes and expectations of the patient and the family (Lindesay 1998; Patel 2000). Sixth, there is a paucity of screening and diagnostic instruments for dementia in BME older people (Shah and MacKenzie 2007). Seventh, bias and prejudice of clinicians can also complicate consultations (Solomon 1992). Finally, well-intentioned family members may withhold information if they feel that it will present the patient in a 'bad light' (Shah 1999; Mukadam *et al.* 2011a, 2011b).

If dementia is identified by the GP, it may or may not be treated, and this is due to several factors. The GP may believe that nothing can be done that ethnically sensitive secondary care services are not available, and may have had previous poor experience of secondary care referrals (Shah *et al.* 2005a). If the dementia presenting to the GP is less severe or lacks troublesome behavioural and psychological signs and symptoms of dementia, then an onward referral to secondary care may be considered unnecessary (Shah *et al.* 2005a). The GP may feel better able to communicate with the patient, particularly if they share the same ethnic background. Also, the GP may wish to refer the patient to secondary care but the patient or the family may be reluctant due to some of the reasons discussed above (Shah *et al.* 2005a). However, all these reasons are speculative, and epidemiological data to support these explanations are generally absent.

SECONDARY CARE FACTORS

All the factors described above equally apply to secondary care (Shah *et al.* 2005a). Only three published studies have specifically examined BME older people in OAPDS. (Bhatkal and Shah 2004; Odutoye and Shah 1999; Redelinghuys and Shah 1997). These studies included older people of Polish and Indian subcontinent origin. At the time that these studies were conducted, services for dementia and 'functional' mental disorders in old age were integrated into one OAPDS, although the model of service delivery is currently moving towards segregated dementia-only services after the implementation of the National Dementia Strategy (DH 2009).

In three cross-sectional evaluative studies of two OAPDS in West London, Indian subcontinent origin (Odutoye and Shah 1999; Redelinghuys and Shah 1997) and Polish (Bhatkal and Shah 2004) older people received individual components of health and social services at the same frequency as indigenous older people, and their prevalence in the OAPDS was consistent with the local population demography, suggesting equitable access to the OAPDS. This was despite the household size and the number of children being higher in the Indian subcontinent group compared to the indigenous group. Access to OAPDS by BME older people originating from Poland and the Indian subcontinent appears to be improving in some UK services. These studies destroyed the traditional myth that extended families in some BME groups look after their older people; similar observations were reported in *Forget Me Not*, the Audit Commission's analysis of mental health services for older people in England and Wales (Audit Commission 2000, 2002).

Caution should be exercised in extrapolating these findings to dementia because these three studies examined all patients in the three services, and only a proportion would have had dementia; there is also a current trend of dementia services being segregated from 'functional' mental illness in old age services.

A population-based study of a mixed group of BME older people in Islington reported similar findings for the use of primary care, secondary care and social services resources, but OAPDS was not specifically considered (Livingston *et al.* 2002). Cholinesterase inhibitors used in the treatment of Alzheimer's disease are less frequently prescribed for BME individuals compared to the general elderly population (Purandare *et al.* 2006).

Reasons for improved service access, in the above three studies, may have been the design, development and delivery of OAPDS being culturally capable, appropriate and sensitive. This included the ethnicity of staff members reflecting the ethnicity of the local population, employment of bilingual nurses on the wards and in the day hospitals, employment of an Indian community psychiatric nurse to specifically cater for patients of Indian subcontinent origin, and locating the two dementia day hospitals in the heart of the community close to population clusters of Indian subcontinent origin and Polish older people (Hoxey, Mukherjee and Shah 1999). Based on this and other evidence, appropriate guidance on the design and delivery of OAPDS, along with examples of good practice, is now available (Bhattacharyya and Benbow 2013; Daker-White *et al.* 2002; Seabrooke and Milne 2003; Shah 2010a, 2010b; Shah *et al.* 2009b), although a detailed description beyond that given here is outside the scope of this chapter. The challenge will be to incorporate these concepts into the new development of memory services in the context of the National Dementia Strategy. Most services are now moving towards pure dementia services, and are being segregated from the traditional service model of a unitary mental health service for older people with any mental health issue. These new dementia services centre on community-based memory services including provision of a memory clinic. Some excellent guidance to meet the needs of BME groups in these new and rapidly evolving services is given in a briefing paper from the Social Care Institute for Excellence (Moriarty, Sharif and Robinson 2011).

'Count Me In' census

The findings of six annual (2005–2010) censuses of all psychiatric inpatients in England and Wales have been published. The findings from the 2007–2010 'Count Me In' census of all psychiatric inpatients specifically reported age-standardised admission rates for different BME groups over the age of 65 and were broadly similar. Using the 2008 census as an example, with the total population aged 65 and over in England and Wales as the standard population, the standardised admission ratio for those aged 65 and older in different BME groups was as follows: higher in the White Irish, Other White, White and Black Caribbean, Other Asian, Black Caribbean, Black African and Other Black groups; lower in the White British and Chinese groups; and there was no difference with the standard population in the White and Black African, White and Asian, Indian, Pakistani and Bangladeshi groups (Commission for Healthcare Audit and Inspection 2008). Superficially, this suggests that nationally there may be equitable access to inpatient OAPDS among BME older people, and this requires careful examination (Shah 2009).

The 'Count Me In' censuses were undertaken on a single census day and they do not therefore measure admission rates; they actually measured bed occupancy on the census day (Shah 2009). Therefore, the use of the term 'standardised admission rates' in the 'Count Me In' census report is misleading (Shah 2009). Bed occupancy is a function of the number of admission rates and length of stay in hospital after admission; bed occupancy will be higher if the admission rates are higher and/or the length of stay is longer (Shah 2009). Therefore, factors that either increase admission rates or length of stay will also increase bed occupancy (Shah 2009). A detailed discussion of these factors is beyond the scope of this chapter, but persuasive arguments suggesting that these findings do not represent equity of access to inpatient services have been described elsewhere (Shah 2009). The findings of the 'Count Me In' censuses need to be interpreted with caution as they may be an artefact of increased length of stay rather than indicating a genuine increase (that is, increased admission rates compared to white British older people) in the uptake of inpatient services. Also they only represents one component of a comprehensive OAPDS, and data for dementia are not separately available. Moreover, the vast majority of people with dementia are cared for in the community.

Screening and diagnostic instruments

Dementia is usually diagnosed by establishing a history of cognitive impairment and decline in function over time. This is usually further supplemented by administering measurement instruments that provide objective data on the type and severity of cognitive impairment. Screening for dementia is becoming increasingly important in order to identify those with dementia at an early stage, and it is usually conducted with brief tests for cognitive impairment; a clinical diagnosis with a more detailed history is reached in those thought to have cognitive impairment on screening.

Screening instruments have been developed for some BME groups. The abbreviated Mental Test Score (Qureshi and Hodkinson 1984) has been developed in several Asian languages for use among Gujarati and Pakistani elders and in English for use among older African Caribbeans in the UK (Rait *et al.* 1997, 2000a, 2000b). Similarly, the Mini Mental State Examination (MMSE) (Folstein, Folstein and McHugh 1975) has been developed in Gujarati, Bengali, Punjabi, Hindi and Urdu (Lindesay *et al.* 1997b; Rait *et al.* 2000a), and in English for use in the African Caribbean group (Rait *et al.* 2000b) in the UK. Selected items from the Consortium to Establish a Registry for Alzheimer's Disease (CERAD) neuropsychological test battery

(Morris *et al.* 1989), the Cambridge Cognitive Capacity Scale (CAMCOG) component of the Cambridge Examination for Mental Disorders of the Elderly (CAMDEX) interview (Roth *et al.* 1986), and the clock drawing test have also been evaluated in older African Caribbeans in the UK (Richards and Brayne 1996; Richards *et al.* 2000; Stewart *et al.* 2001b). Moreover, normative data on some cognitive batteries including the MMSE, the CERAD battery and clock drawing are available for African Caribbean older people (Stewart *et al.* 2001b, 2002) and for MMSE in Gujarati (Lindesay *et al.* 1997b).

The main difficulty with all the screening instruments for dementia is that only bilingual clinicians can use them because the questions are in the BME older person's language (Oommen, Bashford and Shah. 2009). There are no instruments that can be administered by English-speaking clinicians in English, with an interpreter translating the question to the patient and the answer to the clinician, and with the clinician scoring (Oommen *et al.* 2009).

There is, nevertheless, a paucity of screening instruments for dementia for use in BME groups. There are no diagnostic instruments for use with older people from BME groups. Traditionally, in the absence of such instruments, diagnostic conclusions have been reached on good history taking (including collateral history from other informants such as relatives) and mental state examination, and there is no reason why this cannot and should not be pursued with older BME people. Appropriate guidance in the assessment of BME elders with dementia is now available (Shah 2010a, 2010b).

Policy context

Government reports and national guidelines and policies can broadly be divided into those relating to BME mental health in general, and those relating to the mental health of older people with specific mention of BME groups. Dementia appears to be excluded from national guidelines and policies pertaining to BME mental health in general, but the general principles may be of value for dementia. Also, dementia appears to form only a fraction of national guidelines and policies pertaining to the mental health of older people.

These policy documents include: the National Service Framework (NSF) for Mental Health (DH 1999); the NSF for Older People (DH 2001); *Forget Me Not*, the Audit Commission's analysis of mental health services for older people in England and Wales (Audit Commission 2000a, 2002); *Everybody's Business* (DH 2005b), a service development guide, aimed at building on the service models outlined in the NSF for Older People; the *Inside Outside* report (NIMHE 2003); and *Delivering Race Equality in Mental Health Care* – a five-year action plan for achieving racial equality and tackling discrimination in mental health services in England (DH 2005a).

None of the national guidelines and policies described above address the issue of culture and ethnicity specifically in the context of dementia, but this state of affairs is changing. One of the key principles of care outlined in the National Institute for Health and Clinical Excellence's (NICE) clinical guidance on dementia related to diversity (sex, ethnicity, age or religion) with a strong emphasis on 'person-centred care' (NICE 2006). This guidance advocated that the needs and preferences of people with dementia relating to diversity must be identified, and where possible, accommodated, but failed to specifically mention BME groups. There was also recognition of language as a possible barrier to care, with recommendations that interpreters are readily available and that written information is provided in the preferred language and/or an accessible format. NICE's technical appraisal on drugs in the category 'cholinesterase inhibitors used in the treatment of dementia' (NICE 2007) was found to be unlawful because it breached the Race Discrimination Act. It discriminated against people from different ethnic backgrounds, particularly those whose first language was not English, because it relied heavily on an assessment tool developed in English. The latter may explain poor prescription rates for antidementia drugs in some BME groups (Purandare *et al.* 2006). The National

Dementia Strategy for England also recognises the importance of ethnicity, culture and religion in the systematic development of services for dementia (DH 2009).

The vast majority of these policy initiatives have not been formally evaluated, and it is therefore difficult to judge their success in dealing with dementia in the BME context.

Conclusion

The total number of cases of dementia among BME older people is likely to increase because dementia is an age-related disorder; the number of older BME people is increasing; and the prevalence of dementia among BME older people is similar or higher than that in indigenous white British older people. However, there is evidence that BME older people have reduced access to dementia services, although this has improved in some services. Nevertheless, there is clear recognition in governmental policy documents that older people from BME groups with dementia face particular challenges and are especially vulnerable to exclusion, marginalisation and inequality in mental health promotion and mental health service access. Furthermore, there is guidance in the policy documents to facilitate equitable access to services by older people from BME groups with dementia.

There is a clear urgent need to develop and implement practical strategies that will improve access by older people with dementia from BME groups to OAPDS. These strategies will need to be at a national and local service level, and be a collaboration between the statutory primary and secondary health care services, social services, BME groups and the voluntary sector catering for dementia and older people. They will need to address stigma, improve knowledge about dementia, provide information about dementia in a culturally sensitive manner, promote primary prevention earlier in life as a range of cardiovascular risk factors have been identified, encourage BME individuals to take advantage of dementia services (including memory clinics) that have emerged after the implementation of the National Dementia Strategy, and take advantage of help that can be provided by social services. These strategies need to be underpinned by in-built evaluation. The policy framework to meet the needs of BME older people with dementia is there, but the actual implementation of this within service delivery models requires novel and innovative approaches, but it can be achieved.

References

Adamson, J. (1999) 'Carers and dementia among African/Caribbean and South Asian families.' *Generations Review 9*, 12–14.

Adamson, J. (2001) 'Awareness and understanding of dementia in African/Caribbean and south Asian families.' *Health and Social Care in the Community 9*, 391–396.

Adamson, J., Ben-Sholomo, Y., Chutervedi, N. and Donovan, J. (2003) 'Ethnicity, socio-economic position and gender – do they affect reported health-care seeking behaviour?' *Social Science & Medicine 57*, 895–904.

Adelman, S., Blanchard, M., Rait, G., Leavey, G. and Livingston, G. (2011) 'Prevalence of dementia in African Caribbean compared with UK-born white older people: two stage cross-sectional study.' *British Journal of Psychiatry 199*, 119–125.

Age Concern and Help the Aged Housing Trust (1984) *Housing for Ethnic Elders*. London: Age Concern.

APPG (All-Party Parliamentary Group) on Dementia (2013) *Dementia Does Not Discriminate. The Experience of Black, Asian and Minority Ethnic Communities.* July. London: Alzheimer's Society. Available at www.alzheimers.org.uk/site/scripts/download.php?fileID=1857, accessed on 28 February 2014.

Audit Commission (2000) *Forget Me Not: Mental Health Services for Older People.* London: Audit Commission.

Audit Commission (2002) *Forget Me Not.* Developing Mental Health Services for Older People in England. London: Audit Commission.

Barker, J. (1984) *Research Perspectives on Ageing: Black and Asian Old People in Britain.* London: Age Concern Research Unit.

Beattie, A., Daker-White, G., Gilliard, J. and Means, R. (2005) '"They don't quite fit the way we organise our services": results from a UK field study of marginalised groups and dementia care.' *Disability and Society 20*, 67–80.

Balarajan, R., Yuen P. and Raleigh V.S. (1989) 'Ethnic differences in general practice consultation rates.' British Medical Journal 299, 958–960.

Bhalia, A. and Blakemore, K. (1981) *Elders of the Minority Ethnic Groups.* Birmingham: All Faiths for One Race (AFFOR).

Bhatkal, S. and Shah, A.K. (2004) 'Clinical and demographic characteristics of elderly Poles referred to a psychogeriatric service.' *International Psychogeriatrics 16*, 351–360.

Bhatnagar, K.S. (1997) 'Depression in South Asian elders.' *Geriatric Medicine 27*, 55–56.

Bhatnagar, K.S. and Frank, J. (1997) 'Psychiatric disorders in elderly from the Indian subcontinent living in Bradford.' *International Journal of Geriatric Psychiatry 12*, 907–912.

Bhattacharyya, S. and Benbow, S.M. (2013) 'Mental Health Services for black and minority ethnic elders in the United Kingdom: a systematic review of innovative service provision and policy implications.' *International Psychogeriatrics 25*, 359–373.

Bhopal, R. (1997) 'Is research into ethnicity and health racist, unsound or unimportant science?' *British Medical Journal 314*, 1751–1756.

Blakemore, K. and Boneham, M. (1994) *Age, Race, and Ethnicity: A Comparative Approach.* Buckingham: Open University Press.

Bowes, A. and Wilkinson, H. (2003) '"We didn't know it would get so bad": South Asian experiences of dementia and service response.' *Health and Social Care in the Community 11*, 387–396.

Commission for Healthcare Audit and Inspection (2008) *Count Me In 2008. Results of the 2008 National Census of Inpatients in Mental Health and Learning Disability Services in England and Wales.* London: Commission for Healthcare Audit and Inspection.

Daker-White, G., Beattie, A.M., Gilliard, J. and Means, R. (2002) 'Minority ethnic groups in dementia care: a review of service needs, service provision and models of good practice.' *Ageing and Mental Health 6*, 101–108.

DH (Department of Health) (1999) National Service Framework for Mental Health. *National Service Frameworks.* London: Department of Health.

DH (2001) *National Service Framework for Older People. National Service Frameworks.* London: DH.

DH (2005a) *Delivering Race Equality in Mental Health Care. An Action Plan for Reform Inside and Outside Services and the Government's Response to the Independent Inquiry into the Death of David Bennett.* Available at www.dh.gov.UK/assetroot/04/10/07/75/04100775.pdf, accessed on 11 July 2009.

DH (2005b) *Everybody's Business: Integrated Mental Health Services for Older Adults: A Service Development Guide.* London: DH.

DH (2009) *Living Well with Dementia: A National Dementia Strategy.* London: DH. Available at www.dh.gov.uk/en/Publicationsandstatistics/Publications/PublicationsPolicyAndGuidance/DH_094058, accessed on 11 July 2009.

Donaldson, L.J. (1986) 'Health and social status of elderly Asians. A community survey.' *British Medical Journal 293*, 1079–1082.

Folstein, M.F., Folstein, S.E. and McHugh, P.R. (1975) '"Mini Mental State": A practical method for grading the cognitive state of patients for the clinician.' *Journal of Psychiatric Research 12*, 189–198.

Gillam, S., Jarman, B., White, P. and Law, R. (1989) 'Ethnic differences in consultation rates in urban general practice.' *British Medical Journal 299*, 953–958.

Goldberg, D. and Huxley, P. (1981) *Common Mental Disorders. A Biosocial Model.* London and New York: Tavistock and Routledge.

Haider, I. and Shah A. (2004) 'A pilot study of behavioural and psychological signs of dementia in patients of Indian sub-continent origin admitted to a dementia day hospital in the United Kingdom.' *International Journal of Geriatric Psychiatry 19*, 1195–1204.

Hofman, A., Rocca, A., Brayne, C., Breteler, M.M. *et al* (1991) 'The prevalence of dementia in Europe: a collaborative study of 1980–1990 findings.' *International journal of Epidemiology 20*, 736–748.

Hopkins, A. and Bahl, V. (1993) *Access to Care for People from Black and Ethnic Minorities.* London: Royal College of Physicians.

Hoxey, K., Mukherjee, S. and Shah, A.K. (1999) 'Psychiatric services for ethnic elders.' *Old Age Psychiatrist 1*, 44–46.

Jagger, C. (1998) 'Asian elders. An under studied and growing population.' *Old Age Psychiatrist 10*, 8.

Jordanova, V., Stewart, R., Davies, E., Sherwood, R. and Prince, M. (2007) 'Markers of inflammation and cognitive decline in an African Caribbean population.' *International Journal of Geriatric Psychiatry 22*, 966–973.

Jorm, A., Korten, A.E. and Henderson, A.S. (1987) 'The prevalence of dementia: a quantitative integration of the literature.' *Acta Psychiatrica Scandinavica 76*, 465–479.

Lawrence, V., Murray, J., Samsi, K. and Banerjee, S. (2008) 'Attitudes and support needs of Black Caribbean, south Asian and White British carers of people with dementia in the UK.' *British Journal of Psychiatry 193*, 240–246.

Lawrence, V., Samsi, K., Banerjee, S., Morgan, C. and Murray, J. (2011) 'Threat to valued elements of life: the experience of dementia across three ethnic groups.' *Gerontologist 51*, 39–50.

Lawrence, V., Banerjee, S., Bhugra, D., Sangha, K., Turner, S. and Murray, J. (2006) 'Coping with depression in later life: a qualitative study of help-seeking in three ethnic groups.' *Psychological Medicine 36*, 1375–1383.

Lindesay, J. (1998) 'The diagnosis of mental illness in elderly people from ethnic minorities.' *Advances in Psychiatric Treatment 4*, 219–226.

Lindesay, J., Jagger, C., Hibbert, M.J., Peet, S.M. and Moledina, F. (1997a) 'Knowledge, uptake and availability of health and social services among Asian Gujarati and white elders.' *Ethnicity and Health 2*, 59–69.

Lindesay, J., Jagger, C., Mlynik-Szmid, A., Sinorwala, A., Peet, S. and Moledina, F. (1997b) 'The mini-mental state examination (MMSE) in an elderly immigrant Gujarati population in the United Kingdom.' *International Journal of Geriatric Psychiatry 12*, 1155–1167.

Livingston, G., Leavey, G., Kitchen, G., Manela, M., Sembhi, S. and Katona, C. (2001) 'Mental health of migrant elders – the Islington study.' *British Journal of Psychiatry 179*, 361–366.

Livingston, G., Leavey, G., Kitchen, G., Manela, R.M., Sembhi, S. and Katona, C. (2002) 'Accessibility of health and social services to immigrant elders: the Islington study.' *British Journal of Psychiatry 180*, 369–374.

LSE (London School of Economics and Political Science), King's College London and Alzheimer's Society (2007) *Dementia UK. The Full Report.* Available at www.alzheimers.org.uk/News_and_Campaigns/Campaigning/PDF/Dementia_UK_Full_Report.pdf, accessed on 11 July 2009.

Mak, Z., Kim, J.M. and Stewart, R. (2006) 'Leg length, cognitive impairment and cognitive decline in an African Caribbean population.' *International Journal of Geriatric Psychiatry 21*, 266–272.

Manthorpe, J. and Hettiaratchy, P. (1993) 'Ethnic minority elders in Britain.' *International Review of Psychiatry 5*, 173–180.

Marwaha, S. and Livingston, G. (2002) 'Stigma, racism or choice. Why do depressed ethnic elders avoid psychiatrists?' *Journal of Affective Disorders 72*, 257–265.

McCallum, J.A. (1990) *The Forgotten People: Carers in Three Minority Communities in Southwark.* London: King's Fund Centre.

McCracken, C.F.M., Boneham, M.A., Copeland, J.R.M., Williams, K.E. *et al* (1997) 'Prevalence of dementia and depression among elderly people in black and ethnic groups.' *British Journal of Psychiatry 171*, 269–273.

Moriarty, J., Sharif, N. and Robinson, J. (2011) *Black and Minority Ethnic People with Dementia and their Access to Support and Services.* London: Social Care Institute for Excellence. Available at www.scie.org.uk/publications/briefings/files/briefing35.pdf, accessed on 28 February 2014.

Morris, J., Heyman, A., Mohs, R. *et al.* (1989) 'The consortium to establish a registry for Alzheimer's disease (CERAD). Part 1. Clinical and neuropsychological assessment of Alzheimer's disease.' *Neurology 39*, 1159–1165.

Mukadam, N., Cooper, C. and Livingston, G. (2011a) 'A systematic review of ethnicity and pathways to care in dementia.' *International Journal of Geriatric Psychiatry 26*, 12–20.

Mukadam, N., Cooper, C., Basil, B. and Livingston, G. (2011b) 'Why do ethnic elders present later to UK dementia services? A qualitative study.' *International Psychogeriatrics 23*, 1070–1077.

NICE (National Institute for Care and Health Excellence) (2006) *Dementia NICE Guidelines.* London: NICE.

NICE (2007) *Donepezil, Galantamine, Rivastigmine and Memantine for the Treatment of Alzheimer's Disease. NICE Technological Appraisal Guidance 2 (Amended).* London: NICE.

NIMHE (National Institute of Mental Health England) (2003) *Inside Outside – Improving Mental Health Services for Black and Minority Ethnic Communities in England.* London: NIMHE.

Odutoye, K. and Shah, A.K. (1999) 'The clinical and demographic characteristics of ethnic elders from the Indian sub-continent newly referred to a psychogeriatric service.' *International Journal of Geriatric Psychiatry 14*, 446–453.

ONS (Office for National Statistics) (2013) 'DC2101EW – Ethnic Group by Age and Sex.' Available at www.nomisweb.co.uk/census/2011/DC2101EW/view/2092957703?rows=c_ethpuk11&cols=c_age

OPCS (Office of Population Censuses and Surveys) (1983) *1981 Census: Country of Birth. Great Britain.* London: HMSO.

OPCS (1993a) *1991 Census: Ethnic Group and Country of Birth Great Britain.* London: OPCS.

OPCS (1993b) *1991 Census: County Reports.* London: OPCS.

Oommen, G., Bashford, J. and Shah, A.K. (2009) 'Ageing, ethnicity and psychiatric services.' *Psychiatric Bulletin 33*, 30–34.

Patel, N. (2000) 'Care for ethnic minorities: the professionals' views.' *Journal of Dementia Care*, Jan./Feb., 26–27.

Patel, N., Mirza, N.R., Lindblad, P., Amstrup, K. and Samaoli, O. (1998) *Dementia and Minority Ethnic Older People. Managing Care in the UK, Denmark and France.* Lyme Regis: Russell House Publishing Limited.

Pringle, M. and Rothera, I. (1996) 'Practicality of recording patient ethnicity in general practice: descriptive intervention study and attitude survey.' *British Medical Journal 312*, 1080–1082.

Purandare, N., Luthra, V., Swarbrick, C. and Burns, A. (2007) 'Knowledge of dementia among South Asian (Indian) older people in Manchester, UK.' *International Journal of Geriatric Psychiatry 22*, 777–781.

Purandare, N., Swarbrick, C., Fischer, A. and Burns, A. (2006) 'Cholinesterase inhibitors for Alzheimer's disease: variations in clinical practice in the north-west of England.' *International Journal of Geriatric Psychiatry 21*, 961–964.

Qureshi, K.N. and Hodkinson, H.M. (1984) 'Evaluation of a ten-question mental test in institutionalised elderly.' *Age and Ageing 3*, 152–157.

Rait, G. and Burns, A. (1997) 'Appreciating background and culture: the south Asian elderly and Mental Health.' *International Journal of Geriatric Psychiatry 12*, 973–977.

Rait, G., Morley, M., Lambat, I. and Burns, A. (1997) 'Modification of brief cognitive assessments for use with elderly people from the South Asian sub-continent.' *Ageing and Mental Health 1*, 356–363.

Rait, G., Burns, A., Baldwin, R., Morley., M., Chew-Graham C., and St Leger, A.S. (2000a) 'Validating screening instruments for cognitive impairment in older south Asians in the United Kingdom.' *International Journal of Geriatric Psychiatry 15*, 54–62.

Rait, G., Morley, M., Burns, A., Baldwin, R., Chew-Graham, C. and St Leger, A.S. (2000b) 'Screening for cognitive impairment in older African-Caribbeans.' *Psychological Medicine 30*, 957–963.

Redelinghuys, J. and Shah, A.K. (1997) 'The characteristics of ethnic elders from the Indian subcontinent using a geriatric psychiatry service in west London.' *Ageing and Mental Health 1*, 243–247.

Richards, M. and Brayne, C. (1996) 'Cross-cultural research into cognitive impairment and dementia: some practical experiences.' *International Journal of Geriatric Psychiatry 11*, 383–387.

Richards, M., Brayne, C., Dening, T. *et al* (2000) 'Cognitive function in UK community-dwelling African Caribbean and white elders: a pilot study.' *International Journal of Geriatric Psychiatry 15*, 621–630.

Roth, M., Tym, E., Mountjoy, C.Q., Huppert, F.A. *et al* (1986) 'CAMDEX: A standardised instrument for diagnosis of mental disorder in the elderly with special reference to the early detection of dementia.' *British Journal of Psychiatry 149*, 698–709.

Seabrooke, V. and Milne, A. (2003) 'Developing dementia services for an Asian community.' *Nursing and Residential Care 5*, 240–242.

Seabrooke V. and Milne A. (2004) *Culture and Care in Dementia: A Study of Asian Community in North Kent.* Northfleet: Alzheimer's and Dementia Support Services/Mental Health Foundation.

Secretaries of State for Health, Northern Ireland and Scotland (1989) Working for Patients (Cm 555). London: HMSO.

Senior, P.A. and Bhopal, R. (1994) 'Ethnicity as a variable in epidemiological research.' *British Medical Journal 309*, 327–330.

Shah, A.K. (1997a) 'Interviewing mentally ill ethnic minority elders with interpreters.' *Australian Journal on Ageing 16*, 220–221.

Shah A.K. (1997b) Straight talk. Overcoming language barriers in diagnosis. *Geriatric Medicine,* 27, 45-46.

Shah, A.K. (1999) 'Difficulties experienced by a Gujarati psychiatrist in interviewing elderly Gujaratis in Gujarati.' *International Journal of Geriatric Psychiatry 14*, 1072–1074.

Shah, A.K. (2007a) 'Demographic changes among ethnic minority elders in England and Wales. Implications for development and delivery of old age psychiatry services.' *International Journal of Migration, Health and Social Care 3*, 22–32.

Shah, A.K. (2007b) 'Can the recognition of clinical features of mental illness at clinical presentation in ethnic elders be improved?' *International Journal of Geriatric Psychiatry 22*, 277–282.

Shah, AK. (2008) 'Estimating the absolute number of cases of dementia and depression in the black and minority ethnic elderly population in the UK.' *International Journal of Migration, Health and Social Care 4*, 4–15.

Shah, A.K. (2009) 'The "Count Me In" psychiatric inpatient census for 2007 and the elderly: evidence of improvement or cause for concern?' *Psychiatric Bulletin 33*, 201–203.

Shah, A.K. (2010a) *Guide to Mental Health Assessment. PRIAE-ISCRI Managing Better Mental Health Care for Black and Minority Ethnic Elders*. Preston: UCLAN.

Shah, A.K. (2010b) *Elders and Carers Guide. PRIAE-ISCRI Managing Better Mental Health Care for Black and Minority Ethnic Elders*. Preston: UCLAN.

Shah, A.K. and Dighe-Deo, D. (1998) 'Elderly Gujaratis and psychogeriatrics in a London psychogeriatric service.' *Bulletin of the International Psychogeriatric Association 14*, 12–13.

Shah, A.K. and MacKenzie, S. (2007) 'Disorders of ageing across cultures.' In D. Bhugra and K. Bhui (eds) *Textbook of Cultural Psychiatry*. Cambridge: Cambridge University Press.

Shah, A.K., Adelman, S. and Ong, Y.L. (2009b) *Psychiatric Services for Black and Minority Ethnic Older People, College Report 156*. London: Royal College of Psychiatrists.

Shah, A.K., Dennis, M. and Lindesay, J. (2009a) 'Comparison of elderly suicide rates amongst migrants in England and Wales with their country of origin.' *International Journal of Geriatric Psychiatry 24*, 292–299.

Shah, A.K., Lindesay, J. and Jagger, C. (1998) 'Is the diagnosis of dementia stable over time among elderly immigrant Gujaratis in the United Kingdom?' *International Journal of Geriatric Psychiatry 13*, 440–444.

Shah, A.K., Lindesay, J. and Nnatu, I. (2005a) 'Cross-cultural Issues in the Assessment of Cognitive Impairment.' In A. Burns, J. O'Brien and D. Ames (eds) *Dementia*. London: Arnold Hodder.

Shah, A.K., Oommen, G. and Wuntakal, B. (2005b) 'Cultural aspects of dementia.' *Psychiatry 4*, 103–106

Solomon, A. (1992) 'Clinical diagnosis among diverse populations: a multicultural perspective.' *Family in Society: Journal of Contemporary Human Society*, June, 371–377.

Stevens, T., Leavey, G. and Livingston, G. (2004) 'Dementia and hypertension in African/Caribbean elders.' *Age and Ageing 33*, 193–195.

Stewart, R., Prince, M. and Mann, A. (2003) 'Age, vascular risk, and cognitive decline in an older, British, African Caribbean population.' *Journal of the American Geriatric Society 51*, 1547–1553.

Stewart, R., Powell, J., Prince, M. and Mann, A. (2004) 'ACE genotype and cognitive decline in an African Caribbean population.' *Neurobiology of Ageing 25*, 1369–1375.

Stewart, R., Richards, M., Brayne, C. and Mann, A. (2001a) 'Vascular risk and cognitive impairment in an older British, African-Caribbean population.' *Journal of the American Geriatric Society 49*, 263–269.

Stewart, R., Richards, M., Brayne, C. and Mann, A. (2001b) 'Cognitive function in UK community-dwelling African Caribbean elders: normative data for a test battery.' *International Journal of Geriatric Psychiatry 16*, 518–527.

Stewart, R., Johnson, J., Richards, M., Brayne, C. and Mann, A. (2002) 'The distribution of Mini-Mental State Examination scores in older UK African-Caribbean population compared to MRC CFA study norms.' *International Journal of Geriatric Psychiatry 17*, 745–751.

Stewart, R., Russ, C., Richards, M., Brayne, C., Lovestone, S. and Mann, A. (2001c) 'Apolipoprotein E genotype, vascular risk and early cognitive impairment in an African Caribbean population.' *Dementia and Geriatric Cognitive Disorder 12*, 251–256.

Taylor, C., Tillin, T., Chatuvedi, N., Dewey, M. *et al* (2013) 'Midlife hypertension status and cognitive function 20 years later: the Southall and Brent revisited study.' *Journal of American Geriatric Society 60*, 1489–1498.

Thomas, P., Thornton, T. and Shah, A.K. (2009) 'Language, games and interpretation in psychiatric diagnosis: a Wittgensteinian thought experiment.' *Journal of Medical Humanities 35*, 13–18.

Thornton, T., Shah, A.K. and Thomas, P. (2009) 'Understanding, testimony and interpretation in psychiatric diagnosis.' *Medicine, Healthcare and Philosophy 12*, 49–55.

Wild, S.H., Fischbacher, C.M., Brock, A., Griffiths, C. and Bhopal, R. (2007) 'Mortality from all causes and circulatory diseases by country of birth in England and Wales, 2001–2003.' *Journal of Public Health 29*, 191–198.

5

ACCESSING SUPPORT AND SERVICES

Jo Moriarty

> 'I remember my grandmother used to forget things. We thought it was just because she was old. I now think it was dementia.'
>
> 'My mother is elderly. She does not like any outsiders helping with personal care. My wife does everything for her.'
>
> 'We just sat there [in the centre] on our own all day. Other people were dancing and singing. We had a cup of tea and in the evening they dropped us home. There was no one there we could talk to.' (Rehman, cited in APPG on Dementia 2013a, p.5)

This chapter explores the impact of culture and ethnicity on attitudes to dementia, access to diagnosis, and service uptake, and considers their implications for service provision. Although the research evidence base remains comparatively small, two very consistent findings have emerged. The first is that in the UK and internationally people from black and minority ethnic (BME) groups generally access services later, at a stage when their dementia has become more severe (Cooper *et al.* 2010; Mukadam *et al.* 2011b). The second is that, having accessed these services, their experiences tend to be more negative (Bowes and Wilkinson 2002; Bunn *et al.* 2012; Lawrence *et al.* 2008; Milne and Chryssanthopoulou 2005). This chapter discusses some of the reasons why this should be so.

The quotations shown at the beginning of this chapter will resonate with many practitioners and researchers. They come from research commissioned by the All-Party Parliamentary Group on Dementia (a group of representatives from the House of Commons and House of Lords spanning all political parties interested in the topic) as part of its inquiry into dementia services for people from BME groups (APPG on Dementia 2013b). They encapsulate some of the main questions discussed in this chapter, including:

- Do levels of understanding about dementia vary between different ethnic groups? Does this mean people from certain ethnic groups are less likely than others to seek support?
- What role do other factors play in influencing people's decisions about whether to ask for support, such as differing cultural expectations about the help that other members should give?
- What approaches can health and social care practitioners adopt to try to improve access to dementia services for people from BME groups?

The context for these discussions involves three aspects that interlink with other chapters in this book. First, it is important to recognise that ethnicity is not a monolith – there are differences within and between different ethnic groups, as well as experiences that are shared. Second, irrespective of ethnic background, many people with dementia and their families have problems in accessing good quality support. However, for some communities, factors such as language barriers and different cultural expectations act as additional obstacles. Third, everyone possesses multiple identities. In addition to people's ethnic background, other characteristics, such as gender, sexuality, age, personality, and different life events, such as migration history, also influence their experiences. Each aspect needs to be considered simultaneously to ensure that people are supported in ways that acknowledge their uniqueness as individuals while recognising the wider structural barriers that create inequalities in access to support. As Botsford and colleagues have written:

> ethnicity alone cannot account for individual responses to dementia [...] and therefore awareness of cultural factors needs to be balanced with sensitivity to the unique life experience and relationships of the individuals. (Botsford, Clarke and Gibb 2012, p.2207)

Limitations of the existing evidence base

UK government policies have been comparatively late in explicitly acknowledging the impact of culture and ethnicity on the way that people access and use dementia services. This has had implications both in the amount of funding allocated to address ethnic disparities in the use of dementia services, and in researching why these differences exist. The delay means that the evidence base has been slow to expand, and it is still, as Cooper and colleagues have shown (2010), dominated by research originating in the US. In the UK, most of the studies about people with dementia from BME groups tend to be quite small-scale and are mainly undertaken in large urban areas where these populations are most concentrated (Moriarty, Sharif and Robinson 2011).

There is a larger literature that focuses on older people from BME groups' experiences of health and social care services, which often includes a sub-set of participants caring for someone with dementia (see, for example, Katbamna *et al.* 2004; Manthorpe *et al.* 2008) but, as the number of resources written by people with dementia increases (see, for example, Bryden 2005; Swaffer undated), we are becoming more aware of the power of people's own personal accounts. A striking omission from existing published research on ethnicity and dementia is the voice of people with dementia themselves, with some limited exceptions (see, for example, Azam 2007). This means that the perspectives of people with dementia from minority ethnic groups are often relayed by family carers and service providers, and we rarely know through their own words about their views of the barriers they face in accessing support and services.

Estimated number of people with dementia from BME groups

There are currently around 800,000 people with dementia in the UK, but only 48 per cent are thought to have actually received a diagnosis (Alzheimer's Society 2014b). It is estimated that there are currently 25,000 people from BME groups with dementia in England and Wales. This number is expected to grow to nearly 50,000 by 2026 and to over 172,000 by 2051 (APPG on Dementia 2013b).

Although we do not have any precise diagnosis rates by ethnicity, it is likely that proportionally even fewer people with dementia from BME groups have been given a diagnosis. This is because, despite suggestions that vascular dementia is more frequent among Black Caribbean and Asian people because of their higher rates of heart disease, and that rates of young onset dementia appear to be higher among Black Caribbean people (APPG on Dementia 2013b), they are, as mentioned above, under-represented in dementia services in relation to their numbers within the population (APPG on Dementia 2013b; Challis *et al.* 2014; Cooper *et al.* 2010; Moriarty *et al.* 2011; Mukadam *et al.* 2011b; Truswell 2013). A number of reasons have been offered to explain why this has happened, and these are now explored in turn.

Dementia as a disease or a 'normal' part of ageing

Several theories of 'help-seeking' (or health-seeking) behaviour have been developed to explain why people do not always access the health and social care services that have been developed to support them (Cornally and McCarthy 2011; Wacker and Roberto 2008; Walters, Iliffe and Orrell 2001). Among these is the presumption that people only access health and social care services once they recognise that they have a condition for which they need help. People from ethnic and cultural backgrounds who view dementia as a 'normal' part of ageing may be less likely to request support for family members with dementia until a crisis point is reached, because they do not think they have an illness.

Until the mid-1970s, the idea that dementia was a 'normal' part of ageing was widespread, even within the medical profession (Downs 2000). Since then, biomedical advances in the causes and manifestations of dementia have largely changed this viewpoint across Europe, North America and Australasia, but it continues to predominate in many other parts of the world. In her seminal study of Black Caribbean and South Asian carers of people with dementia, Adamson (2001) found that participants tended to associate dementia with 'normal' ageing, a finding that has been replicated consistently in other studies undertaken with a range of ethnic groups in the UK (Bowes and Wilkinson 2002; Johl, Patterson and Pearson 2014; La Fontaine *et al.* 2007; Turner, Christie and Haworth 2005; Uppal and Bonas 2014), and in countries such as Australia (Alzheimer's Australia Vic 2008) and the US (Liu *et al.* 2008). 'Normal' ageing in this context encompasses different trajectories of ageing, some more and some less desired (Liu *et al.* 2008), which is why it often sits uncomfortably with the dichotomous way dementia and 'normal' ageing are presented in Western medicine.

Language of dementia

Understanding these wider socio-cultural aspects of dementia is important because they affect the way that people with dementia experience their condition. Another well-known explanation for the under-representation of people from minority ethnic groups in dementia services is the lack of an equivalent word for 'dementia' in most South (Seabrooke and Milne 2004) and East Asian languages (Fung *et al.* 2014). Furthermore, the words that do exist to describe the changes associated with dementia tend to be derogatory. The shame associated with having a condition that is viewed so negatively is thought to be a major factor resulting in people delaying asking for help as long as possible (APPG on Dementia 2013b; Bowes and Wilkinson 2002;

Bunn *et al.* 2012; Cooper *et al.* 2010; Jolley 2009; La Fontaine *et al.* 2007; Mackenzie 2006; Moriarty *et al.* 2011; Mukadam *et al.* 2011b).

Different approaches have been adopted to try to overcome this problem. In Taiwan, health and social workers, people with dementia, and family carers led a campaign to change the traditional Chinese term *Chi Dai Zheng*, which was based on the concept of 'stupidity and slow-witted brain with psychosis-like features', to a new term, *Shi Zhi Zheng*, which means 'disorder with dysfunction of intelligence or loss of wisdom'. Similarly, in Japan, the local word for dementia, *Chiho*, which implied that the person was foolish and absentminded, was replaced by *Ninchi-Sho*, which means 'major cognition disorder' (Fung *et al.* 2014). An alternative approach undertaken in an information programme for South Asian people with dementia and their families run by the Alzheimer's Society was to bypass issues around translation by using the English word 'dementia' alongside a simple explanation in the relevant language (Capper 2014).

In considering the negative associations of words used to describe dementia in different languages, we should not forget that the English word 'dementia' is derived from Latin, and it, too, was originally associated with 'madness' and loss of judgement. Although its meaning has since changed and the original definition has fallen into disuse, people with dementia still experience stigma and discrimination, as discussed in more detail below.

Policy-makers and practitioners trying to improve support for people with dementia from minority ethnic groups rightly emphasise the barriers caused by the absence of an equivalent word for dementia in many languages, but we also need to consider if other commonly used phrases, such as 'sufferer', 'living death' and 'victim', also perpetuate negative perceptions (George 2010). At the broader level, this is a wider issue that involves aspects such as the values taught on professional qualifying education, and how dementia is represented in the media. More specifically, health and social care professionals sometimes find themselves speaking to people with dementia and their families through interpreters, or using translated materials, without knowing precisely what has been said or written. In Chapter 4 Shah and Zarate Escudero discuss the challenges of diagnosing dementia among people whose primary language is not English. However, as well as the need for professional interpreters who are knowledgeable about dementia and familiar with medical terminology (Shah 2007), we also need interpreters and translators who can use sensitive, as well as technically accurate, language. This leads on to the next section that considers how lack of fluency in written and spoken English can create further barriers to accessing support and services.

Language barriers

There seems little doubt that people who are not fluent in the main languages used in the country in which they live are at a disadvantage when using all types of health and social care services and other public services, compared with native speakers or those who are bilingual (Botsford, *et al* 2012). In the first place, they may know less about diagnostic services such as memory clinics and other resources. In the second, even if they do access these services, they may find it hard to comprehend care plans, or they may not wish to use services where they feel isolated from other staff and service users because of language barriers.

The overwhelming majority of the current generation of older people with dementia from a BME group living in the UK was born overseas. Their levels of written and oral fluency in English are variable, particularly among women. Others may lose the ability to speak English as their dementia progresses, particularly if they learned the language as an adult.

The Alzheimer's Society and Alzheimer Scotland have translated a number of their factsheets into the main community languages, although existing research about the needs of older people from BME groups has suggested that DVDs tend to be more popular than leaflets, especially among those who have limited literacy in their primary language or in English (Moriarty and Manthorpe 2012), and so a number of organisations have created DVDs in different languages (Scottish Dementia Clinical Research Network 2010) as an alternative or to supplement written information.

People also need opportunities to discuss what they have read and seen. In our recently completed study of social care support for family carers (Moriarty, Manthorpe and Cornes 2014), an outreach worker who spoke several community languages explained the need for a home visit to a woman from a BME group who cared for her husband with dementia so that they could talk through the information she had been given:

> trying to get [this carer] to understand the terminologies that are being used [...] is really difficult on the phone. Hence [I am] going to [...] take [...] leaflets that have information about the diagnosis that [her husband] has [...] I think I need to go and do a home visit and sit down and do a face to face and get her to understand a little bit. (Ifrah, worker, 20)

Another project (Moriarty 2013) drew on interviews undertaken with outreach workers employed by Age UK to support people from BME groups. These workers commented that providing information about dementia was an increasingly important part of their work. As well as running information sessions and meeting with community groups, they also welcomed chances to appear on local radio stations broadcasting programmes aimed at people from BME groups. They saw these as providing an increasingly important avenue for improving awareness about dementia, particularly for those who did not watch or listen to English language television or radio programmes or read newspapers or magazines printed in English.

Established generic methods to reach ethnic groups that are currently under-represented in dementia services, such as outreach workers, interpreters and providing translated versions of information and publicity material, can be augmented by different techniques tailored towards reaching specific communities. For example, the Los Angeles-based El Portal project for Latino people with dementia printed postcard-sized brochures for distribution in local laundrettes, beauty salons and *botánicas* (shops selling alternative medicine and other products such as candles and incense found in many Latino communities) (Aranda *et al.* 2003).

Stigma

Stigma reflects an external process by which a person's social contribution or value is denigrated by the pejorative labels that are attached to them (Sutton *et al.* 2014). It exists in all cultures, although the way it is expressed varies between them (Weiss, Ramakrishna and Somma 2006). Stigma towards people with dementia is a global problem (Batsch and Mittelman 2012), and many people with dementia report distressing experiences of being treated differently as a result of their condition (Williamson 2008). Stigma is an important reason for delays in accessing dementia support as people may seek to conceal, minimise or ignore the early signs and symptoms (Vernooij-Dassen *et al.* 2005).

For groups who have experienced discrimination, as have many people from BME groups, and whose life chances may have been affected by structural disadvantages, such as higher rates of poverty and/or employment or poorer health, developing a stigmatising illness or condition might amplify these disadvantages even further. In particular, the shame associated with having, or being associated with someone who has, a stigmatising illness (La Fontaine *et al.* 2007; Liu *et al.* 2008; Mackenzie 2006) may deter people from accessing resources within their community, meaning that people with dementia and their families may become very isolated. In cultures where arranged marriages are more common, people may not wish to disclose they have a relative with dementia in case it reduces family members' chances of making a good marriage (Bowes and Wilkinson 2002; Liu *et al.* 2008). Liu and colleagues (2008) also question whether stigma poses an additional risk for people with dementia in cultures where they are viewed as 'child-like' because their opportunities to make decisions are more likely to be taken from them.

Because stigma takes different forms within different ethnic and cultural groups, attempts to improve service uptake need to be tailored. In their study of health and social care providers in Scotland, Bowes and Wilkinson (2002) reported that practitioners found it was more successful to emphasise the physical changes to the brain associated with dementia with people from South Asian backgrounds because of the stigma surrounding mental illness. By contrast, the Federation of Irish Societies chose 'memory loss' as part of its initiative to create more 'dementia-friendly' Irish community organisations.

Box 5.1: *Cuimhne*, the Irish Memory Loss Alliance

Cuimhne (pronounced 'queevna') is the Irish word for 'memory'. It is an initiative aimed at developing training and support to Irish clubs and community organisations that provide a variety of different social events and support services to older people so that the staff and volunteers will develop confidence to interact with people with memory loss. Dementia and Alzheimer's are terms that can be frightening and stigmatising. We also know that the Irish community are much more comfortable talking about memory loss, thus enabling conversations which will help to inform improvements to services. (Adapted from Federation of Irish Societies 2012)

Knowledge about dementia

Lack of knowledge about dementia is thought to contribute to stigma. As a result, the dementia strategies that have been developed in different parts of the world generally share a common aim to improve understanding among the general public (Batsch and Mittelman 2012). This is based on research suggesting that the general public's knowledge of dementia tends to be variable, and that some groups tend to have poorer knowledge than others.

Purandare and colleagues (2007) surveyed white British and South Asian older people attending day centres in Manchester who were not known to have dementia. While knowledge of dementia was generally poor across both groups, it was worse among respondents from a South Asian background. A study undertaken in Japan (which is, of course, more ethnically homogeneous) also concluded that there were gaps in the public's knowledge (Arai, Arai and Zarit 2008). In this study, middle-aged women tended to know most, mainly because of their experience of family caregiving, and because they knew more about long-term care and ageing issues in general.

In Australia, people from all ethnic groups appear to hold some misconceptions about dementia. However, among indigenous Australians, where rates of dementia seem to be higher than among the non-indigenous population, gaps in knowledge appeared to be greater, particularly among younger people (Garvey *et al.* 2011).

By contrast, research undertaken in Northern Ireland found that the general public as a whole had a reasonably good understanding of dementia, but that their views could be quite stereotyped. Many agreed with the statement that 'people with dementia are like children' and failed to differentiate between what people in the early stages and later stages of dementia might be able to do. The proportion of people interviewed from a minority ethnic group was too small to compare results by ethnicity, but there did seem to be some associations between education and age, with younger, more educated respondents being more in favour of sharing a diagnosis of dementia with the person affected, while older ones were more knowledgeable about the benefits of diet and exercise. Knowing someone with dementia was, not surprisingly, also associated with greater knowledge (Dowds *et al.* 2012; McParland *et al.* 2012).

Taking these studies as a whole, differences in sampling and in the measures used to test knowledge of dementia mean that extreme caution is needed in comparing results between them. However, they show the need to develop information resources that are culturally sensitive and that specifically address the information needs of different groups. It has also been suggested that helping people to understand dementia in the context of the social model of disability might result in less paternalistic attitudes to people with dementia (Gilliard *et al.* 2005; Nolan *et al.* 2006).

A number of national and local campaigns have been developed to raise awareness of dementia across the population. In England, the most famous of these currently is the Dementia Friends campaign, based on the Nationwide Caravan to Train One Million Dementia Supporters in Japan:

Box 5.2: Dementia Friends

The Dementia Friends initiative developed by Public Health England and the Alzheimer's Society aims to recruit a million people who have attended the Dementia Friends training and then gone on to share their knowledge with other people within their network. (Adapted from Alzheimer's Society 2014a)

Religion

Religion, whether in the form of adherence to an organised religion or a personal belief system, may influence the way people perceive dementia and choose to access support. It is increasingly recognised that in some circumstances, religious beliefs may be more important than ethnic group in determining people's attitudes to dementia (Regan 2013; Regan *et al.* 2012; Uppal and Bonas 2014). Different reported examples of this include beliefs that dementia is a punishment from God (Adamson 2001), or for behaviour in a past life (Hinton *et al.* 2008), that a person with dementia is possessed, or a victim of witchcraft (Jett 2006; Mackenzie *et al.* 2003), and that caring for someone with dementia is a religious obligation (Mackenzie 2006), sacrifice (Hinton *et al.* 2008), or expression of filial piety (Liu *et al.* 2008).

Cultural expectations around caring

Because so many people access dementia services as a result of anxieties expressed by other family members rather than themselves, cultural beliefs around the obligation to care often act as a barrier to seeking support until there is a crisis or family members experience extreme pressure in their caring role (Botsford, Clarke and Gibb 2011; Mukadam *et al.* 2011b). Carers from BME groups seem to be more likely to espouse what has been defined as the 'traditional caregiver ideology' and to consider that care should be provided from within the family (Lawrence *et al.* 2008). This means that they often access services at a later point than their white British counterparts (Bowes and Wilkinson 2002; Mukadam, Cooper and Livingston 2011a; Mukadam *et al.* 2011b; Uppal and Bonas 2014). They may also feel under greater pressure within their community to care for a family member without asking for outside support (Mackenzie 2006), and to feel less trust that services will be able to provide suitable support for the person for whom they care (Jolley 2009; Mukadam *et al.* 2011b).

There is evidence of some convergence between different ethnic groups, especially among women, in terms of expectations around caring (Lawrence *et al.* 2008). More women from BME groups are in paid employment, and some minority ethnic groups are becoming more geographically dispersed so that adult children are less likely to live near their parents than previously (Moriarty *et al.* 2011). However, carers of people from BME groups do appear to be more vulnerable in terms of expectations that they will provide support, both from within their community and from health and social care professionals.

Discussion and implications for the future

In presenting the different aspects of ethnicity and culture on attitudes to dementia, access to diagnosis, and service uptake, there is a risk that the onus for delays in access to treatment is placed on people with dementia and their families, while the responsibility for health and social care services to develop accessible and culturally sensitive services is not emphasised enough. Although previous negative perceptions and experiences of health and social care services may cause delays in accessing dementia services (Mukadam *et al.* 2011a), and we should never underestimate the existence of stereotyping and even racism among professionals (Worth *et al.* 2009), this is a very under-researched area in dementia care.

As this chapter has tried to show, language barriers, lack of awareness about dementia, stigma, and different cultural expectations about caring all seem to have contributed to delays in accessing services among people from different ethnic groups. This has important implications in terms of creating ethnic inequalities in access to support and services. This is becoming increasingly important in the context of earlier recognition of dementia, access to drug treatments, and the opportunity to plan care in the future. However, the chapter has also tried to convey how it is important not to regard stigma and discrimination in dementia as something that is restricted to people from certain ethnic or cultural groups. In their analysis of the different ways that dementia has been conceptualised, Bartlett and O'Connor (2007) make the argument that citizenship may provide a different lens than personhood from which to explore certain aspects of people's experiences of dementia. 'Personhood', they write, 'cannot fully explain the essence of power relations and citizenship cannot fully recognise the essence of individuality' (p.115). This is a powerful argument for making stronger links between research on culture and ethnicity in dementia care and the broader health inequality agenda. This would mark an important step in translating what is already known about the impact of culture and ethnicity on access to dementia services into the creation of services in which culture and ethnicity are not markers of inequalities in access to the types of support that people with dementia and their families want.

References

Adamson, J. (2001) 'Awareness and understanding of dementia in African/ Caribbean and South Asian families.' *Health and Social Care in the Community 9*, 391–396.

Alzheimer's Australia Vic (2008) *Perceptions of Dementia in Ethnic Communities*. Hawthorn, VIC: Alzheimer's Australia Vic.

Alzheimer's Society (2014a) *Dementia Friends* [Online]. Available at www.alzheimers.org.uk/site/scripts/documents_info.php?documentID=2070, accessed on 15 July 2014.

Alzheimer's Society (2014b) *Early Diagnosis Campaign* [Online]. Available at www.alzheimers.org.uk/earlydiagnosis, accessed on 20 June 2014.

APPG (All-Party Parliamentary Group) on Dementia (2013a) APPG Meeting Transcript Day 2. Web-based publication. Alzheimer's Society.

APPG on Dementia (2013b) *Dementia Does Not Discriminate: The Experiences of Black, Asian and Minority Ethnic Communities*. July. London: Alzheimer's Society. Available at www.alzheimers.org.uk/site/scripts/download_info.php?downloadID=1186, accessed on 11 December 2014.

Arai, Y., Arai, A. and Zarit, S.H. (2008) 'What do we know about dementia? A survey on knowledge about dementia in the general public of Japan.' *International Journal of Geriatric Psychiatry 23*, 433–438.

Aranda, M.P., Villa, V.M, Trejo, L., Ramírez, R. and Ranney, M. (2003) 'El Portal Latino Alzheimer's Project: model program for Latino caregivers of Alzheimer's disease-affected people.' *Social Work 48*, 259–271.

Azam, N. (2007) *Evaluation Report of the Meri Yaadain Dementia Project*. Bradford: Bradford District Health and Social Care Communications Team.

Bartlett, R. and O'Connor, D. (2007) 'From personhood to citizenship: broadening the lens for dementia practice and research.' *Journal of Aging Studies 21*, 107–118.

Batsch, N.S. and Mittelman, M.S. (2012) *World Alzheimer Report 2012: Overcoming the Stigma of Dementia*. London: Alzheimer's Disease International.

Botsford, J., Clarke, C.L. and Gibb, C.E. (2011) 'Research and dementia, caring and ethnicity: a review of the literature.' *Journal of Research in Nursing 16*, 437–449.

Botsford, J., Clarke, C.L. and Gibb, C.E. (2012) 'Dementia and relationships: experiences of partners in minority ethnic communities.' *Journal of Advanced Nursing 68*, 2207–2217.

Bowes, A. and Wilkinson, H. (2002) '"We didn't know it would get that bad": South Asian experiences of dementia and the service response.' *Health & Social Care in the Community 11*, 387–396.

Bryden, C. (2005) *Dancing with Dementia: My Story of Living Positively with Dementia*. London: Jessica Kingsley Publishers.

Bunn, F., Goodman, C., Sworn, K., Rait, G. *et al* (2012) 'Psychosocial factors that shape patient and carer experiences of dementia diagnosis and treatment: a systematic review of qualitative studies.' *PLOS Medicine* [Online], 9. Available at www.plosmedicine.org/article/info%3Adoi%2F10.1371%2Fjournal.pmed.1001331

Capper, C. (2014) 'Dementia services must not culturally discriminate.' *The Guardian*, 23 April 2014.

Challis, D., Jolley, D., Giebel, C., Zubair, M. *et al* (2014) *South Asian Voices Enabling Dementia Care (SAVE-D)*. Manchester: Personal Social Services Research Unit.

Cooper, C., Tandy, A.R., Balamurali, T.B.S. and Livingston, G. (2010) 'A systematic review and meta-analysis of ethnic differences in use of dementia treatment, care, and research.' *American Journal of Geriatric Psychiatry 18,* 193–203.

Cornally, N. and McCarthy, G. (2011) 'Help-seeking behaviour: a concept analysis.' *International Journal of Nursing Practice 17*, 280–288.

Dowds, L., McParland, P., Devine, P. and Gray, A.M. (2012) *Attitudes to and Knowledge of Dementia in Northern Ireland 2010*. Belfast: University of Ulster.

Downs, M. (2000) 'Dementia in a socio-cultural context: an idea whose time has come.' *Ageing and Society 20*, 369–375.

Federation of Irish Societies (2012) *Cuimhne – The Irish Memory Loss Alliance* [Online]. Available at http://in-gb.co.uk/cuimhne-the-irish-memory-loss-alliance, accessed on 15 July 2014.

Fung, H., Chiu, K., Sato, M., Kua, E.H., Lee M.S., Yu, X., Ouyang, W.-C., Yang, Y.K. and Sartorius, N. (2014) 'Renaming dementia – an East Asian perspective.' *International Psychogeriatrics 26*, 885–887.

Garvey, G., Simmonds, D., Clements, V., O'Rourke, P., *et al* (2011) 'Making sense of dementia: understanding amongst indigenous Australians.' *International Journal of Geriatric Psychiatry 26*, 649–656.

George, D.R. (2010) 'Overcoming the social death of dementia through language.' *Lancet 376*, 586–587.

Gilliard, J., Means, R., Beattie, A. and Daker-White, G. (2005) 'Dementia care in England and the social model of disability: lessons and issues.' *Dementia 4*, 571–586.

Hinton, L., Nhauyen Tran, J., Tran, C. and Hinton, D. (2008) 'Religious and spiritual dimensions of the Vietnamese dementia caregiving experience.' *Hallym International Journal of Aging 10*, 139–160.

Jett, K.F. (2006) 'Mind-loss in the African American community: dementia as a normal part of aging.' *Journal of Aging Studies 20*, 1–10.

Johl, N., Patterson, T. and Pearson, L. (2014) 'What do we know about the attitudes, experiences and needs of black and minority ethnic carers of people with dementia in the United Kingdom? A systematic review of empirical research findings.' *Dementia* [Online]. Available at http://dem.sagepub.com/content/early/2014/05/12/1471301214534424.abstract, accessed on 15 July 2014.

Jolley, D. (2009) 'The "Twice a Child" projects: learning about dementia and related disorders within the black and minority ethnic population of an English city and improving relevant services.' *Ethnicity and Inequalities in Health and Social Care 2*, 5–9.

Katbamna, S., Ahmad, W., Bhakt, P., Baker, R. and Parker, G. (2004) 'Do they look after their own? Informal support for South Asian carers.' *Health & Social Care in the Community 12*, 398–406.

La Fontaine, J., Ahuja, J., Bradbury, N.M., Phillips, S. and Oyebode, J.R. (2007) 'Understanding dementia amongst people in minority ethnic and cultural groups.' *Journal of Advanced Nursing 60*, 605–614.

Lawrence, V., Murray, J., Samsi, K. and Banerjee, S. (2008) 'Attitudes and support needs of Black Caribbean, South Asian and White British carers of people with dementia in the UK.' *British Journal of Psychiatry 192*, 240–246.

Liu, D., Hinton, L., Tran, C., Hinton, D. and Barker, J.C. (2008) 'Reexamining the relationships among dementia, stigma, and aging in immigrant Chinese and Vietnamese family caregivers.' *Journal of Cross-Cultural Gerontology 23*, 283–299.

Mackenzie, J. (2006) 'Stigma and dementia – East European and South Asian family carers negotiating stigma in the UK.' *Dementia: The International Journal of Social Research and Practice 5*, 233–248.

Mackenzie, J., Coates, D., Ashraf, F., Gallagher, T. and Ismail, L. (2003) *Understanding and Supporting South Asian and Eastern European Family Carers of People with Dementia.* Bradford: University of Bradford, Bradford Dementia Group.

Manthorpe, J., Moriarty, J., Rapaport, J., Clough, R. *et al* (2008) '"There are wonderful social workers but it's a lottery": older people's views about social workers.' *British Journal of Social Work 38*, 1132–1150.

McParland, P., Devine, P., Innes, A. and Gayle, V. (2012) 'Dementia knowledge and attitudes of the general public in Northern Ireland: an analysis of national survey data.' *International Psychogeriatrics 24*, 1600–1613.

Milne, A. and Chryssanthopoulou, C. (2005) 'Dementia care-giving in black and Asian populations: reviewing and refining the research agenda.' *Journal of Community & Applied Social Psychology 15*, 319–337.

Moriarty, J. (2013) *Review of Age UK's Services for Black and Minority Ethnic Older People.* Internal report for Age UK. London: King's College London, Social Care Workforce Research Unit. [Unpublished].

Moriarty, J. and Manthorpe, J. (2012) *Diversity in Older People and Access to Services – An Evidence Review.* London: Age UK.

Moriarty, J., Manthorpe, J. and Cornes, M. (2014) 'Reaching out or missing out: approaches to outreach with family carers in social care organisations.' *Health & Social Care in the Community, 23*, 1, 42–50.

Moriarty, J., Sharif, N. and Robinson, J. (2011) *Black and Minority Ethnic People with Dementia and their Access to Support and Services.* SCIE Research Briefing 35. London: Social Care Institute for Excellence.

Mukadam, N., Cooper, C. and Livingston, G. (2011a) 'A systematic review of ethnicity and pathways to care in dementia.' *International Journal of Geriatric Psychiatry 26*, 12–20.

Mukadam, N., Cooper, C., Basit, B. and Livingston, G. (2011b) 'Why do ethnic elders present later to UK dementia services? A qualitative study.' *International Psychogeriatrics 23*, 1070–1077.

Nolan, L., McCarron, M., McCallion, P. and Murphy-Lawless, J. (2006) *Perceptions of Stigma in Dementia: An Exploratory Study*. Dublin: Trinity College Dublin, School of Nursing and Midwifery.

Purandare, N., Luthra, V. and Swarbrick, C. (2007) 'Knowledge of dementia among South Asian (Indian) older people in Manchester, UK.' *International Journal of Geriatric Psychiatry 22*, 777–781.

Regan, J.L. (2013) 'Redefining dementia care barriers for ethnic minorities: the religion–culture distinction.' *Mental Health, Religion & Culture 17*, 345–353.

Regan, J.L., Bhattacharyya, S., Kevern, P. and Rana, T. (2012) 'A systematic review of religion and dementia care pathways in black and minority ethnic populations.' *Mental Health, Religion & Culture 16*, 1–15.

Scottish Dementia Clinical Research Network (2010) 'NHS Tayside launch Coping with Dementia DVD for Carers' [Online]. Perth: Scottish Dementia Clinical Research Network. Available at www.sdcrn.org.uk/news-and-events/news/nhs-tayside-launch-coping-dementia-dvd-carers, accessed on 14 July 2014.

Seabrooke, V. and Milne, A. (2004) *Culture and Care in Dementia: A Study of the Asian Community in North West Kent*. Northfleet: Alzheimer's and Dementia Support Services/Mental Health Foundation.

Shah, A. (2007) 'Can the recognition of clinical features of mental illness at clinical presentation in ethnic elders be improved?' *International Journal of Geriatric Psychiatry 22*, 277–282.

Sutton, E., Pemberton, S., Fahmy, E. and Tamiya, Y. (2014) 'Stigma, shame and the experience of poverty in Japan and the United Kingdom.' *Social Policy and Society 13*, 143–154.

Swaffer, K. (undated) *Creating Life with Words: Inspiration, Love and Truth* [Online]. Available at http://kateswaffer.com/, accessed on 20 June 2014.

Truswell, D. (2013) *Black, Asian and Minority Ethnic Communities and Dementia – Where Are we Now?* A Race Equality Foundation Briefing Paper. *Better Health Briefing 30*. London: Race Equality Foundation.

Turner, S., Christie, A. and Haworth, E. (2005) 'South Asian and white older people and dementia: a qualitative study of knowledge and attitudes.' *Diversity in Health and Social Care 2*, 197–209.

Uppal, G. and Bonas, S. (2014) 'Constructions of dementia in the South Asian community: a systematic literature review.' *Mental Health, Religion & Culture 17*, 143–160.

Vernooij-Dassen, M.J.F.J., Moniz-Cook, E.D., Woods, R.T., Lepeleire, J.D. *et al.* (2005) 'Factors affecting timely recognition and diagnosis of dementia across Europe: from awareness to stigma.' *International Journal of Geriatric Psychiatry 20*, 377–386.

Wacker, R.R. and Roberto, K.A. (2008) *Community Resources for Older Adults: Programs and Services in an Era of Change.* Thousand Oaks, CA: Sage Publications, Inc.

Walters, K., Iliffe, S. and Orrell, M. (2001) 'An exploration of help-seeking behaviour in older people with unmet needs.' *Family Practice 18*, 277–282.

Weiss, M.G., Ramakrishna, J. and Somma, D. (2006) 'Health-related stigma: rethinking concepts and interventions.' *Psychology, Health & Medicine 11*, 277–287.

Williamson, T. (2008) *Dementia: Out of the Shadows.* London: Alzheimer's Disease Society.

Worth, A., Irshad, T., Bhopal, R., Brown, D. *et al.* (2009) 'Vulnerability and access to care for South Asian Sikh and Muslim patients with life limiting illness in Scotland: prospective longitudinal qualitative study.' *British Medical Journal 338*, b183.

Section Two

ENGAGING AND WORKING WITH PEOPLE WITH DEMENTIA AND THEIR FAMILIES

6

DEMENTIA AND CAREGIVING IN SOUTH ASIAN COMMUNITIES IN THE UK

Karan Jutlla

Overview

This chapter explores the experiences of caring for a family member with dementia for those from South Asian communities living in the UK. The barriers and challenges faced have resulted in a low service uptake, with families often presenting themselves to services at crisis point. Existing research in this area has highlighted that experiences of South Asian people are influenced by cultural norms associated with roles and positions in South Asian families, dementia being understood as a mental illness and its associated stigma, and prior experiences of health and social care services. Based on existing research, this chapter explores each of these areas in depth, making recommendations for dementia policy and practice initiatives, and highlighting areas worthy of further investigation.

Introduction

Caring at home for a family member living with dementia is known to be demanding. While some family members report satisfaction in caregiving, and indeed are able to continue to work together and maintain meaningful relationships (Hellström, Nolan and Lundh 2007; Keady and Nolan 2003), many family members involved in caregiving experience high levels of stress, depressive symptoms, poor physical health, social isolation and financial problems (Alzheimer's Society 2014a; Brodaty, Gresham, and Luscombe 2007). Furthermore, evidence suggests that levels of stress and distress increase over time, as the dementia progresses and the effects become more wide-ranging in their impact on the person living with dementia (Froelich *et al.* 2009; Kannan *et al.* 2011). Important to a person's experiences of caring for a family member with dementia will be their gender, age, social class and ethnicity (Botsford, Clarke and Gibb 2011).

As evidenced by the 2011 Census, the UK has become more ethnically diverse, with rising numbers of people identifying with minority ethnic groups. Census findings on international migration found that South Asian countries (India, Pakistan and Bangladesh) continued to rank highly within the most common non-UK countries of birth. South Asian communities have a strong presence in the UK, and the numbers continue to rise; the Asian and Asian British ethnic group categories had some of the largest increases between the 2001 and 2011 Censuses (ONS 2012). There is a corresponding increase in the numbers of South Asian people with dementia. Consequently, there is an increasing service demand for people with dementia and their carers and family members from South Asian communities, and this will continue to increase as communities age in place.

There are a number of studies that inform us about the experiences of caring for a person with dementia from South Asian communities in the UK (Bowes and Wilkinson 2003; Buffin, Shah and Syed 2009; Jutlla and Moreland 2007; Mackenzie 2006; Moreland 2001, 2003; Rochfort 2008; Seabrooke and Milne 2004). These studies have included Muslim, Hindu, Buddhist, Gujarati, Bangladeshi and Sikh carers. Research evidence about the experiences of dementia and caregiving within and between these specific ethnic groups remains limited, but any assumption that South Asian communities are one homogeneous cultural group needs to be challenged. Research with Sikh carers of a family member with dementia, undertaken by the author, highlighted the internal heterogeneity of the Sikh community in Wolverhampton, the findings of which have been included in this chapter.

Over the years there have been changes in the way in which the experience of dementia has been conceptualised by researchers (Ablitt, Jones and Muers 2009). Initially the research focus was exclusively on caregiving, and tended to concentrate on the burden experienced as a consequence of caring, and emphasised outcomes such as depression and physical ill health. During this time, the person with dementia was largely absent from research and frequently conceptualised in terms of the problems created for family caregivers. Unfortunately, the experiences of people with dementia from minority ethnic communities in the UK is still largely absent from research (Jutlla 2013a). Both cultural and language barriers have made it methodologically difficult for researchers wanting to explore this area (Shah, Oommen and Wuntakal 2005).

Despite this knowledge gap, we know that the journey through dementia involves considerable changes and challenges, and each family's journey is unique, for the family as a whole and for each person within it. According to existing research, experiences of caring for a family member with dementia for those from South Asian communities are largely influenced by cultural norms associated with roles and positions in the family; the stigma of mental illness; and experiences of health and social care services. Research with Sikh carers of a family member with dementia has also brought our attention to how migration experiences impact on caregiving experiences.

Roles and positions in the family

In South Asian communities there are cultural norms about the different roles and positions within the family that determine informal care responsibilities. Although this is a concept relevant to *all* communities, those from a South Asian background have made evident the pertinence of gendered divisions of labour, and the impact this has on the caregiving role and the reliance on children to care for their parents at home, a responsibility that falls heavily on daughters-in-law. Research with Sikh carers of a family member with dementia highlighted the expectation to adhere to the responsibilities associated with their relational role to the cared-for person by members of the Sikh community, an external pressure which further impacted on their experiences.

In South Asian communities there is a strong cultural tradition that children will look after their elders, and, more importantly, that they will look after them in their own homes (APPG on Dementia 2013; Jutlla 2013b). In the extended South Asian family, sons are expected to be responsible primarily for the material support of their parents, whilst their wives are expected to provide physical care, except, perhaps, for the personal hygiene of adult males in the family (Ahmad and Atkin 1997; Mand 2006; Seabrooke and Milne 2004). Although some husbands and sons are classed as the registered carer (the carer known to services), they frequently defer to their wives, daughters and sisters for practical help. Consequently, the majority of hidden carers (carers unknown to services) are often daughters-in-law whose husbands are officially classed as the registered carer (Dwyer and Coward 1992; Globerman 1996; Jutlla 2011; Yeo and Gallagher-Thompson 1996). As Blakemore and Boneham (1994, p.83) note, when considering daughters-in-law, 'it is quite possible to be isolated in a large family group, to be treated in an offhand or condescending way, to be denied freedom of movement and basic rights to one's own money or goods'. This situation appears to apply more to women, and can be a reason for feeling trapped and powerless in the family (Blakemore and Boneham 1994; Jutlla 2011). Daughters-in-law, who have never worked in the UK post-migration, experience this inequality even more, creating tensions and contrary pulls whereby they often find themselves in powerless positions (Bhachu 1988; Lamb 2000). Although employment often gives women more confidence, and a sense of independence (Bhachu 1988; George 2005), evidence confirms that cultural norms about gendered roles and positions in the family have remained strong in South

Asian families in the UK (Mand 2006; Jutlla 2103b; Singh and Tatla 2006).

The greater reliance on sons and daughters-in-law reflects the tradition that a daughter's priority, once she is married, is with her husband's family, as she is 'given away' on marriage (Lamb 2000, p.83). This cultural norm is where 'women are temporary members and guests in their natal household and, following marriage are seen as outsiders' (Mand 2006, p.5). This has caused complex situations and compromised loyalties for Sikh women who are married and caring for a biological parent (Jutlla 2011). Although it is widely acknowledged that women leave natal households to join and care for their husband, and, by extension, his household, research has indicated that women contest such ideological constructs (Jutlla 2011; Raheja and Gold 1994). Being 'given away' often means that a husband's mother has significant power over her daughters-in-law, as is the norm in their homeland (Lamb 2000). Although there is some evidence that this is starting to change, and women are becoming more independent, research with Sikh carers reveals the complexities of this situation when an older family member has developed dementia and consequently returns to such traditional norms (Jutlla 2011).

Gendered divisions of labour between older South Asian couples have also resulted in a greater reliance on children for support when their spouse becomes in need of care. Older South Asian female spousal carers, for example, often need guidance to manage family finances, previously a male responsibility (Jutlla 2011; Moreland 2001). Whilst older South Asian women may be able to manage the caring responsibilities at home, they often do not have access to wider social networks to help them to manage this care better. This is due to the ideological division in South Asian norms between the public and domestic space (Mand 2006). In Sikh families, for example, activities involving rituals and care provision performed in the context of the household are conceptualised as women's work, whereas those performed in the public sphere are traditionally thought of as men's work (Jutlla 2011; Mand 2002).

Boneham's (1989) study of older Sikh women in Leamington Spa showed, initially, that this group was well integrated in supportive family networks, although Boneham found a surprisingly high number of problems stemming from isolation and loneliness. Those Sikh older women who lived with their 'aspiring middle-class' sons and their families often reported being left alone, and away from their friends and the temple, which is an important place of congregation for Sikh women (Blakemore and Boneham 1994; Singh and Tatla 2006). These women were also discouraged from meeting out of doors in the UK, not only due to prevailing social norms, but also the adverse climate.

Many older South Asian women have thus remained in the home post-migration to the UK. The UK in the 1960s was reported as a 'hard and hostile environment in which to live' (Ballard and Ballard 1979, p.30), with many racist encounters on arrival (Jutlla 2014). This was another reason for women being encouraged to remain in the home post-migration, as it was not considered safe for them to be in the public domain. It is no surprise, therefore, that to care for their spouse with dementia, they relied heavily on their children for support with daily activities such as grocery shopping and attending hospital appointments (Jutlla 2011). This supports Bhachu's (1988) claim that whilst there may be geographical distance between family members, reciprocal obligatory relationships between independently resident siblings and parents and children may continue.

Research on male carers suggests that many have difficulties with domestic tasks such as cooking and cleaning, particularly those who have had to learn from scratch (Hamdy *et al.* 1998; Ribeiro and Paul 2008). Social isolation is also common amongst male carers (McDonnell and Ryan 2011; O'Brien, Ames and Burns 2000), particularly older South Asian men, who quite frequently mention wandering the streets, visiting parks or chatting in town precincts as ways of passing time and socialising (Blakemore and Boneham 1994; Jutlla 2011; Mand 2006). Whilst men are becoming more visible in caregiving research, there are still few studies that focus expressly on the extent to which the caring role has made positive contributions to their life and has been rewarding (Ribeiro and Paul 2008).

When considering the caregiving experiences of South Asian older men, research with the Sikh community in Wolverhampton evidenced how their migration experiences equipped Sikh older men with the skills to be able to manage the responsibilities associated with caring for their spouse with dementia (Jutlla 2014; Jutlla and Moreland 2009).

The industrial economic boom in Wolverhampton in the 1960s attracted large numbers of Sikh men from the Punjab who were prepared to do 'tedious and unpleasant jobs for very long hours' (Ballard and Ballard 1979, p.29). Although Sikh women also migrated to the UK for better employment opportunities, mainly to work in textiles (Hall 2002), men significantly outnumbered them (Papastergiadis 2000). Consequently, there arose a high proportion of all-male households whereby migrants lived in communal residences as a way of saving money (Ballard and Ballard 1979; James 1974). Such experiences meant that men very quickly learnt domestic skills, such as cooking and cleaning, before they called for their wives to join them to set up home. Consequently, those caring for their wives with dementia reported being able to cope effectively with taking over domestic chores, as these are skills they acquired post-migration.

Their self-efficacy and transferrable resiliency skills proved useful for helping them to manage the responsibilities associated with caring with their wives with dementia. Although the Sikh male carer experience may, in this respect, run counter to that of male carers in general, Sikh migrant men do appear to share the difficulties of social isolation experienced by other men caring for wives with dementia.

Caregiving for a person with dementia is often conceptualised as a separate role by mainstream services, perhaps due to the challenges and demands it carries with it. However, for most people, caring for a person with dementia is largely seen as an extension of one's relational role to the cared-for person (Heron 2000; Jutlla 2011; La Fontaine and Oyebode 2013; O'Connor 2007). As stated earlier, cultural norms about gendered roles and divisions of labour in the family are particularly strong in minority ethnic communities who, as a result of migration, have strengthened such norms (Jutlla 2011). Research with migrant communities has made evident the need for them to maintain their cultural identities (Gardner 2002; Jutlla 2011; Levitt 2001). Consequently, maintaining the responsibilities associated with their position in the family is considered a priority, especially when an older member of the family needs care (Jutlla 2011).

Because the Sikh community creates additional pressures for carers to have to cope with their situations, ambivalence arises about cultural norms. This was illustrated in the research I carried out in Wolverhampton (Jutlla 2011), where participants referred to 'the urban village culture'. Drawing out the experiences of the Sikh community in Wolverhampton reinforces the importance of locality when researching minority ethnic communities. The experiences of those who live in an area highly populated by their own community members (such as the Sikhs in Wolverhampton) may be different to those who live in an area populated predominantly by members of a different community, although more research is needed on this.

Although the community itself can create an additional pressure for South Asian carers, the desire to care for a family member at home is one that resonates with most people. Evidence from the All-Party Parliamentary Group (APPG) enquiry suggests that children from South Asian communities are beginning to understand that caring for older family members at home may not be practical (APPG on Dementia 2013). However, we must not forget that if the appropriate support is in place, there is no reason why caring for a family member with dementia at home could not be practical.

Dementia policy and practice literature has little considered how care might be negotiated within the family based on the different roles and positions and their associated responsibilities. Previous research has identified assumptions that families will 'look after their own' (DH 1998). The APPG on Dementia (2013) suggests that the risk of this stereotyping is a failure by services to reach out to minority ethnic communities and to ensure support is in place. Whilst there is evidence of South Asian families becoming more fragmented and nuclear (Jutlla 2013b; Moriarty and Webb 2000), care is still largely negotiated between family members (Jutlla 2011). The family as a resource is particularly important for those from minority ethnic communities, as they tend to either not be recognised by services, or lack knowledge of the services available to them (APPG on Dementia 2013; Jutlla 2011; Jutlla and Moreland 2007; Moriarty, Sharif and Robinson 2011). Another important factor in the experiences of South Asian carers is associated with the connotations of dementia as a condition.

Dementia and the stigma of mental illness

There is no word for 'dementia' in any of the South Asian languages (Punjabi, Hindi, Urdu, Gujarati and Bangladeshi), making it difficult to conceptualise dementia as the destruction of brain cells (Jutlla and Moreland 2007; Mackenzie 2006; Seabrooke and Milne 2004). Consequently, the behavioural symptoms of the person with dementia are often misunderstood as the effects of old age (Jolley *et al.* 2009; Jutlla and Moreland 2007; Seabrooke and Milne 2004). As the dementia progresses, the person will present symptoms beyond memory loss dependent on the type of dementia they are living with.

Vascular dementia is common in South Asian communities due to higher incidences of hypertension and diabetes (Moriarty *et al.* 2011). In addition to memory problems, the symptoms of vascular dementia include the following: problems with the speed of thinking, concentration and communication;

seizures; periods of severe (acute) confusion; hallucinations; and psychological symptoms such as becoming more obsessive (Alzheimer's Society 2014b). Without an understanding that these symptoms are the result of the lack of blood supply to brain cells, the existence of such symptoms can be seen as a person being possessed or consumed by an evil spirit – thus leading families to seek spiritual healing (APPG on Dementia 2013; Jolley *et al.* 2009; Jutlla and Moreland 2007).

Whilst there is a stigma of mental illness in society in general, the particular stigma of mental illness in South Asian communities has been well reported (Jutlla and Moreland 2007; Mackenzie 2006; Seabrooke and Milne 2004; Turner and Benbow 2002). Although this is due, in part, to a general lack of knowledge and understanding about dementia and what it involves, my research with Sikh carers of a person with dementia highlighted the need for further investigation about the concept of mental illness in South Asian communities. Those participants who were well educated about the symptoms of dementia and what it involves considered it an illness triggered by a traumatic event in the person's life. Furthermore, events that were considered traumatic were those that opposed certain cultural norms. For example, a British-born Sikh woman believed that her mother's dementia was triggered by the fact that all her sisters (with the exception of herself) married white British men. A Sikh man from rural Punjab caring for his wife similarly believed that his wife's dementia was triggered when their son got divorced. Both individuals were well educated about the prognosis of dementia.

This area is worthy of further investigation than was possible in this research. An in-depth understanding of the concept of mental health in South Asian communities will better inform practice initiatives that seek to raise awareness and improve knowledge of dementia in such communities. For example, it was recently suggested that dementia should be presented as a medical condition to reduce the stigma of the illness in South Asian communities (EFID Workshop on Empowerment and Inclusion 2014). Consequently, South Asian families may seek help from services prior to reaching crisis point, as is currently the case (Saad, Smith and Rochfort 2008; Seabrooke and Milne 2009).

It has been suggested that South Asian families are reluctant to seek help from services due to wanting to portray an image of wellbeing to those outside of the family (Jutlla 2011; Jutlla and Moreland 2007; Seabrooke and Milne 2004). According to Mackenzie (2006), this is largely due to arranged marriages that are still practised in the UK today and involve the joining of two families. Proposals are made from within the community based on a family's status, reputation and respect. Illnesses such as dementia thus remain hidden from the community, as there is concern that exposure could lead to the refusal of a marriage proposal, especially where there is an unmarried daughter in the family (Mackenzie 2006; Mackenzie *et al.* 2003). Some may fear that seeking help from services may reveal their circumstances within their community. That is not to say that all South Asian families do not seek help, and those that have, have experiences of health and social care services that are important to consider.

Experiences of health and social care services

Inspectorial evidence about the experiences of health and social care services for those from minority ethnic communities has revealed the presence of language and cultural barriers within services, making it difficult for South Asian communities to both access and make use of services efficiently (APPG on Dementia 2013; Moriarty *et al.* 2011; Rauf 2011). South Asian carers of people with dementia have reported services as culturally inappropriate due to a lack of awareness associated with their various faiths, cultural norms and dietary requirements (Jutlla 2011; Jutlla and Moreland 2007). As for most people, the first port of call for guidance and assistance with a health problem is the general practitioner (GP). As many older members of South Asian communities, particularly women, do not have access to wider social and support networks, the GP is not just the *first* port of call, but for some, the *only* port of call.

Research with South Asian carers of a person with dementia in Wolverhampton revealed that these communities held a hierarchy of creditability amongst health professionals, with medical doctors considered the most knowledgeable (Jutlla and Moreland 2007). Further research revealed that although many families reached services at crisis point, they had previously contacted their GP several times, and the GP had reinforced the misconception that the symptoms presented were the effects of old age (Jutlla 2011). In-service education for GPs about dementia is thus crucial to improve early detection of dementia in South Asian communities, and to ensure there is a timely diagnosis (Jolley *et al.* 2009; Moriarty *et al.* 2011).

South Asians may well be socially excluded as service users due in part to institutionalised racism that has led to the mistrust of health and social care services in the UK (Jutlla 2014; Patel *et al.* 1998). Moreover, according to Blakemore and Boneham (1994, p.78), 'Asian people's social lives and priorities are often seen as "too different" from majority norms, incomprehensible and insufficiently adapted.' Research with Sikh carers revealed that experiences of hostility and white racism on arrival to the UK have continued rather than changed over time, causing migrant Sikh carers to connect their experiences of health and social care services in the UK with their particular experiences of white racism and exclusion recalled from their past. Consequently, the self-efficacy and resiliency accrued from their individual experiences of migration were employed to cope with and manage caregiving (Jutlla 2014).

A small-scale action research project was recently conducted with health and social care staff to identify issues they faced when working with people with dementia from minority ethnic communities (Jutlla and Lillyman 2014). This study revealed a lack of communication and trust with family members. This not only resulted in limited information about the needs and wants of the person with dementia, but also caused staff to feel marginalised and excluded. Such feelings often led to a lack of motivation and self-worth amongst staff working with such people, particularly as it created an additional barrier to supporting the person with dementia to live well. The need to improve communication between health and social care staff and minority ethnic families is a key area that needs to be addressed.

Using real-life case examples from the participants, this study also identified how cultural norms are both cross-cutting and accumulative, depending on a person's attributes and personal history. Consequently, notions of homogeneity were questioned, and the need for education and training on the person-centred approach to dementia care (Brooker 2007; Kitwood 1997) was identified.

Recommendations for policy and practice

An in-depth exploration of the experiences of South Asian carers of a family member with dementia in the UK has highlighted a number of recommendations for dementia policy and practice initiatives. First, services need to 'reach out' to South Asian families and ensure that support is in place that helps the cared-for person to live well with dementia at home. Although this should be the case for all families, regardless of ethnic background, services should understand that care may be negotiated between family members depending on their role and position in the family. For example, cultural norms associated with roles and positions in the family may mean that some carers, particularly daughters-in-law, remain hidden from services. With this in mind, assumptions should not be made that members of South Asian communities choose, or prefer, to 'look after their own', and consequently do not require support from services.

Second, there is a need to raise awareness and improve knowledge about dementia amongst South Asian communities, and this is beginning to be addressed (see, for example, Alzheimer's Society 2013). Third, there needs to be in-service education about dementia for GPs to promote timely diagnosis and early intervention, and to subsequently reduce the number of people from South Asian communities who are reaching services at crisis point. Although it is necessary to improve communication and rapport between health and social care staff and family members to reduce language barriers, education and training should also include information about the issues and challenges for those from minority ethnic communities in the UK, which will include their experiences of migration.

Life histories are important for understanding possible complex behaviours, and are an essential component for providing person-centred dementia care. Whilst South Asian communities share a similar experience and face particular challenges in getting the support they need, there are some differences, both within and between these communities. With this in mind, services should acknowledge and respond to the differences within and between all minority ethnic communities and, at an individual level, ensure a person-centred approach is taken.

Conclusion

South Asian carers' experiences of caring for a family member with dementia are influenced by a number of factors. Firstly, there are cultural norms associated with roles and positions in South Asian families that impact on the way that caring tasks are managed and negotiated. Secondly, dementia can be understood as a mental illness and therefore its associated stigma can often lead to carers not making use of services to maintain an image of well being within their community. Thirdly, it is often difficult for South Asian Carers to access and make efficient use of health and social care services, especially where there are language and cultural barriers. Research with Sikh carers of a family member with dementia further revealed how migration experiences can impact on caregiving experiences, including their experience of health and social care services.

In addition to the recommendations for dementia policy and practice initiatives made earlier, this chapter has also highlighted some areas that would be worthy of further investigation. A deeper understanding of the concept of mental illness in South

Asian communities would better inform practice initiatives seeking to raise awareness about dementia in such communities. It would also be useful to investigate whether the cultural norms reported in this chapter are pertinent for members of South Asian communities who live in areas that are less populated by members of their own community, in order to understand whether they have an impact (or not) on experiences of caregiving in the same way they do for carers who are part of well-established communities in a given area.

Overall, policy-makers and practitioners are advised to remain sensitive to the issues and challenges faced by members of South Asian communities caring for a family member with dementia, but at the same time, they are also advised not to make generalisations. We should not forget that at the essence of person-centred dementia care is the need to respect, appreciate and understand the uniqueness and diversity of individuals, families and communities.

References

Ablitt, A., Jones, G.V. and Muers, J. (2009) 'Living with dementia: a systematic review of the influence of relationship factors.' *Aging and Mental Health 13*, 4, 497–511.

Ahmad, W.I.U. and Atkin, K. (eds) (1997) *'Race' and Community Care.* Buckingham: Open University Press.

Alzheimer's Society (2013) *Alzheimer's Society Launches Volunteer Project Reaching Out to BME Communities in London.* London: Alzheimer's Society. Available at www.alzheimers.org.uk/site/scripts/news_article.php?newsID=1478, accessed on 21 January 2014.

Alzheimer's Society (2014a) *Caring for a Person with Dementia.* London: Alzheimer's Society. Available at www.alzheimers.org.uk/site/scripts/home_info.php?homepageID=53, accessed on 21 January 2014.

Alzheimer's Society (2014b) *What is Vascular Dementia?* London: Alzheimer's Society. Available at www.alzheimers.org.uk/site/scripts/documents_info.php?documentID=161, accessed on 12 May 2014.

APPG (All-Party Parliamentary Group) on Dementia (2013) *Dementia Does Not Discriminate: The Experiences of Black, Asian and Minority Ethnic Communities.* July. London: Alzheimer's Society. Available at www.alzheimers.org.uk/site/scripts/download_info.php?downloadID=1186, accessed on 11 December 2014.

Ballard, R. and Ballard, C. (1979) 'The Sikhs: The Development of South Asian Settlements in Britain.' In J.L Watson (ed.) *Between Two Cultures: Migrants and Minorities in Britain.* Oxford: Basil Blackwell.

Bhachu, P. (1988) 'Apni Marzi Kardhi: Home and Work, Sikh Women in Britain.' In S. Westwood and P. Bhachu (eds) *Enterprising Women: Ethnicity, Economy, and Gender Relations.* London: Routledge.

Blakemore, K. and Boneham, M. (1994) *Age, Race and Ethnicity: A Comparative Approach.* Buckingham: Open University Press.

Boneham, M. (1989) 'Ageing and ethnicity in Britain: The case of elderly Sikh women in a Midlands town.' *New Community 15*, 3, 447–459.

Botsford, J., Clarke, C.L. and Gibb, E. (2011) 'Research and dementia, caring and ethnicity: a review of the literature.' *Journal of Research in Nursing 16*, 5, 437–449.

Bowes, A. and Wilkinson, H. (2003) '"We didn't know it would get that bad": South Asian experiences of dementia and the service response.' *Health and Social Care in the Community 11*, 5, 387–396.

Brodaty, H., Gresham, M. and Luscombe, G. (2007) 'The Prince Henry hospital dementia family caregivers training programme.' *Revista Română de Psihiatrie, seria a III-a 15*, 5, 425–434.

Brooker, D. (2007) *Person-Centred Dementia Care: Making Services Better.* London: Jessica Kingsley Publications.

Buffin, J., Shah. A. and Syed, A. (2009) *Managing Better Mental Health Care for BME Elders.* June. Preston: Policy Research Institute on Ageing and Ethnicity and University of Central Lancashire.

DH (Department of Health) (1998) *They Look After Their Own Don't They? Inspection of Community Care Services for Black and Minority Ethnic Older People.* London: DH.

Dwyer, J.W. and Coward, R.T. (eds) (1992) *Gender, Families and Elder Care.* London: Sage.

EFID Workshop on Empowerment and Inclusion (26 March 2014) *Involving People with Dementia from Ethnic Minority Groups and their Families in the Community.* Brussels: Philanthropy House.

Froelich, L., Andreasen, N., Tsolaki, M., Foucher, A. *et al.* (2009) 'Long-term treatment of patients with Alzheimer's disease in primary and secondary care: results from an international survey.' *Current Medical Research and Opinion 25*, 12, 3059–68.

Gardner, K. (2002) *Age, Narrative and Migration.* Oxford: Berg.

George, S.M. (2005) *When Women Come First. Gender and Class in Transnational Migration.* London: University of California Press.

Globerman, J. (1996) 'Motivations to care: daughters- and sons-in-law caring for relatives with Alzheimer's disease.' *Family Relations 45*, 1, 37–45.

Hall, R.A. (2002) 'When is a wife not a wife? Some observations on the immigration experiences of South Asian women in West Yorkshire.' *Contemporary Politics 8*, 1, 65–68.

Hamdy, R.C., Turnbull, J.M., Edwards, J. and Lancaster, M.M. (1998) *Alzheimer's Disease. A Handbook for Caregivers.* 3rd edn. Mosby, MO: Missouri.

Hellström, I., Nolan, M. and Lundh, U. (2007) 'Sustaining "couplehood": Spouses' strategies for living positively with dementia.' *Dementia 6*, 3, 383–409.

Heron, C. (2000) *Working with Carers.* London: Jessica Kingsley Publishers.

James, A.G. (1974) *Sikh Children in Britain.* London: Oxford University Press.

Jolley, D., Moreland, N., Read, K., Kaur, H., Jutlla, K. and Clark, M. (2009) 'The "Twice a Child" projects: learning about dementia and related disorders within the black and minority ethnic population of an English city and improving relevant services.' *Journal of Ethnicity and Inequalities in Health and Social Care 2*, 4, 4–9.

Jutlla, K. (2011) 'Caring for a Person with Dementia: A Qualitative Study of the Experiences of the Sikh Community in Wolverhampton.' November. PhD thesis, Keele University.

Jutlla, K. (2013a) 'Ethnicity and cultural diversity in dementia care: a review of the research.' *Journal of Dementia Care 21*, 2, 33–39.

Jutlla, K. (2013b) 'Cultural norms about the roles of older people in Sikh families.' In A. Singh (ed.) *Indian Diaspora: Voices of Grandparents and Grandparenting.* Boston, MA: Sense Publishers.

Jutlla, K. (2014) 'The impact of migration experiences and migration identities on the experiences of services and caring for a family member with dementia for Sikhs living in Wolverhampton, UK.' *Ageing and Society*, 18 July 2014.

Jutlla, K. and Lillyman, S. (2014) 'An action research study engaging in the use of story boarding as research based approach to teaching to identify issues faced when working with people with dementia from ethnic communities.' *Worcester Journal of Learning and Teaching*, 9. Available at www.worc.ac.uk/edu/documents/Action_Research_engaging_in_the_use_of_storyboarding_Jutlla_and_Lillyman.pdf, accessed on 30 January 2015.

Jutlla, K. and Moreland, N. (2007) *Twice a Child III: The Experiences of Asian Carers of Older People with Dementia in Wolverhampton.* March. West Midlands: Fordementiaplus.

Jutlla, K. and Moreland, N. (2009) 'The personalisation of dementia services and existential realities: understanding Sikh carers caring for an older person with dementia in Wolverhampton.' *Journal of Ethnicity and Inequalities in Health and Social Care 2*, 4, 10–21.

Kannan, H., Bolge, S.C., Del Valle, M., Alvir, J. and Petrie, C.D. (2011) 'The association between Alzheimer's disease symptom severity and caregiver outcomes: a cross-sectional study.' *The Primary Care Companion to CNS Disorders 13*, 3, 995–1006. Available at http://europepmc.org/abstract/PMC/PMC3184568, accessed on 30 January 2015.

Keady, J. and Nolan, M. (2003) 'The dynamics of dementia: working together, working separately or working alone?' In M. Nolan, U. Lundh, G. Grant and J. Keady (eds) *Partnerships in Family Care: Understanding the Caregiving Career.* Buckingham: Open University Press.

Kitwood, T. (1997) *Dementia Reconsidered: The Person Comes First.* Buckingham: Open University Press.

La Fontaine, J. and Oyebode, J.R. (2013) 'Family relationships and dementia: a synthesis of qualitative research including the person with dementia.' *Ageing & Society 34*, 7, 1243–1272.

Lamb, S. (2000) *White Saris and Sweet Mangoes: Aging, Gender, and Body in North India.* London: University of California Press.

Levitt, P. (2001) *The Transnational Villagers.* London: University of California Press.

Mackenzie, J. (2006) 'Stigma and dementia - East European and South Asian family carers negotiating stigma in the UK.' *Dementia: The International Journal of Social Research and Practice 5*, 2, 233-248.

Mackenzie, J., Coates, D., Ashraf, F., Gallagher, T. and Ismail, L. (2003) *Understanding and Supporting South Asian and Eastern European Family Carers of People with Dementia.* Bradford: Bradford Dementia Group, University of Bradford.

Mand, K. (2002) 'Place, gender, power in transnational Sikh marriages.' *Global Networks: A Journal of Transnational Affairs 2*, 3, 233–248.

Mand, K. (2006) *Social Capital and Transnational South Asian Families: Rituals, Care and Provision.* Families and Social Capital ESRC Research Group. Working Paper No. 18. March. London: London South Bank University.

McDonnell, E. and Ryan, A.A. (2011) 'Male caregiving in dementia: a review and commentary.' *Dementia 12*, 2, 238–50

Moreland, N. (2001) *Twice a Child: Dementia Care for African-Caribbean and Asian Older People in Wolverhampton.* West Midlands: Fordementiaplus.

Moreland, N. (2003) *Twice a Child II: Dementia Care for African-Caribbean and Asian Older People in Wolverhampton.* West Midlands: Fordementiaplus.

Moriarty, J. and Webb, S. (2000) *Part of their Lives: Community Care for Older People with Dementia.* Bristol: Policy Press.

Moriarty, J., Sharif, N. and Robinson, J. (March 2011) *Black and Minority Ethnic People with Dementia and their Access to Support and Services. Research Briefing.* London: Social Care Institute for Excellence.

ONS (Office for National Statistics) (2012) 'Ethnicity and National Identity in England and Wales 2011.' December. London: ONS. Available at www.ons.gov.uk/ons/dcp171776_290558.pdf, accessed on 26 February 2014.

O'Brien, J., Ames, D. and Burns, A. (eds) (2000) *Dementia.* 2nd edn. London: Arnold.

O'Connor, D. (2007) 'Developing a caregiver identity: the positioning process.' *Journal of Aging Studies 21*, 2, 165–174.

Papastergiadis, N. (2000) *The Turbulence of Migration.* Cambridge: Polity Press.

Patel, N., Mirza, N.R., Lindbald, P., Amstrup, K. and Samaoli, O. (1998) *Dementia: Minority Ethnic Older People. Managing Care in the UK, Denmark, and France.* Lyme Regis: Russell House Publishing Ltd.

Raheja, G. and Gold, A. (1994) *Listen to the Heron's Words: Reimagining Gender and Kinship in North India.* Berkeley, CA: University of California Press.

Rauf, A. (2011) *Caring for Dementia: Exploring Good Practice on Supporting South Asian Carers through Access to Culturally Competent Service Provision.* Bradford: Meri Yaadein Dementia Team.

Ribeiro, O. and Paul, C. (2008) 'Older male carers and the positive aspects of care.' *Ageing and Society 28*, 2, 165–183.

Rochfort, M. (2008) *The 9th Darzi Clinical Pathway Group.* West Midlands: Care Services Improvement Partnership.

Saad, K., Smith, P. and Rochfort, M. (2008) *Caring for People with Dementia: It's Really Time To Do Something Now!* West Midlands: West Midlands Strategic Health Authority.

Seabrooke, V. and Milne, A. (2004) *Culture and Care in Dementia: A Study of the Asian Community in Northwest Kent.* January. London: Mental Health Foundation.

Seabrooke, V. and Milne, A. (2009) 'Early intervention in dementia care in an Asian Community. Lessons from a dementia collaborative project.' *Quality in Ageing 10*, 4, 29–36.

Shah, A., Oommen, G. and Wuntakal, B. (2005) 'Cross-cultural aspects of dementia.' *Psychiatry 4*, 2, 103–106.

Singh, G. and Tatla, D.S. (2006) *Sikhs in Britain: The Making of a Community.* London: Zed Books.

Turner, S.J. and Benbow, S.M. (2002) 'Dementia, stigma and the general practitioner.' *Hospital Update 64*, 1, 45–47.

Yeo, G. and Gallagher-Thompson, D. (eds) (1996) *Ethnicity and the Dementias.* London: Taylor & Francis.

7

ACCESS, ASSESSMENT AND ENGAGEMENT

Vincent Goodorally

This chapter discusses issues associated with access, assessment and engagement. It explores some of the challenges which health and social care services should address in meeting the needs of people from some black and minority ethnic (BME) communities in relation to dementia. Highlighting the importance of a meaningful assessment process, it introduces a specific assessment tool – the modified Culturagram – which has been adapted for use in the UK and which offers a framework to assist practitioners in learning about the cultural needs of the people with whom they are in contact.

Challenges of service provision

In the UK people living with dementia use a range of care services, from points of pre-diagnosis through to end of life. Their family carers may also need support in their caring role and also after the person with dementia has died. A range of organisations provide services: the National Health Services (NHS), social care services, social enterprises, and the private sector and voluntary sector (large charitable organisations and small BME-specific groups).

Access to various services is complicated by their funding and provision. Health services, subject to immigration status (European citizenship and evidence of a National Insurance number), are free at the point of entry. In England and Wales social care services (subject to immigration status) are needs-led, means-tested and chargeable. However, personal/social and nursing care is currently free in Scotland, whereas the private sector is available to anyone with the financial means to pay for it. The voluntary sector subsidises the real costs of their services to the individual. Both health and social care (as purchasers) commission services from social enterprises, the private and voluntary sector (providers). Health and social care systems are very complex. They have their own policies, procedures and information systems. Integrated health and social care older people's mental health teams, whilst claiming to provide more holistic approaches for people with dementia, remain ad hoc in their existence, and are not equitably available in all areas.

All health and social care institutions and services are regulated and inspected by the Care Quality Commission (CQC), an independent quality monitoring body. Providers are expected to comply, with the set CQC standards inspection reports being publicly accessible. It is generally acknowledged that there is wide variation in the quality of dementia care services, with the public perception often one that is negative. The negative experiences of people with dementia from BME communities were recognised over 30 years ago (Glendenning 1982). They face the same challenges as any other service user, but may additionally experience problems associated with language, stigma and racism.

At a national level a raft of policies, for example, the National Dementia Strategy (DH 2009) and legislation, the Equality Act 2010, have sought to address the identified issues that affect BME groups. At a regional level, the newly formed Clinical Commissioning Groups (CCGs) can commission services specifically for BME needs as identified by the Joint Strategic Needs Assessment (JSNA) of people with dementia. However, there is evidence that the JSNA was not used effectively in understanding the needs of BME populations (APPG on Dementia 2013). There are many challenges to delivering culturally appropriate dementia care services in the UK, and whilst there are examples of truly innovative services (APPG on Dementia 2013), these are few and far between.

Challenges can exist at macro and micro levels. At a macro level the concept of *customer care* is underdeveloped in health and social care compared to that in the retail industry. The tendency in health care is to commission a service or fulfil an obligation rather than provide a quality experience. Often the approach in dementia care is to bring people with dementia together, to deliver a communal service with an assumption that they all have the same interests (Cox and Flood 2013). An example might be to bring all socially isolated BME people together in an ethnic-specific day centre when a befriender may be more appropriate.

BME people with dementia may benefit from a variety of care options, such as extra care or sheltered housing, or the shared lives scheme. However, they are not always offered these opportunities equitably to other groups. Large well-established BME-specific voluntary organisations, for example, Jewish Care, are able to provide a wide range of culturally appropriate services (including dementia care). Smaller BME generic or dementia-specific organisations are often very popular with the families affected by dementia, although they struggle to survive, not just from lack of funding and unsuitable buildings for older people, but also support from mainstream services and infrastructure. As a result they may be forced to discontinue a service with no other provider being able to take on that role.

In England and Wales dementia care is generally the remit of mental health institutions rather than neurological services, whereas in Scotland the reverse is the norm. In addition, within the wider field of mental health, working with people with dementia is not seen as an attractive proposition from a career perspective or in pay and remuneration. Recruitment and retention across dementia services, whether health or social, is a major issue. Bilingual and bicultural staff with a general nursing qualification may have excellent dementia care skills but cannot work in older people's mental health services as they do not have a mental health qualification. As a result, many positions cannot be filled, despite funding being available.

The National Audit Office (NAO 2007) highlighted the maze that many families affected by dementia have to navigate. Such navigation is even harder for someone with language or other communication difficulties. Admiral Nurses (qualified nurses specialising in dementia care) and dementia navigators are of enormous help to people living with dementia and their families. Admiral Nurses have an excellent understanding of the care system, and their services have consistently been highly praised by families affected by dementia from all backgrounds. However, access to such a service is patchy, their numbers being few across the country. Truswell (2013) has demonstrated the particular economic benefits of having a dementia navigator dedicated to working with ethnic communities. At practice level the challenges are different, and Sewell's (2009) model helps to illuminate what might be the associated issues. Sewell's model comprises of '4 Ps' (patient/service users, practitioners, physical interventions, and psychosocial supports), which are centrally glued by relationships.

Building relationships and developing trust to deliver person-centred care to families from BME communities takes time, knowledge and specific skills. Hard-pressed practitioners can often end up taking a task-orientated approach and making certain cultural assumptions, such as those made about the individual based on their real or perceived ethnic identity – for example, 'they look after their own' can prevail and remain unchallenged if supervision and reflective practice is not in place.

The patient factors surrounding lack of engagement with services can be varied. Some may simply not be aware of the existence of health, social and voluntary sector services; they may believe services are culturally inappropriate or insensitive; they may have had a poor experience of services (Lindesay *et al.* 1997); they may perceive the psychiatrist to be unhelpful and the GP to have insufficient time (Lawrence *et al.* 2006). Physical co-morbid conditions, such as diabetes and high blood pressure, are treatable risk factors for dementia, but are also more common in some BME communities, so access to sympathetic and knowledgeable medical support is essential. Services to treat dementia and co-morbidities are not well integrated, and finding the funding for health promotion initiatives for such at-risk groups is a challenge when resources are scarce.

Psychosocial interventions, for example, cognitive stimulation therapy and reminiscence therapy, have been shown to be effective in improving the quality of life of people with dementia. However, these interventions may need to be adapted to meet identified cultural needs. Finally, BME groups may have experienced disadvantages associated with race, culture and ethnicity, not just in the UK, but also from their country of origin. However, when they do use mainstream services, their expectation is that they are treated with respect, feel safe and staff should behave with integrity.

Engaging effectively with people from minority ethnic groups

Engagement, by definition, is a two-way process, involving listening and interaction with a goal that is one of mutual benefit. The main approaches to effective engagement include informing, consulting and collaborating. The people with dementia, their families and the communities in which they live should be seen as partners in care by service providers. Staff engagement in finding solutions to care issues is a key tenet of the NHS constitution (DH 2013), with meaningful engagement of users being one of the building blocks of delivering race equality (DH 2005). Wenger, McDermott and Synder (2002) suggest the use of a stakeholder analysis template to assist with the engagement and participation process. The template sets out to record the names of the stakeholders, their level of power and influence, and the best, or preferred, way of communication, for example, face-to-face. Community profiles and JSNAs provide a wealth of information to support this engagement process. However, an understanding of the target communities' attitudes, beliefs and values about dementia is essential to the success of such a process. This can be gained through a variety of means: from academic articles, community partners, or within the organisation through bilingual and bicultural practitioners. However, Dominelli (1992) warns against the danger of using team members from a BME background to find and implement solutions.

Involving a community through their spiritual representatives, for example, an imam, is also important. They are often willing to share a basic understanding of their culture with professionals by explaining a few greeting words, how to show respect, etc. Other practitioners, such as trusted community development workers, can assist with any engagement initiative.

Practitioners could use events such as Black History Month to help reduce barriers and generate trust. Providing dementia awareness-raising sessions to local BME champions, including interpreters and businesses, will help with the collaborating process. Finally, using terms and meanings that the community find more acceptable, for example, 'memory loss' instead of 'dementia', and 'caring for an ageing family member' instead of the term 'carer', may help in engaging the audience in the first instance.

Approaches to outreach

Making change happen requires planning. Various local community stakeholders will assist with the change process. Some groups, for example, South Asian people, are under-represented in dementia services. Voluntary sector organisations such as the Alzheimer's Society and Friends of the Elderly, with additional funding from mainstream commissioners, have sought to address this imbalance by employing outreach workers and volunteers from the target communities. The aims of such projects are to raise awareness of dementia in the communities, to develop health promotion approaches and inform local commissioning. Whilst such projects have been successful in meeting their objectives, they tend to operate in areas where there is already a significant BME population. However, where there are small numbers of BME people, for example, in rural areas, there is a danger that these people may end up very isolated. Specialist dementia workers, such as Admiral Nurses, are in a good position to undertake such outreach work.

The Dementia Local Implementation (DLI) group provides an excellent opportunity for networking and garnering support from others. The intranet and local BME media and business community may offer invaluable practical support, such as advertising events, funding for dementia awareness-raising sessions, leaflets translated for the target audience, bilingual professionals, etc. Services must develop trust and credibility in the communities they serve, as such outreach work will only be successful if staff in all dementia care services are attuned to the needs of people from diverse backgrounds (Daker-White *et al.* 2002).

Assessment

Assessment is a holistic process that involves gaining an overview of any given situation; this has been referred to as the *helicopter vision* (Thompson 2009). It is more than just gathering information or identifying needs and what services should be provided; it is also a collaborative effort that involves undertaking an interview as part of the assessment process (Sewell 2009); thus, assessment is not a neutral experience, as the assessor brings a lot of himself/herself into the process. Gutheil and Heyman (2005) discuss that cultural issues are a crucial but often overlooked component of the assessment process, and point out that a narrow assessment can lead to considerable difficulties later.

Addressing cultural and ethnicity issues in social work practice dates back to the 1980s, and is now included in the curriculum for social work training. The nursing profession, on the other hand, seems to have taken the person-centred approach, with some ascribing to trans-cultural nursing practice. People from BME communities living with dementia are likely to be supported by different family members. Therefore, an understanding of the family systems and dynamics will assist the practitioner in gaining the helicopter vision.

Assessing cultural needs

A literature search conducted by the author in 2011 identified a lack of validated family assessment tools in use in the UK that specifically addressed culture and ethnicity in dementia. The search identified a generic assessment framework in use in adult social care in the US that appeared to have the potential to be adapted for this use. The 'Culturagram' (Congress 2008) is an assessment tool/framework developed in the US to help health care professionals to recognise and address the needs of culturally diverse people. Whilst it has received some interest outside the US, its use in the UK has been limited. For example, Chau (2008) claimed that using the Culturagram helped health care professionals explore the needs of the Chinese community (and other minority ethnic groups) in the UK. The tool is sensitive to the culture and ethnic background of individuals, and fits with the concept of cultural competence (Laird 2008), but would need modification for use in the UK, where different health care systems apply (Parker and Bradley 2011).

In its presentation, the Culturagram is a diagrammatic aid to assessment, and addresses ten important factors, with the family at the centre.

Modified UK Culturagram

The author made a successful application to the Foundation of Nursing Studies (FoNS) Patients First Programme[1] to carry out a practice development project looking at improving the experiences of the assessment process in dementia care. A detailed description of the project as a whole can be found elsewhere (see Goodorally 2014), but one element within the broader project was to explore the use of the Culturagram tool and to adapt it for use within dementia care settings in the UK.

1 See www.fons.org/programmes/patients-first.aspx

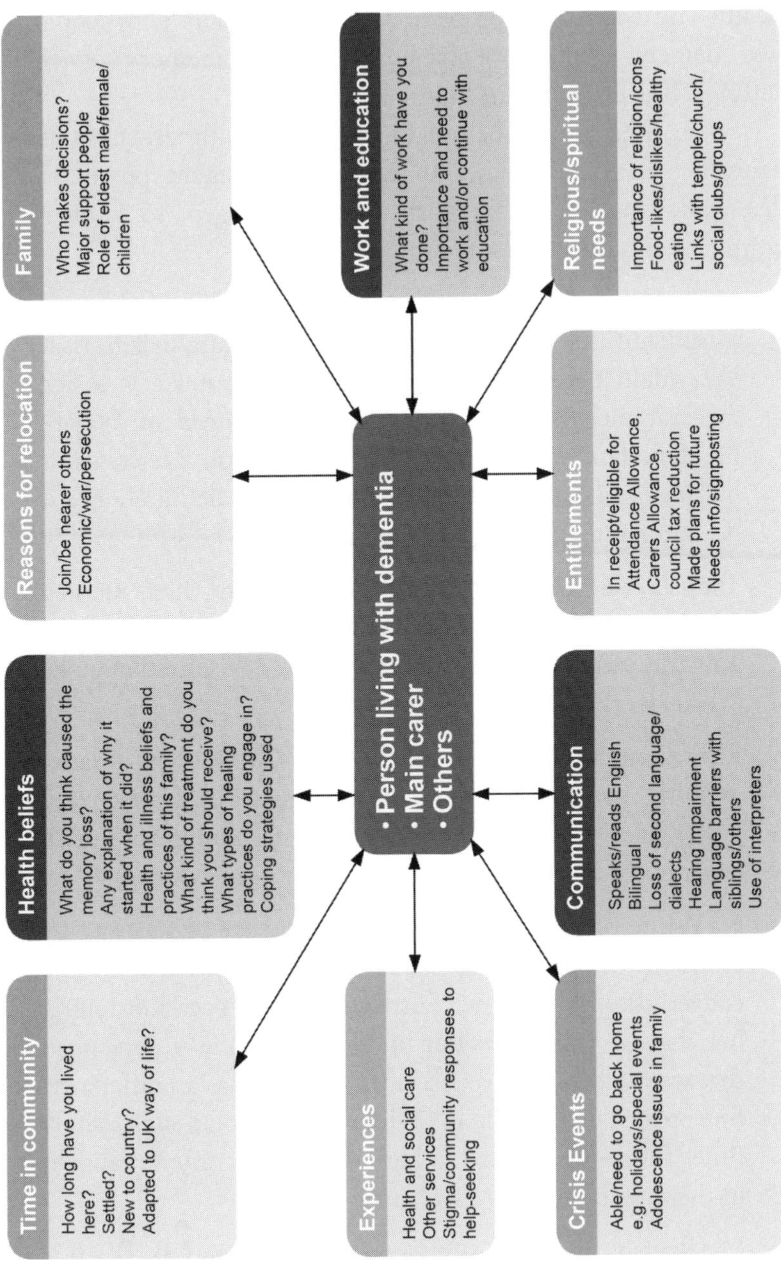

Source: Adapted from Congress, E. and Kung, W. (2005) 'Using the Culturagram to assess and empower culturally diverse families.' In E. Congress and M. Gonzalez *Multicultural Perspectives in Working with Families.* New York: Springer Publishing Company, pp.3-21.

The modified Culturagram was developed in consultation with health and social care professionals, family carers and people with dementia, within mental health care and memory service settings. It is presented in Figure 7.1.

So far, it has proved helpful in promoting culturally sensitive assessments, as an adjunct to existing assessment processes. The following feedback, with names changed to protect confidentiality, illustrates its perceived value:

> M. [a White Irish man with memory impairment] found it difficult to grasp the concept of culture/belief/crisis. We would need a stock list of phrases to make it easier, for example, the word 'understanding' instead of 'belief'. He definitely enjoyed being seen as a person. He said this has made him think about his faith. I will definitely use it [Culturagram] again.' (Social worker)

> The service user [White British woman] had marked cognitive impairment [...] difficult to explain to her. I can see how this can help us work in a more person-centred manner. (Social worker)

> Easy enough to use with service user [Greek Cypriot lady] as all the questions we would ask in an assessment any way. I particularly liked the questions about community, health experiences and faith. (Community psychiatric nurse)

> S. [White British woman with dementia] can be very prickly especially when talking about her memory. Most of the conversation is with her husband, on this occasion telling her that we want to better understand you as a person, so that we can best help you, seem[s] to have made a difference. She opened up and told me I did not know all in such a short time. They both seemed to have enjoyed the interest shown in them. (Community psychiatric nurse)

> L. [British Asian] is supporting her husband B. [British Asian with dementia]. L. has been stressed in her caring role but has been reluctant to let B. attend the local day centre,

> although he enjoyed the days out. I now realise how lonely she is. Perhaps another approach is needed. (Admiral Nurse)

As the quotes above show, using the Culturagram in practice was found by staff to aid the assessment process, in particular around cultural issues that might otherwise have been missed. However, a comprehensive and systematic evaluation of its use is now needed. Whilst these results are encouraging, in the case of its use here, additional factors may also have been at play, not least the fact that staff sensitivities around cultural issues had been heightened because of involvement in a broader practice development project on assessment, culture and ethnicity, and furthermore, because users may have felt a sense of ownership of the tool as a result of their direct input in the process of refining it. What seems important is that spotlighting cultural issues, in this case around the use of the Culturagram tool, can have very positive consequences in ensuring that cultural issues are addressed within the assessment process.

Conclusion

This chapter has explored some of the challenges faced by people from BME groups in accessing dementia services, and has focused on the need to develop positive approaches to promote engagement. One specific cultural assessment framework has been presented here. Ideally, however, all assessments would be conducted in culturally competent ways, and practitioners and the services they work within would be open to seeing and responding to the cultural needs in prospective and existing service users.

References

APPG (All-Party Parliamentary Group) on Dementia (2013) *Dementia Does Not Discriminate: The Experiences of Black, Asian and Minority Ethnic Communities.* July. London: Alzheimer's Society. Available at www.alzheimers.org.uk/site/scripts/download_info.php?downloadID=1186, accessed on 11 December 2014.

Chau, R.C.M. (2008) *Health Experience of Chinese People in the UK.* A Race Equality Foundation Briefing Paper, Briefing 10.

Congress, E.P. (2008) 'Visual Assessment tools – the Culturagram.' Available at http://socialworkpodcast.blogspot.co.uk/2008/12/visual-assessment-tools-culturagram.html, accessed on 31 January 2014.

Congress, E.P. and Kung, W. (2005) 'Using the Culturagram to assess and empower culturally diverse families.' In E. Congress and M. Gonzalez (eds) *Multicultural Perspectives in Working with Families.* New York: Springer Publishing Company.

Cox, C. and Flood, R. (2013) *Design Challenge: Living Well with Dementia.* Supplementary Information Report. London: Design Council.

Daker-White, G., Beattie, A., Gilliard, J. and Means, R. (2002) 'Minority ethnic groups in dementia care: a review of service needs, service provision and models of good practice.' Aging and Mental Health 6, 2, 101–108.

DH (Department of Health) (2005) *Delivering Race Equality in Mental Health Care: An Action Plan for Reform Inside and Outside Services and the Government's Response to the Death of David Bennett.* London: DH.

DH (2009) *Living Well with Dementia: A National Dementia Strategy.* London: DH.

DH (2013) *NHS Constitution for England and Wales.* London: DH.

Dominelli, L. (1992) 'An Uncaring Profession?' In P. Abraham, A. Rattansi and R. Skellington (eds) *Racism and Antiracism: Inequalities, Opportunities and Policies.* London: Sage Publications.

Goodorally, V. (2014) *Culturagram: Developing and Implementing a Culturally and Ethnically Sensitive Family Assessment Tool for People Living with Dementia and their Families.* Available at http://fons.org/library/report-details.aspx?nstid=55736, accessed on 28 August 2014.

Glendenning, F. (1982) 'Ethnic Minority Elderly People.' In J. Cheetham (ed.) *Social Work and Ethnicity.* London: George Allen & Unwin.

Gutheil, I.A. and Heyman, J.C. (2005) 'Working with Culturally Diverse Older Adults.' In E.P. Congress and M.J. Gonzalez (eds) *Multicultural Perspectives in Working with Families* (Chapter 6). 2nd edition. New York: Springer Publishing Company.

Laird, S. (2008) *Anti-oppressive Social Work: A Guide for Developing Cultural Competence.* London: Sage.

Lawrence, V., Banerjee, S., Bhugra, D., Sangha, K., Turner, S. and Murray, J. (2006) 'Coping with depression in later life: a qualitative study of help-seeking in three ethnic groups.' *Psychological Medicine 36*, 1375–1383.

Lindesay, J., Jagger, C., Hibbert, M.J., Peet, S.M. and Moledina, F. (1997) 'Knowledge, uptake and availability of health and social services among Asian Gujarati and White elders.' *Ethnicity and Health 2*, 59–69.

NAO (National Audit Office) (2007) *Improving Services and Support for People with Dementia.* London: NAO.

Parker, J. and Bradley, G. (2011) 'Tools and Diagrammatic Aids to Assessment.' In J. Parker and G. Bradley (eds) *Social Work Practice. Assessment, Planning, Intervention and Review*. 3rd edition. Exeter: Learning Matters Ltd.

Sewell, H. (2009) *Working with Ethnicity, Race and Culture in Mental Health: A Handbook for Practitioners*. London: Jessica Kingsley Publishers.

Thompson, N. (2009) *Understanding Social Work: Preparing for Practice*. Basingstoke: Palgrave Macmillan.

Truswell, D. (2013) *Black, Asian and Minority Ethnic Communities – Where Are We Now? Better Health Briefing 30*. A Race Equality Foundation Briefing Paper. London.

Wenger, E., McDermott, R. and Synder, W.M. (2002) *Cultivating Communities of Practice: A Guide to Managing Knowledge*. Boston, MA: Harvard Business School Press.

8

COMMUNICATION AND WORKING WITH INTERPRETERS

CULTURAL COMPETENCE IN DEMENTIA RESEARCH AND PRACTICE

Julia Botsford

Introduction

There is increasing ethnic diversity within the older UK population. This fact, along with recognition that cultural differences in attitudes and responses have a corresponding impact on access to diagnosis and support, means that the imperative to ensure that dementia services and those working within them are equipped to address needs across the spectrum is becoming more and more urgent.

Cultural and ethnic background play a major role in determining a person's beliefs about health and illness as well as their attitudes and preferences when it comes to accessing treatment and care. Health practitioners therefore need not only knowledge and skills to address specific health issues, but also abilities that ensure these can be delivered appropriately and with cultural sensitivity. Researchers, equally, need to be culturally competent in their approach to the design, conduct and interpretation of studies.

This chapter explores the challenges of working within or across ethnicities (conceptualised here as the insider/outsider debate), and also considers in depth the issues associated with effective communication and working across cultures and language differences, principally in a research context, but also in relation to clinical practice. In discussing the issues, some illustrative examples are drawn from a research study conducted by the author between 2007 and 2010 with Black Caribbean and Greek Cypriot communities in North London. Aspects of this study have previously been published elsewhere (see Botsford, Clarke and Gibb 2012). Details of the study can be found in Box 8.1.

Box 8.1: Dementia and relationships: experiences of Greek Cypriot and African Caribbean partners (Botsford *et al.* 2012)

The study set out to explore in depth the experiences of partners of people with dementia in the Greek Cypriot and African Caribbean populations of a London borough – Haringey.

A constructivist grounded theory approach was adopted. In the first phase individual and group interviews were conducted with Greek Cypriot and Caribbean people who were members of the local Cypriot and Caribbean community centres. In the main phase a series of interviews were conducted with seven Greek Cypriot and six African Caribbean partners of people with an established dementia diagnosis. Up to four interviews took place with each participant, where necessary with an interpreter present.

The outcomes of the study revealed partners of people with dementia engaged in an ongoing process of 'redefining relationships', encompassing both positive and negative effects. Three relationship orientations – 'I' (individual-centred), 'We two' (couple-centred) and 'We as a family' (family-centred) – were identified. There were similarities and differences between the experiences of the Greek Cypriot and Caribbean participants that influenced how people related to their partners, families and formal services. Within and across each group different ways of viewing the dementia-associated changes, of appraising and dealing with the associated threat, and of making practical changes were seen through a series of processes – recognising, reacting and adjusting. Shielding processes, acquired over a life course that included relocating to England, and incorporating resilience and coping strategies, also appeared to influence the impact of the dementia-associated changes on the partner.

The findings of this study support and extend existing theory around how couple relationships evolve when one partner develops dementia, by demonstrating the additional significance of wider family relationships alongside that of the couple. The process of redefining relationships appears to be influenced by the knowledge, attitudes and circumstances of the individual, as well as by their unique journey in life and their existing relationships, factors that appear to be at least in part influenced by ethnic background.

Ethnicity and dementia: a developing evidence base?

Health care practice is expected to be based on up-to-date and robust evidence, and yet much of the research, where it exists at all, either does not include participants from minority ethnic groups or does not give enough weight to ethnicity in the analysis of results (Hussain-Gambles 2003).

In relation to dementia, the relative lack of a UK evidence base has previously been highlighted (Botsford, Clarke and Gibb 2011; Milne and Chryssanthopoulou 2005), with commentators noting that most of the studies that have been published to date have focused on South Asian and Black Caribbean communities, with very little on other minority ethnic groups such as white minorities. Milne and Chryssanthopoulou have also highlighted a lack of rigour in the definition of groups that could undermine validity. For example, the blanket term 'South Asian' may be used to refer to studies of Pakistani, Sikh, Gujarati or other 'South Asian' 'sub'-groups, with the implication that results apply across all, and with scant regard for the differences that actually exist. Furthermore, much of the existing research evidence concerns carers rather than people with dementia, explores experiences of services, and is small-scale and local (Jutlla 2013; Moriarty, Sharif and Robinson 2011).

There are, however, grounds for cautious optimism that the situation is changing, with greater interest now being shown in the area. The 2013 G8 Dementia Summit, along with the *Dementia Does Not Discriminate* report (APPG on Dementia 2013), confirms that researchers, politicians, service planners and providers have now woken up to the imperative for dementia services to recognise, understand and address the needs of the UK's increasing numbers of black and minority ethnic (BME) families affected by dementia.

Nevertheless, there are challenges associated with conducting high-quality research in relation to dementia and ethnicity. Many of these issues parallel the challenges faced in clinical practice by health and social care teams.

Access and engagement in a research setting

Chapter 7 considered approaches to assessment and engagement with ethnic populations. There are similar operational issues when it comes to carrying out research. The very fact that people with dementia may tend to be especially stigmatised and hidden within some ethnic populations represents a challenge to the researcher. The researcher will need to develop proactive strategies to encourage participation. For example, it is important to recognise and respect the terms of reference of the potential participants. Forbat (2003) described the importance of using terms and language that are acceptable and meaningful, for example, citing the fact that the term 'looking after' was preferable to 'carer' and 'caring' to potential participants, and those she approached to help her gain access to them, in her study of people identifying as South Asian and African Caribbean.

Clearly language issues are important and need to be addressed. Not only must attention be paid to the conceptual appropriateness of the terms being used, for example, being conscious of where to use and where to avoid technical medical terms, but also, where applicable, how to communicate with non-English-speaking participants, or with participants for whom English may not be a first language. It may be necessary to use written materials in translation, for example, but care needs to be taken here to ensure that they are high quality, accurate, and applicable to the target population. For example, in relation to Greek Cypriots, there are subtle but significant differences in language use compared with mainland Greek, and these need to be factored in when using Greek written materials or interpreters, even if they are used for pragmatic reasons.

Clearly, conducting research in different languages is likely to be more costly (involving, as it does, paying for translations of written information and interviewing recordings etc.), and significantly more time-consuming. Further consideration of language and communication issues will be given later on in this chapter.

Insider/outsider debate: issues in research and practice

Many of the same issues apply both to research and practice. Issues around this debate have been articulated in relation to research, but in many ways apply equally or perhaps even more acutely within the realm of clinical practice.

Essentially, the insider/outsider debate refers to a discussion of the advantages and disadvantages of being a member of the group being researched or receiving health care. In this case the question concerns whether one is a member of the same ethnic group or not. Three main advantages for insider research have been outlined:

- significant understanding of a group's culture
- the ability to interact naturally with group members
- previously established relational intimacy with the group (Bonner and Tolhurst 2002).

Being a member of the same ethnic group could promote easier access, assist in the development of trust and rapport, and promote a sense of 'on the same wave length' that could enable understanding and reduce scope for misunderstandings. Speaking the same language is clearly a major advantage. On the other hand, insider research may run the risk of sacrificing the sense of distance that may be viewed as necessary for objectivity and balance.

In the research study outlined earlier, my role as researcher was, from an ethnicity perspective, as an 'outsider', in that I was a White British person researching African Caribbean and Greek Cypriot people. It is worth considering the pros and cons in a little more detail.

There have been criticisms, particularly within the sphere of feminist research, that white researchers' findings may not apply to minority ethnic groups, or may misrepresent them, and that issues may not have been given the attention they ought to have been (Phoenix 1988). In a discussion focusing on a simplistic white/black dichotomy, Rhodes (1994) suggests that the concern may not only be that black people may be inhibited when talking to a white researcher, but also that a white person is unable to enter into a black person's worldview since they possess neither the language nor the cultural equipment to do so.

Clearly, in conducting research interviews it is essential to create a context in which participants feel comfortable enough to talk as freely as possible, and where the researcher will be able to hear and understand as much as possible of what is said. Acknowledgement of the impact of perceived difference is important. The extract below, taken from an interview I carried out with an African Caribbean woman during the first part of the study, demonstrates that my perceived difference from her was significant, although not enough to inhibit her entirely. She clearly identified me as different from her (that is, English), but is apparently reluctant to personalise her generalisation about English people by including me – hence a move from 'you' (that is, 'you English') to 'they're' (that is, 'English people in general', but not necessarily 'you' personally):

> Black Caribbean woman: I find that the…no disrespect to you…
>
> Julia: Be honest…
>
> Black Caribbean woman: I find that English people is different to us. You know, you know they don't speak to you like how we would speak to you. Like when we meet you on the street, we look at you and we'll say hello. You know? But they're not like that.

One might speculate about what she might have said, or gone on to say, had she perceived me as another Black Caribbean person.

Other white British researchers have expressed similar concerns. For example, one white feminist researcher, reflecting on her experience of interviewing African Caribbean women, wrote:

> I worried that my assumptions about Black women's family lifestyles and cultural practices might be based on false understandings. I also worried (as it turns out with good reason) that Black women would not relate to me woman-to woman, but as a Black person to a white person, and that this would affect the information I received from them. (Edwards 1990, p.483)

Papadopoulos (2006) identifies four key elements in culturally competent research. These are cultural awareness, cultural knowledge, cultural sensitivity, and cultural competence, expressed in the ability to 'recognise and challenge racism and other forms of discrimination and oppressive practice' (p.18).

Within this framework, cultural awareness incorporates self-awareness and recognition of one's own cultural frame of reference (seen as essential to understanding the values of others, and achieved through reflecting on one's own cultural frames of reference), as well as knowledge and understanding of the history, norms and values of the studied group. Cultural knowledge, Papadopoulos proposes, must take in recognition of how external forces, such as how society is structured, can impact on the experiences of cultural groups, in order to avoid essentialism, which, in this case, would assume that every single thing about a person is due to their ethnicity rather than to any other aspect of their being. This is an approach that could lead to stereotyping and discrimination.

Similar cultural competence is also necessary in clinical practice. It needs to be treated as an ongoing process, and cannot be reduced to a tick box exercise of completing mandatory training on 'equality and diversity'.

Papadopoulos (2006) advocates 'insider' research, and proposes that true sensitivity is best achieved by matching the ethnicity of the researcher with that of the participant. Echoing Ram (1996), she suggests that this encourages a more equal context for interviews to take place in, and allows 'more sensitive and accurate information to be collected' (Papadopoulos 2006, p.90). Some of the benefits have been outlined by a number of researchers (Bhopal 1995; Douglas 1998).

However, the alignment of researcher ethnicity with that of participants is by no means unproblematic. Determining a person's ethnic identity is not as straightforward as it might initially appear. Ethnicity and cultural identity are subjective, and potentially shifting, aspects of a person, a point discussed in Chapter 3. Indeed, authors such as Song and Parker have raised the issue of mixed descent researchers, and where they may or may not fit along the continuum of commonality and difference (Song and Parker 1995).

Furthermore, the strategy of matching researcher and participants could be criticised in that it seems to imply that ethnic identity is the only significant element (Ramji 2008), thus failing to take account of other important aspects of social identity and lived experience. In the earlier interview extract, the focus was on 'Englishness' and 'non-Englishness', but this was only one of a number of differences between researcher and participant. Differences related to age, socio-economics, and in some cases gender, as well as power and status, are just as important. If we are going to match for ethnicity, should we also match for age, gender, class, or any other aspects of identity? This is not only impractical, but also absurd.

In addition, Brah (1996) suggests that shared ethnicity does not in itself assure a vantage point of privileged insight. In an account of her own experience of being a British Asian researcher researching British Asians, Ramji (2008) described her relationships with interviewees as characterised by a 'persistent tension between commonality and difference regarding shared cultural identities' (p.104). She noted that her shared 'Indianness' was helpful in recruiting people to take part in the study, but that throughout interviews participants sought to establish how similar or dissimilar to them she was, and that this seemed to influence the rapport and interactions between them.

Walton (1986) claims that since it is impossible for any researcher, whatever their cultural identity, to belong to all the multiplicity of groups she or he studies, so there should be some freedom to comment on aspects of the life of groups one is not actually a member of.

Some researchers have highlighted that not being from the same ethnicity as interviewees does not have to be a handicap, and indeed may be a benefit. Rhodes found that as a white researcher interviewing African Caribbean women about their experiences of fostering, she had the advantage of 'stranger value' (Rhodes 1994, p.551). Participants identified with her as a non-social worker and non-insider, and thus appeared more able to speak freely without fear of being judged negatively or what they said getting out to others. In many cases, they provided information that they would have assumed was taken for granted by another black person, opening up access to details that might have otherwise been left unsaid. Going even further, she found her whiteness was relevant but acted as a stimulant to communication rather than a block. I found that participants wanted to explain aspects of their stories and did not assume prior knowledge, which meant that they brought into the open aspects of their experience, for example, in the case of several

African Caribbean participants, having experienced racism and prejudice in the past.

In the main, the people who took part in this study seemed to relish the opportunity to open up about themselves over a series of meetings, and indicated that it had been an enjoyable experience for them, despite the fact that for some there were feelings of sadness and uncertainty at times. Whilst it is possible that my ethnic background influenced the decision about whether to take part in the study, for some people my initial concerns that Greek Cypriot and African Caribbean people would not want to talk to an 'outsider' were not borne out in the interviews that took place:

> I don't mind talking with people. I talk with anyone, anyone. You see the point is you have to look at people as human beings. I like having civilized conversation you see. You can go and do your research, you're gathering research and that's fine. (African Caribbean man)

As we have seen, the issue of how the characteristics of the researcher, and in this case the researcher's distinct ethnicity, impacts on the process and outcomes of the research remains a contested area. Several commentators have highlighted the importance of being reflective, and, self-awareness as key to maintaining the integrity of the research.

Ideally, cross-cultural research should involve members of the ethnic community being researched. There is some strength in having mixed insider/outsider research teams. Where the researchers do not share ethnicity, it would be important to consistently work alongside members of the relevant community to check the cultural appropriateness of the research design and implementation, as well as the cultural resonance of the findings.

Importance of effective communication

Good communication is always central to ensuring that cross-cultural encounters are successful, whether in a research or a practice setting. There is always scope for misunderstandings to occur, whether due to mishearing the words of someone speaking with an unfamiliar accent, or as a result of misreading non-verbal behaviours, through to the potential for misinterpretation of culturally bound metaphors and concepts.

Anyone working clinically with people with dementia and their families will be acutely aware of the importance of good communication skills. One of the features of dementia is a progressive reduction in language and the ability to express ideas as words, as well as a reduction in the ability to recognise the meanings of spoken and written words. In the early stages, people with dementia will often retain the ability to speak and understand English, even if this is not their mother tongue, but in the later stages, they may no longer be able to communicate verbally in English. This may lead to increasing problems with accessing services and engaging with paid carers. Take the example of Maria, a Turkish woman with advanced dementia. She is able to recognise some words in Turkish but is no longer able to communicate in English at all. Her family are struggling to manage her care at home, but reluctant for her to go into a residential setting where there are no Turkish-speaking carers, as they fear she will become isolated and her needs will not be understood.

Language and working with interpreters

Ideally, people who do not have English as a first language will have the option of communicating in their own language. As in the example of Maria, above, this may not always be practical on an everyday basis, and this can be a very real problem.

However, in research or in clinical practice, the use of interpreters is a practical way to share vital information between the person with dementia and the health provider, or researcher and interviewee. This will be essential in encounters where significant information is being gathered or shared, for example, during the process leading to diagnosis or where significant decisions are taking place. In everyday situations, practical steps can be taken, such as using picture boards or making sure that carers know how to say certain key words so they can use them during personal care, for example.

In some families, a pattern of relatives acting as interpreters will have developed over time. Perhaps the son or daughter of a non-English-speaking immigrant will have taken on the role of agent in relation to dealing with officials or bureaucracy because they speak English better than their parents. This is certainly a familiar pattern in my clinical practice as an Admiral Nurse working with families in a culturally diverse borough in London.

However, while some people may prefer to have relatives as interpreters, and feel most comfortable with this, there is inevitably a concern about whether the nature of the relationship between the person with dementia and relative/interpreter will influence what gets said and how it gets said. Perhaps the relative has his or her own agenda, and will prioritise this over and above that of the person with dementia. Coupled with this is a real risk that either the person with dementia will not be able to talk freely in front of their relative, for example, about sensitive issues, or that the relative will not translate accurately either through a lack of language ability or because they are censoring communication for some reason of their own. Where the relative is also a carer, it is also important to recognise that they will have needs in their own right, and may therefore be caught between expressing their own views and those of the person with dementia. For these reasons it is recommended that the use of relatives as interpreters is discouraged, especially for significant interactions, for example, where important information is being discussed, such as where bad news is being given or important decisions need to be made.

Working with interpreters

Working with and through interpreters is an experience that can be rather off-putting for both interviewer and interviewee. The conversational flow is interrupted as the translation occurs, and this means that as an interviewer, one will be observing body language, but having to wait for the accompanying words that go along with it. It also means that interjections or clarifications cannot be spontaneous, and there is a danger that the flow and direction of the interview is controlled via a third party. The overall impact can be a sense of being on the outside, looking in.

On the positive side, interpreters can act as what Ravel calls 'Cultural brokers and cultural consultants' (2003, p.122). There are different approaches to working with interpreters. An interpreter may either be a translator (where the words in one language are substituted for those in another in as neutral and impartial a way as possible), or able to assist the clinician/researcher in understanding cultural meanings. What Miller (1986) describes as the myth of the interpreter as 'postman' is articulated well by Messant (2003). He suggests that the Western view of communication as a relay between two people, of words which convey the meaning of an idea from one person to another, and where the interpreter's role would be to supply the right words which can stand in for the ideas, is unrealistic and inaccurate. In this 'postman' model the personhood of the interpreter would be irrelevant and insignificant. He suggests, however, that interpreting involves not just words, but shared meaning systems. In other words, the reality of interpreting is about more than simply swapping words with the same meanings. Words are imbued with meanings, and there are not always exact substitutes available. Furthermore, families relate to the interpreter.

Interpreters in research: ensuring rigour

Within research it is especially important to achieve results that are rigorous and accurate. Squires (2009) reviewed 40 cross-language qualitative research studies and produced recommendations for how researchers managed translators and interpreters in their studies. She identified only 6 out of the 40 studies she reviewed which met all the criteria for trustworthy results, and emphasised the need for researchers to address the methodological issues more systematically. Key points she raised were the importance of highlighting the role of translator and interpreter, pilot testing questions in the participant's language, stating the translator and interpreter's credentials, acknowledging translation as a limitation of the study, and the use of an appropriate methodological framework.

In order to ensure accuracy of translation and that crucial meanings are not missed, Papadopoulos (2006) suggests getting any recordings of interviews retranslated at a later date. This process of 'back-translation', she suggests 'ensures that translation was not an exercise of mere lexical equivalence but one of conceptual equivalence too' (2006, p.94).

The way this process can work is illustrated here in reference to the research study referred to earlier (Box 8.1). Adamson and Donovan (2002) recommend that where interpretation is needed in a research project, the fewer interpreters involved, the better. Preferably one interpreter should take part in the data collection where possible. This can facilitate the development of good working relationships between researcher and interpreter, leading to enhanced quality in the conduct of the study.

All the Greek Cypriot participants were offered the opportunity to have an interpreter involved in their interviews. All the first phase interviews occurred in the presence of an interpreter. In the second phase some felt, and indeed were, fluent in English, and so did not take this up. Of the others, all except one were interviewed in the presence of the same interpreter as had been involved in the earlier phase. One interviewee insisted on his daughter acting as interpreter and participating in the interviews.

All the research interviews were recorded and transcribed. For the purpose of retrospective review (back-translation), a different interpreter was asked to review the Greek Cypriot audio files to determine accuracy and consistency. Since it was not practical or financially viable to retranslate the entire collection of interpreted sound files (which comprised roughly 21 hours out of a total of 59 hours of audio material in phase two), a number of extracts were selected for scrutiny. Some were selected at random, and others were selected on the basis of specific criteria including where there appeared to be scope for the interpreter to have missed some of what was being said (for example, where the interviewee and interpreter were talking simultaneously), where the sound quality was poor and therefore transcription was hampered, or where the content contained conceptual ideas rather than pure facts. In addition, several extracts from interviews where the daughter had interpreted for her father were included.

A second interpreter was employed to carry out this exercise. The audio files were played to him and he commented on what he heard. In some cases he provided his own translation, and in others he made comments. Overall, this exercise confirmed that the original interpretations had been extremely accurate. Although it revealed a small amount of missed data in some cases, what had been lost was by no means central to the study topic, and the key points were conveyed in full, thus preserving the integrity of the original process.

In the case of the interviews carried out via the daughter, it also confirmed that she was accurately translating the questions and supplying accurate translations of her father's responses. A review of the sound files showed, however, that she would often add her own supplementary comments after her father's. It was already evident, even without recourse to retranslation, where this happened. The following excerpt gives a flavour of this. The italicised sections, originally uttered in Greek, have been translated into English by the interpreter, and the underlined sections show the daughter's additions:

> Julia: What other sort of things is she different from how she used to be before?
>
> Greek Cypriot daughter: [Greek] *What other things have changed about her?*
>
> Greek Cypriot man: [Greek] *What things have changed? I don't know. She picks at her clothes …*
>
> Greek Cypriot woman: She picks at her clothes <u>all day. He finds that quite disturbing …</u>

> Greek Cypriot man: [Greek] *'I'm gonna tear them – I'm gonna throw them away.' Brand new things. 'What are these, I'm supposed to be wearing these?' She goes…*
>
> Greek Cypriot daughter: 'I'm gonna tear them – I'm gonna throw them away.' Brand new things. 'What are these, I'm supposed to be wearing these?' She goes. He's very good. He takes her shopping and he buys her, she's got brand new… she's got more clothes than I have [laughs]. He's very good.

In relation to more conceptual translations, the process demonstrated some areas of mild controversy. This is illustrated by the use of the Greek word *koumera*, for which there is no direct equivalent in English. This word was interpreted as 'friend' by the original interpreter and 'Best woman at a wedding' by the second. Subsequent inquiry has revealed that while the official dictionary definition is closer to the latter, older Greek Cypriots tend to use the word much more broadly. The original interpreter was able to apply the spirit of what was being conveyed in respect of the context, in the absence of an exact English match. During the interview, when the word was used, the interpreter informed me that the interviewee had been the lady's son's godmother and thus the term *koumera* was used to reflect that she was a friend but that also there was an 'official' link between them.

It is an interesting exercise which confirms the potential for meanings to be 'lost in translation', but also suggests that with care and attention it is possible to make sure that important abstract and culturally specific meanings can be projected across language and culture. It also, however, illustrates that where the topics are complex and involve a lot of culturally specific and abstract terms, there is value in ensuring that interpreters are from a similar cultural background as well as simply able to speak the same language (thus a Greek Cypriot person who speaks English is preferable to an English person who has learned to speak Greek).

Guidance for working with interpreters in the dementia care setting

The recommendations below are based on both practical experience and other sources including Minas, Stankovska and Ziguras (2001) and Culley and Dyson (2010).

WHEN TO USE AN INTERPRETER

- Where English is not the person with dementia/carer's first language and he or she is unable to communicate effectively in English or does not feel confident in his or her English.
- When a person with dementia/carer is deaf and uses sign language.

PRIOR TO BOOKING AN INTERPRETER

- Find out the specific language and, very importantly, the dialect spoken by the person with dementia/carer.
- Allow yourself time to plan the interview in advance. This may be especially important if more than one person will be present, for example, if you will be meeting a person with dementia along with one or more family carers.
- Inform the interpreting service of the specific needs of the person with dementia/carer and the nature of the appointment.
- Use an interpreting service that works according to explicit professional and ethical codes (including confidentiality).
- Be prepared to negotiate appointment times. This may need to be done by the interpreting service by phone or in writing. Make sure to inform the interpreting service/interpreter of any changes or cancellations.
- Allow up to twice as much time as usual for the appointment.

- Book the same interpreter for repeat appointments wherever possible, *if* all have been satisfied with the interpreter.

BEFORE THE APPOINTMENT

- Meet with the interpreter just prior to the interview where possible. Brief them on the nature of the meeting.
- Confirm the interpreter's knowledge and understanding of important terminology and concepts. For example, how will they translate 'dementia', 'Alzheimer's disease' or other terms?
- Clarify your expectations of how the meeting will be conducted.
- Pay attention to the set-up of the room and where everyone will sit.
- Consider the power relationship. Are there any gender or class dynamics, or any other factors that may affect how the person with dementia will relate to the interpreter (and vice versa)? For example, is there a possibility that the interpreter and person with dementia might have been on opposing sides of a civil war, or is there an issue associated with caste membership?

DURING THE APPOINTMENT

- Introduce yourself and the interpreter, and explain respective roles including the issue of confidentiality.
- Double-check that the interpreter is actually speaking the same language or dialect as the person with dementia/carer – do not just assume this is the case.
- Speak directly to the person with dementia/carer, maintaining eye contact with them as you do so.

- Look for and take note of both the person with dementia and the interpreter's non-verbal communication and body language.
- Be aware of your own non-verbal communication and body language.
- Encourage the interpreter to clarify anything they are unsure of in what you are saying – try to avoid technical jargon or abbreviations.
- Try to break up what you are saying into manageable chunks.
- Allow the interpreter time to speak and receive the response.
- Encourage the interpreter to tell you if they are expressing their own opinions of what is being said so it is clear what exactly the person with dementia is saying, and what is the interpreter's perspective.
- Ask the interpreter to let you know when they have to ask subsidiary questions or rephrase a question for the person with dementia.
- Allow time for the person with dementia/carer to ask questions.
- Remember, you are in control of the interview.
- Seek to set up further appointments in the presence of the interpreter where needed.

AFTER THE APPOINTMENT

- Ask the interpreter for feedback – including their perception of the person with dementia's use of language.
- Debrief the interpreter if necessary – especially where there has been sensitive or upsetting content.

THINGS TO AVOID

- Where possible, avoid using family members to interpret. They may have a conflict of interest and are also not bound by the same confidentiality codes as a professional interpreter. Family members do have an important role in supporting and advocating for the person with dementia, however.
- Do not leave the interpreter alone with the person with dementia. This is to help interpreters remain impartial.
- Avoid excluding the person with dementia/carer by engaging in a lengthy discussion with the interpreter. If it is necessary to talk to them, explain to the person with dementia/carer what you are doing.

Conclusion

This chapter has examined some of the issues of working within and across ethnic groups, and has explored communication issues with particular regard to the challenges of working with people who speak different languages, and who may see the world from different points of reference. Whether a researcher, clinician or care worker, from the same ethnic background as the community being researched or receiving a service, attention needs to be given to the development of positive relationships based on an understanding and acknowledgement of the cultural issues that are at play. Cultural competence is an essential component in both the development of a robust and inclusive evidence base, and in the delivery of positive clinical practice in dementia care.

References

Adamson, J. and Donovan, J.L. (2002) 'Research in black and white.' *Qualitative Health Research 12*, 816–825.

APPG (All-Party Parliamentary Group) on Dementia (2013) *Dementia Does Not Discriminate: The Experiences of Black, Asian and Minority Ethnic Communities.* July. London: Alzheimer's Society. Available at www.alzheimers.org.uk/site/scripts/download_info.php?downloadID=1186, accessed on 11 December 2014.

Bhopal, K. (1995) 'Women and feminism as subjects of black study: the difficulties and dilemmas of carrying out research.' *Journal of Gender Studies 4*, 2, 153–168.

Bonner, A. and Tolhurst, G. (2002) 'Insider-outsider perspectives of participant observation.' *Nurse Researcher 9*, 7–19.

Botsford, J., Clarke, C.L. and Gibb, C.E. (2011) 'Research and dementia, caring and ethnicity: a review of the literature.' *Journal of Research in Nursing 16*, 5, 437–449.

Botsford, J., Clarke, C.L. and Gibb, C.E. (2012) 'Dementia and relationships: experiences of partners in minority ethnic communities.' *Journal of Advanced Nursing 68*, 10, 2207–2217.

Brah, A. (1996) 'Re-framing Europe: en-gendered racisms, ethnicities and nationalisms in contemporary Western Europe.' *Feminist Review 45*, 9–25.

Culley, L. and Dyson, S. (2010) *Ethnicity and Healthcare Practice*. London: Quay Books.

Douglas, J. (1998) 'Developing appropriate research methodologies with black and minority ethnic communities. Part 1: reflections on the research process.' *Health Education Journal 57*, 329–338.

Edwards, R. (1990) 'Connecting method and epistemology: a white woman interviewing black women.' *Women's Studies International Forum 13*, 477–490.

Forbat, L. (2003) 'Concepts and understandings of dementia by "gatekeepers" and minority ethnic "service users".' *Journal of Health Psychology 8*, 645–655.

Hussain-Gambles, M. (2003) 'Ethnic minority under-representation in clinical trials: whose responsibility is it anyway?' *Journal of Health Organisation and Management 17*, 2, 138–143.

Jutlla, K. (2013) 'Ethnicity and cultural diversity in dementia care: a review of the research.' *Journal of Dementia Care 21*, 2, 33–39.

Messant, P. (2003) 'From Postmen to Makers of Meaning: A Model for Collaborative Work between Clinicians and Interpreters.' In R. Tribe and H. Ravel (eds) *Working with Interpreters in Mental Health*. Hove: Brunner-Routledge.

Miller, G. (1986) 'What we say and what we do.' *New York Times Book Review*, p.37.

Milne, A. and Chryssanthopoulou, C. (2005) 'Dementia care-giving in black and Asian populations: reviewing and refining the research agenda.' *Journal of Community Applied Social Psychology 15*, 319–337.

Minas, H., Stankovska, M., and Ziguras, S. (2001) *Working with Interpreters: Guidelines for Mental Health Professionals*. Available at: www.vtmh.org.au/docs/interpreter/VTPU_GuidelinesBooklet.pdf, accessed on 30 January 2014.

Moriarty, J., Sharif, N. and Robinson, J. (2011) 'Black and minority ethnic people with dementia and their access to support and services.' *Research Briefing 35*. London: Social Care Institute for Excellence. Available at www.scie.org.uk/publications/briefings/files/briefing35.pdf, accessed on 30 January 2014.

Papadopoulos, I. (2006) 'The Papadopoulos, Tilki and Taylor model of developing cultural competence.' In I. Papadopoulos (ed.) *Transcultural Health and Social Care – Development of Culturally Competent Practitioners*. London: Churchill Livingstone Elsevier.

Phoenix, A. (1988) 'Narrow definitions of culture: the case of early motherhood.' In S. Westwood and P. Bachu (eds) *Enterprising Women: Ethnicity, Economy and Gender Relations*. London: Routledge.

Ram, M. (1996) 'Ethnography, ethnicity and work: unpacking the West Midlands clothing industry.' In Lyon, E. & Bushfield, J. (eds). *Methodological Imaginations*. Basingstoke: Macmillan.

Ramji, H. (2008) 'Exploring commonality and difference in in-depth interviewing: a case-study of researching British Asian women.' *The British Journal of Sociology 59*, 99–116.

Ravel, H. (2003) 'Applying theoretical frameworks to the work with interpreters.' In R. Tribe and H. Ravel (eds) *Working with Interpreters in Mental Health*. Hove: Brunner-Routledge.

Rhodes, P. (1994) 'Race-of-interviewer effects: a brief comment.' *Sociology 28*, 2, 547–558.

Song, M. and Parker, D. (1995) 'Commonality, difference and the dynamics of disclosure in in-depth interviewing.' *Sociology 29*, 241–256.

Squires, A. (2009) 'Methodological challenges in cross-language qualitative research: a research review.' *International Journal of Nursing Studies*, 46, 277–287.

Walton, H. (1986) *White Researchers and Racism*. Manchester: Faculty of Economic and Social Studies, University of Manchester.

9

WORKING POSITIVELY WITH CULTURE, ETHNICITY AND DEMENTIA

—— Julia Botsford and Karen Harrison Dening ——

Introduction

Several chapters in this book have presented the epidemiological statistics on dementia and black and minority ethnic (BME) populations, as well as the issues in various care settings. Policy and guidance that aim to positively influence such care have also been highlighted. *Living Well with Dementia: A National Dementia Strategy* (DH 2009) set 17 recommendations for the NHS, local authorities and others to improve dementia care services, and focused on three key themes: raising awareness and understanding; early diagnosis and support; and living well with dementia. Central to developing services and care for people affected by dementia from BME populations is the need to raise dementia awareness and to overcome obstacles such as stigma, inequitable access to services, and to develop services that are culturally acceptable.

This chapter explores how local communities and individuals have tackled the recommendations of the strategy. Many projects have started by raising awareness and exploring understandings of dementia in a specific BME community, which have, in turn, made a positive impact on access to diagnosis and care services.

We present various projects and initiatives from around the UK that demonstrate how local communities and individuals are developing services and care to meet the needs of families affected by dementia from BME groups. We particularly wanted this chapter to reflect work across a range of BME communities and from around the country. Locating projects, such as are detailed in the following pages, was in itself a challenge. Some were identified by word of mouth and personal knowledge, others by endless searching on the internet, in journals and media coverage. Interestingly, several showed a reluctance to write about their work, or felt that it was not sufficiently developed yet to present in such a way. However, such projects are often very inspiring in their ability to show what is possible in circumstances that are often seemingly against the odds.

Contributors describe how they have placed culture and ethnicity at the heart of their work to address key aspects of need. Each in their different way reminds us how important it is to see beyond superficial stereotypes about culture and ethnicity, and to connect with the unique and complex individual. We need to see beyond the obvious to ensure that there is real equal access to support and services.

There are always challenges to small, local initiatives, especially when funding is short term. This is a point made by David Truswell. There is a risk that community organisations will lose interest, perhaps because of the discontinuation of the project or a key individual moving on to other work. The community members could also lose trust in the services if their needs are not being adequately met in the future. It is important to make sure that the project is well documented, and that key stakeholders within a community are onboard and involved.

Each of the contributions to this chapter, in their different ways, highlights practical ways of promoting access and engagement within communities who may be less well represented in terms of service uptake, and illustrates why it is important and worthwhile working with ethnic community groups. Specific projects presented here include: a Singing for the Brain group tailored to South Asian people; a Somali dementia cafe; a connecting communities project aimed at promoting awareness in minority ethnic communities in London; a Carer Information and Support Programme adapted for South

Asian people; a wide-reaching project aimed at promoting awareness and good practice in the Irish community; a social group for South American older people; and a project to develop dementia-friendly Sikh Temples (Gurudwaras). Each of these projects is different, and approaches need in its own way, but all of them show that a targeted intervention can make a big difference.

CONNECTING COMMUNITIES IN LONDON

ALLI ANTHONY

'I thought dementia only affected white people'

The Alzheimer's Society was awarded three-year funding by the Department of Health for a pilot project to raise awareness of dementia for Black, Asian and other minority ethnic groups (BAME) across eight London boroughs. The project's aims are to engage volunteers from BAME communities in designing and delivering awareness-raising activities that are appropriate to diverse communities. The project will ultimately produce a commissioning toolkit for dementia awareness-raising with BAME communities to take the programme beyond our current pilot boroughs. The team will also produce guidelines for best practice on volunteering with diverse communities. This funding offers the opportunity to focus on organisational diversity in dementia service provision and volunteering. The project team includes four full-time volunteering officers (VOs) and a half-time project manager.

At the beginning of the project we undertook basic desk research so the whole team was aware of the particular issues that this project faces – namely, there are many diverse communities represented in London, each with unique identities, migration histories, cultural norms, languages, food customs and cultural values, communities with varied perspectives on both volunteering and dementia, communities with variable access to local support services, both mainstream and culturally specific. We know that there is no word for dementia or volunteering in many languages, and that there are many culturally based myths surrounding dementia, sometimes making it even more stigmatised in BAME communities. The new staff team thus had many significant challenges to consider and face in order to make the project manageable in the short term and successful in the long term.

Each VO was assigned two boroughs and was tasked with more detailed research into each borough's population profiles, looking at older population groups in particular. The staff took time to read key academic literature, and were lucky enough to attend the All-Party Parliamentary Group (APPG) on Dementia and Ethnicity. The evidence presented drew together many of the key topics surrounding BAME groups and dementia, with evidence from people with dementia, family carers, service providers and academics in a way that provided the new VOs with a serendipitous training session.

As a team we then devised an illustrated talk to include the main issues. This has been tested and refined over the first year of the project. In essence we maintain:

- Dementia is nobody's fault; anyone can get it – a point reinforced by images of well-known people from different communities who have experienced dementia.
- Dementia is the result of diseases of the brain, of which there are many different types (we highlight the most common of these and their most common symptoms).
- Dementia is not an inevitable consequence of ageing – however, there is an anticipated increase in the numbers of people from BAME communities liable to experience dementia over the next half-century.
- Knowing the stigmatised nature of dementia, it is important to stress how it *is* possible to live well with the condition and remain part of the community, by highlighting the importance of community inclusion.
- When tackling some of the myths surrounding dementia particular to a community, we emphasise how an individual with dementia remains an adult with feelings, emotions and a lifetime of experience.

Previous work to engage with communities identified the need to look at communities individually. The tendency to place all BAME communities under one heading has been unhelpful. In undertaking awareness-raising work it has been critical to research the community in question beforehand. This is achieved initially through Google searches, and then developed through significant time spent with community leaders and/or elders in order to learn more about that particular group. In practice, the initial meetings may take several weeks to arrange, especially where groups have no paid staff and often no email access. This simple process can therefore be time-consuming and sometimes frustrating for staff, and so patience and perseverance are necessary. Once we meet with key community figures, we have found a warm reception and an eagerness for everyone involved with the ageing population to be better informed.

We discuss the importance of dementia awareness with that leader, and take their lead on what approach may work best with that group. Thus with some groups we might hold a large conference-style event with invited speakers, while for others who prefer it, small group work, with several sessions taking place over three or four months, often in the evening or at weekends. Again, this requires staff to be flexible and adaptable.

'My mother has dementia because her daughter married a white man'

In some groups we have found that people have heard of dementia and may know someone with the condition. This can also lead to different misconceptions. The most common question we are asked is the difference between dementia and Alzheimer's disease. We leave plenty of time for questions and answers and are developing an 'FAQ' for facilitators working with BAME groups. This will, for example, include research evidence on coconut oil, information on dementia and Chinese medicinal herbs, and any other culturally endorsed health regimens we may learn of. Seeking feedback from groups is thus an essential part of the process, as is the need for the team to be responsive, prepared to change and to take on board suggestions for improvement and new approaches.

'Pictures can say to people "this happens in our community"'

Traditionally, so many of our images at the Alzheimer's Society have been UK culturally specific, and greater diversity in printed materials is needed. As the project progresses we are refining our materials to include many more varied images as we have found visual communication is more powerful when so many groups we work with have not reached fluency in written English.

We have developed a number of activities that we are currently including with community groups to make our sessions more memorable as well as meaningful for that particular group. Working with a particular faith group in a faith setting, for example, we might focus on a group activity based on Kitwood's flower[1]. Working with very small community groups we might find two or three short sessions over a few weeks have more impact. Many groups are visited by third sector organisations covering a whole variety of health issues, be that diabetes, obesity, smoking cessation or HIV, so it is important to work with colleagues and to ensure dementia is clearly understood. Dementia is clearly a serious subject, and we have found that using interactive activities to convey complex information in memorable ways leaves our participants better informed, and hopefully not too downcast.

'English food is a real turn-off for older Asian people. They won't eat it and won't attend events where it is served because food is such an important part of our identity and culture'

Very early on in the project we realised that the public perception of the Alzheimer's Society is of it being a large and well-

1 Kitwood designed a simple diagram based on a flower, with each petal representing an essential quality of human existence, namely: inclusion, identity, occupation, comfort and attachment with the petals of the flower held together by love.

financed organisation. Some of the very small and often unfunded groups that we approached felt we would need to offer some financial incentives to encourage the community to participate in dementia awareness sessions. As this would not be feasible, we instead managed to obtain good support by ensuring that culturally appropriate refreshments are available. Equally, by tailoring images for each cultural group, we explain how to reduce the risks of vascular dementia, for example, while using pictures of the particular foods important to that community. This is simple to achieve with very little cost since materials can be easily accessed on the internet. It cannot be stressed enough that preparation time has proved to be the key in successful engagement.

Conclusion

For our original targets we were tasked with enabling 1950 people from BAME communities over the three-year life of the project to receive accessible information about dementia, to know how to get a diagnosis to appreciate the benefits of getting a diagnosis and to be able to access local services. Within the first year of the project team being in place we had already reached well over 3000 people, demonstrating how there is a clear need – and a desire – in people to learn more about this condition.

As we move into the next phase of the project we will be looking to consider sustainability, sharing our learning and working with the University of Worcester to evaluate our impact.

If you would like more information, please contact the Project Manager, Alli Anthony, at alli.anthony@alzheimers.org.uk.

CULTURE AND ETHNICITY IN DEMENTIA: DEMENTIA FRIENDLY GURUDWARAS PROJECT

RAJINDER SINGH AND BHAJNEEK KAUR GREWAL

Introduction

A Gurudwara (Sikh Temple) is a place where Sikhs come together for congregational worship. Its primary purpose is to disseminate the eternal teachings of Sri Guru Granth Sahib Ji, the living Guru of the Sikhs. It is also a place to learn Sikh ethics, philosophy, theology, customs, traditions, languages and texts. Besides this, it is a community centre, and offers food, shelter and companionship to all those who need it irrespective of their race, caste, religion, creed or sexual orientation.

A significant proportion of the congregation is made up of the elderly. As longevity is the most important risk factor for developing Alzheimer's disease – the most common form of dementia – it was recognised that some of the Gurudwara's focus should be to raise awareness of dementia, improve accessibility for those with dementia, and provide support to carers and their families.

From the outset in 2012, a core group of Sikh health care professionals who were passionate about making a difference to those affected by dementia came together to spearhead this initiative. A decision was made to initially work with only one Gurudwara with a view to presenting it nationally as a model of a Dementia Friendly Gurudwara. Our local Gurudwara, the Ramgharia Gurudwara Sahib in Bradford, was selected for this purpose. With the aid of Cathy Henwood, Bradford Dementia Friendly Communities coordinator, an action plan was constructed. This was presented to the organisational leaders of the Gurudwara.

Aims and objectives

A systematic review of the physical environment and the current practices at the Gurudwara was undertaken, which allowed us to develop the following objectives that formed the basis of our action plan:

1. Establishing the baseline understanding of dementia within the Sikh community in Bradford through surveys and questionnaires.
2. Tackling the stigma and lack of knowledge about dementia and its implications through the use of tailored workshops, courses, lectures and physical and virtual information portals, both in English and Punjabi.

3. Modifying the environment at the Gurudwara to make it easier for people with dementia to have interaction with it.
4. Liaising with other organisations and dementia groups to share ideas and learn from each other.
5. Encouraging more members of the congregation to take an active role in the Dementia Friendly Gurudwara initiative.
6. Designating a Gurudwara dementia lead to act as a face-to-face contact for members of the Sikh congregation.
7. Reassessing the impact of our work to guide future interventions.

Challenges

The philosophy of the Sikh faith actively encourages social support for those in need. One of the founding principles of Sikhism is to recognise the light of God in all, with no exceptions, and it is regarded as a great honour for a Sikh to serve the needs of others and positively contribute to society. It is important to note that the majority of Sikhs in Britain come from a South Asian background, with many families tracing their origins back to the Punjab in India. Quite separately from the principles of Sikhism, Punjabi culture has a significant influence on day-to-day living in Sikh families. Over the centuries, many Sikh families have woven aspects of Punjabi culture into the fabric of family life. For the most part, the Sikh way of life and the positive influences from Punjabi culture marry well together. However, this complex relationship provided unique challenges when implementing the Dementia Friendly Gurudwaras' action plan.

Promoting change within any well-established institution is often received with initial scepticism. In order for the initiative to be successful, it was crucial to positively engage with the organisational committee and the congregation. Speaking to individuals in both groups on an informal basis proved a powerful tool to encourage engagement with the project. It was noted that many Sikhs at the Gurudwara were concerned about the possibility of developing dementia, and fear was exacerbated by stories of relatives 'losing their minds'. These fears were compounded by a lack of knowledge regarding the condition. Stories of Sikh carers being blamed for their relatives' physical and mental decline, as a consequence of the natural progression of dementia, were especially poignant. By listening to these stories, the Dementia Friendly Gurudwaras team was able to obtain a unique perspective on how the project could be shaped to help those affected by dementia in the Sikh community. Yaad da ghar (House of Memories) is a monthly memory cafe that has been established at the Gurudwara. It serves to encourage open discussion about dementia, and to provide an opportunity for those people affected by dementia in any way to share their stories and experiences. These sessions are free for anyone to attend, and it is hoped that the creation of this safe and friendly environment encourages members of the congregation to open up.

Sikhism is very much a family faith as opposed to a faith of hermits, and indeed, the Sikh teachings strongly encourage involvement in family life. Similarly, Punjabi culture places emphasis on preserving a strong family unit. In the event of illness or tragedy, a family comes together in unison to manage the event. For many, it is regarded as a matter of honour that one looks after one's elders. The image of a family that is united and cares for its members is an important one. In the Punjab, one rarely finds the elderly in nursing homes; rather, they are cared for in times of illness by their family members. Punjabi Sikhs in Britain do not adopt strict practices in this respect, and many have adopted elements of British culture in also seeking help from care facilities if needed. However, for many, the underlying sentiment of family honour is subtle but significant. In 2014 the Dementia Friendly Gurudwaras project received positive media coverage that highlighted the work that was being done in the Gurudwara. Journalists were naturally keen to hear the experiences of those families and carers affected by dementia. However, there was a palpable reluctance for members of the congregation to speak out about their experiences, even in families where those who had suffered with dementia had passed away. This in itself highlights the need to encourage open discussion within the Punjabi and Sikh communities to tackle the powerful stigma associated with dementia.

Dementia affects cognition and behaviour, and therefore carers can be confronted with extremely challenging situations. In Punjabi Sikh families, the acknowledgement that external help is required to care for relatives with dementia may be held at bay, due to the feeling that this is a family failing in itself. The environment at the Gurudwara has an important social component – meals are eaten together as a congregation, worship is congregation-led and the Gurudwaras provides families with an opportunity to catch up with each other. The memory loss and behavioural problems that can affect people with dementia may prevent these members of the congregation from taking part in these important exchanges. Relatives reported feeling embarrassed if their elderly family members could not maintain these social interactions. A feeling of shame within these families has been identified, the underlying causes of which are complicated and multifaceted. These issues can result in Punjabi Sikhs with dementia becoming increasingly isolated as they gradually stop coming to the Gurudwara.

One of the fundamental aims of the Dementia Friendly Gurudwaras project was to ensure that the environment of the Gurudwara was dementia friendly, making it easier for people with dementia to navigate, and thereby encouraging them to continue attending. Although there has been a surge in purpose-built Gurudwaras in the UK, many are often converted from churches and other listed buildings. While each Gurudwara will always have a prayer hall, communal kitchen and dining hall, the layout of each individual Gurudwara may vary significantly. Dementia-friendly signage was introduced to help both new members of the congregation and those with memory problems find their way around. These signs included English and Punjabi directions, with a pictogram representing the area in question. This measure, despite its simplicity, proved to be more complex to execute than initially expected. For example, in the same way that English has multiple words for 'female' (such as woman or lady), the Punjabi language has multiple words for man and woman, each with different connotations. When designing signs for the restrooms at the Gurudwara we had to seek advice from the Punjabi-speaking priests to ensure we chose the most appropriate, neutral and respectful words.

Although many factors contribute to the stigma associated with dementia in the Punjabi Sikh community, the most significant causative factor for this is lack of education and awareness. The language barrier was particularly important to address in this respect. Although the majority of Punjabi Sikhs can understand English, the preference is often to speak Punjabi, especially within the Gurudwara walls. The Dementia Friendly Gurudwaras team ensured that Punjabi information leaflets on dementia and Alzheimer's disease were present in the Gurudwara for people to read in their leisure. These received a very positive response. A virtual information portal was established for people with dementia and their carers. It includes podcasts about dementia in English and Punjabi, and contains links to other dementia resources that can be accessed by carers and others affected by dementia. A suggestion box was introduced in the Gurudwara to encourage those members of the congregation and their carers who are affected by dementia to share their suggestions anonymously as to how we can improve the facilities in the Gurudwara, so that they can shape our goals. To date, the Gurudwara has facilitated dementia-friendly training courses in English only, which limits the target audience. We are currently working together with other local groups to develop a dementia training programme that can be delivered in Punjabi at the Gurudwara.

Looking to the future

The progress made by the Dementia Friendly Gurudwaras initiative has encouraged a dialogue on dementia to begin within the local Sikh community in Bradford. In order for the project to serve the community, it was important to identify areas that needed attention. A survey using the Alzheimer's Disease Knowledge Scale was performed in the spring of 2014 to collect information on the congregation's knowledge of dementia. After implementation of the aforementioned action plan in the pilot Gurudwara, the survey can be repeated to assess whether dementia awareness has improved.

It is hoped that the Ramgarhia Gurudwara in Bradford can act as a role model for other Gurudwaras, both across Bradford and also nationally. The Gurudwaras in Bradford are linked through an electronic mailing group that provides a local network through which to disseminate information and advertise the initiative and its events. The Gurudwaras in Bradford also come together to organise several joint events each year, which provides an opportunity to share ideas. Congregations at the Gurudwaras often respond positively to familiar faces encouraging local projects, and it is hoped that each Gurudwara will have a small Dementia Friendly team to act as a point of contact for those affected by dementia.

To share ideas and learn from other communities, Dementia Friendly Gurudwaras is organising a Dementia Friendly Interfaith Conference within Bradford. This will provide an opportunity for representatives from all faiths to come together and share their experiences of dementia in their respective communities. For more information, see www.dementiafriendlygurudwaras.com or contact Rajinder Singh at rajinder21@hotmail.com.

WHY WE NEED TO WORK MORE WITH BLACK AND MINORITY ETHNIC COMMUNITY ORGANISATIONS

DAVID TRUSWELL

Working with the community intelligence found in the smaller black and minority ethnic (BME) community third sector organisations is an important way of getting information about dementia out into those communities, and also of supporting community voices in speaking out against the stigma attached to dementia. The reach of community organisations into the communities they support is substantial, and often they can be the only 'safe space' in the community to enable discussion about a health issue as misunderstood and discriminated against as dementia often is.

Community organisations are often characterised by the committed and resilient work of community volunteers who carry on despite the volatility of funding in the sector. However, they have few resources for publicising the essential role they play across a range of health information issues. With the emphasis on early diagnosis and community-based support services in the UK National Dementia Strategy (DH 2009), the statutory sector and large national charities now have a significant opportunity to invest in working more effectively with those black and minority organisations focusing on dementia, to make substantial improvements in the lives of people from BME communities living with dementia.

One such organisation is Culture Dementia UK based in West London for the past 15 years. Initially starting with the African Caribbean community, it has built to providing information, a crisis line, and a support group in a service that responds to the wide range of communities typical of the capital. The organisation has a rich network of informal contacts, particularly with the Black African Caribbean faith community. Mobilising these contacts helped the organisation to stage an excellent conference in November 2013, well attended by a multigenerational and diverse audience of carers and others. Giving prominence to the higher incidence of dementia in the African Caribbean, Indian Asian and Irish populations, the conference presentations ranged from identifying symptoms and accessing a general practitioner (GP) to a carer's personal journey with her father, illustrated by a photography portfolio. Statutory sector personnel have much to gain in understanding the emotional issues for communities by attending such events and visibly supporting them as part of their health promotion strategies.

Despite the considerable impact of recent funding constraints, on the organisation itself and those it supports, Culture Dementia UK continues to pursue a dynamic commitment to spreading the word about dementia to BME communities, participating in the Public Health England initiative in June 2014 to increase the number of Dementia Friends in the BME communities by speaking on community radio programmes. The organisation also brought its passion to Luton Council's Annual Dementia Conference in

July 2014, showcasing a young African Caribbean dementia peer support worker speaking of her experience of living with early onset dementia. The challenge for mainstream commissioning is to support the vibrancy and ability to create a memorable emotional message for all ethnicities that Culture Dementia UK supports. This needs to be done in a sustainable way that takes the organisation beyond a hand-to-mouth existence of small time-limited funding to being commissioned for a longer-term strategic communication role that utilises the organisation's community reach in order to achieve significant policy objectives such as dementia-friendly communities and early diagnosis. Find out more at www.culturedementiauk.org.

The challenge of engaging some of the substantial minority communities that unfortunately find themselves 'off the radar' of existing commissioning strategies is taken up by organisations such as the Chinese National Healthy Living Centre (CNHLC), an organisation that was established in 1987 in the Chinese community in London with a role that includes challenging and working with the stigma of mental illness. Although based in London, it has reached out across the UK to provide information and support services to Britain's dispersed Chinese community. Mental health problems generally are highly stigmatised in the Chinese community, with dementia often being strongly denied or dismissed, and carers frequently being unsupported with information and finding themselves and family members with dementia marginalised. CNHLC has secured funding for a three-year pan-London Chinese Dementia and Alzheimer's Awareness and Support Project. Since being set up in January 2014, the project has translated into Chinese the *Defeating Dementia* booklet published by Alzheimer's Research UK. Copies of this have been distributed free of charge to local community centres in various London boroughs. The project has organised workshops on Alzheimer's and dementia presented (by professionals from Alzheimer's Society UK) at a number of Chinese community organisations across London, and is developing a Chinese approach to dementia support groups, the Reminiscence Tea House. Find out more at www.cnhlc.org.uk/en.

Harnessing the competence of organisations such as Culture Dementia UK and the CNHLC is essential to developing affordable strategies for improving early access to diagnosis, disseminating health information and planning culturally informed support services for the growing number of people from BME communities living with dementia. Their ability to deliver significant health information interventions that are emotionally powerful, well organised and thoughtfully designed, with the potential to have a high impact on key groups known to have late presentation to dementia services and significant cultural needs in relation to 'living well' with dementia in the community, is unmatched by any other source and vital to promoting early diagnosis and raising awareness in these communities.

DEVELOPING AN INFORMATION PROGRAMME FOR SOUTH ASIAN FAMILIES

DIANA BARBOSA

Background

In March 2013 the Alzheimer's Society completed a three-year project to develop, pilot and evaluate a Carer Information and Support Programme (CrISP) across the UK. One of its aims was to address accessibility issues for black and minority ethnic (BME) communities. However, whilst the programme was delivered 100 times and reached approximately 1000 carers, only 2.5 per cent of participants were from BME groups.

A literature review and a number of consultation meetings were undertaken to scope a service model that would address the information and support needs of BME communities in the UK, particularly those with a rapidly ageing population, including groups originating from South Asia – India, Pakistan, Bangladesh and Sri Lanka. This led to the development of the Information Programme for South Asian Families (IPSAF).

Aims

The principal aims of IPSAF were to:

- adapt the content, format and delivery of the existing CrISP for a South Asian audience
- develop, test and support the implementation of a collaborative service delivery model, enabling partnerships between the Alzheimer's Society and local community and faith organisations
- co-deliver the programme in 20 locations, to a minimum of 200 family members and friends of people living with dementia
- develop an audio-visual resource that is educational, portable and transferable, and create a DVD containing a series of films to support delivery of the programme in face-to-face sessions and enable the dissemination of information to extended families and the wider South Asian community
- identify and support the development of learning resources to increase the cultural competence of Alzheimer's Society staff, volunteers and partner organisations.

Designing the programme

An initial literature review was followed by a series of consultation meetings that involved approximately 250 South Asian family members and other stakeholders. The feedback gathered informed the cultural tailoring of CrISP, ensuring that IPSAF would be fit for purpose.

Some of the practical adaptations included:

- providing information in an accessible format and in the language of the target audience, ensuring it reaches decision-makers, care providers and extended family
- factoring in the option to deliver the programme for 'women only' or 'men only' or using separate tables for women
- where necessary, allowing time in sessions for interpretation to take place

- pathfinder managers allocating a substantial window of time to engage with local South Asian faith and community organisations and to establish partnership working arrangements.

Programme implementation

A number of core tasks were identified:

1. *To assist staff in developing the skills needed to develop effective partnerships.* Delivery of information services in partnership with local community and faith organisations was identified as a critical success factor for IPSAF. The Alzheimer's Society provided information and partnership agreement documents to clarify expectations. Partners were invited to attend cultural competence training and a programme familiarisation day, and had the opportunity to make use of Alzheimer's Society resources to develop their knowledge of dementia.
2. *To produce a high-quality audio-visual resource* according to the Alzheimer's Society's brand guidelines, that communicated in images a rather extensive and specific script with a modest budget. From the outset it was clear that it would be essential to base the delivery of the programme on audio-visual resources rather than written ones. A DVD was produced with the following quality criteria: educational, divided into chapters, engaging different age groups, transferable and containing Bollywood elements. The chapter themes would coincide with the themes of face-to-face sessions: (1) Understanding dementia; (2) Legal and financial matters; (3) Looking after yourself; (4) Looking after others.
3. *To identify which competences were needed to deliver the programme and how to support their acquisition.* One of the aims of IPSAF was to identify and support the development of learning resources to increase the cultural competence of the Alzheimer's Society and partner organisation staff. With this in mind, an experienced Culture and Diversity consultant was commissioned to develop and deliver a two-day cultural

competence training course and introduce IPSAF facilitators to: (1) Cultural dimensions; (2) Unconscious bias; (3) Brief characterisation of South Asian cultures in the UK – religion, values, beliefs, family structure, naming, diet, dress codes; (4) Demographics; (5) Communication skills; (6) Working with interpreters.

4. *To develop robust evaluation methods*. The programme outcomes are to increase and support:

    - coping strategies and practical skills
    - knowledge of dementia
    - access of services
    - planning for the future
    - peer support.

Each programme is evaluated at the beginning and end, through participant feedback collected by the programme facilitators. In addition, the Bradford Dementia Group (BDG) is carrying out an external evaluation of the project as a whole. The BDG evaluation makes use of methods such as a multiple-choice quiz, small focus groups, and interviews with family members, facilitators and representatives of partner organisations. It will also carry out a follow-up interview three months after an initial one, during the first quarter of 2015. Importantly, BDG will facilitate an advisory group of South Asian people to guide their work.

The BDG evaluation, coupled with the internal reviews of each programme, will provide a measure of outcomes and inform the continuing improvement of the programme.

Implementation and next steps

Five IPSAF programmes were piloted in 2013/14 and reached a total of 46 South Asian carers. The average of attendance at pilot sites was 9.2 people per session. We estimated that each carer was supporting at least one person and sharing the programme information with other family members using the DVD. In this way the information is expected to reach over 120 South Asian family members of people with dementia. So far, the IPSAF programme sessions have been delivered in Bradford, Coventry, Leicester, Rochdale and Enfield.

In 2014/15 the programme will be piloted in a further 15 locations and reach up to 360 South Asian people across England. This is being made possible through the 'Live Well Campaign' and funds raised by Lloyds Banking Group.

If you would like more information about the project, contact the Service Development Team at the Alzheimer's Society central office, or email the Programme Development Manager, Diana Barbosa, at diana.barbosa@alzheimers.org.uk.

ACCESSIBLE DEMENTIA SERVICES: ENGAGING THE SOMALI COMMUNITY IN TOWER HAMLETS

SOPHIE LEATHERLAND AND ALLI ANTHONY

A local consultation carried out by Alzheimer's Society Tower Hamlets in July 2013 found that there were 641 Somali men and women over 65 registered with a general practitioner (GP) in the London Borough of Tower Hamlets, and that there were likely to be many more Somali residents over 65 who were not registered with a surgery.

National prevalence figures project that around 1 in 3 of these residents may develop dementia, so the number of Somali people in the borough requiring dementia-specific services will be further increased by the family members and friends of those affected, who will also need advice and support. This is a significant proportion of the borough's Black African population.

The Somali community draws strength from its strong cultural ties, but these can also act as a barrier to engagement with health care and advice services. There are high levels of stress in the community, often due to lack of understanding about how to access appropriate health care, but also because of a reluctance to seek help due to fears that this will lead to stigma, harassment, family breakdown and isolation. There are broader factors contributing to the high levels of mental illness within the older Somali population, in the form of traumas resulting from many years of war, life in refugee camps and forced migration. Together, these issues contribute to low take-up of dementia support services within Tower Hamlet's Somali community.

> Lack of information about health issues is an existing problem in the Somali community, and this disease (dementia) is one of the less known diseases to the Somali people. (Staff member, Somali Culture and Education Project)

Alzheimer's Society Tower Hamlets is addressing this lack of engagement in a number of ways through its Somali Project. Its focus is a culturally sensitive, Somali-specific outreach and awareness-raising service. They have recruited Somali members of staff, a male and a female worker, in order to adhere to social and cultural customs, to work within the community and to raise awareness. Two Somali dementia cafes have been established, based on a gender segregation model, so that peer support and open, safe discussion of dementia might take place.

Awareness-raising is a key route to addressing the lack of engagement with dementia services by Somalis in the borough, as it is often not seen as a disease but as a mental illness – it is even referred to as a form of 'madness'. There is no word in the Somali language for 'dementia'. The Alzheimer's Society is working with Somali community groups to raise awareness of dementia in the borough, providing faith and community leaders with awareness training so that the myths surrounding dementia can be dispelled by those in respected community positions.

Raising awareness also helps to develop positive contact between the older Somali community and their GPs. We know that obtaining a formal diagnosis is absolutely crucial to accessing ongoing support. If the Somali community has an informed view of dementia, they are more likely to recognise the early signs and symptoms and to seek advice. Through better informing GPs' understanding of the Somali community, the likelihood of their signposting to appropriate support services once a formal diagnosis has been made is increased. This is part of a much bigger drive by the Alzheimer's Society, across all communities, to better inform GPs about dementia and the benefits of early diagnosis.

The materials used to facilitate this increased awareness are also a focus for the Somali Project. The Somali community has a tradition of oral, rather than written, communication, meaning that some promotional activities such as branded leaflets are not appropriate in disseminating information or advertising services. This has made it even more vital that awareness-raising and support services are taken out to the community, so that word of mouth and a visual presence increases service take-up. The dementia cafes are a perfect example of this, as talking, listening, watching and sharing are put to the forefront of accessing and benefiting from support, rather than reading and writing.

> The community has to be helped to understand that in relation to health issues the symptoms must be related to the illness and not the person and that help is available. (Staff member, mental health worker, Family Action)

The Somali Project team found that when the Somali dementia cafes were held in environments familiar to the older Somali population, for example, a sheltered housing scheme or day centre, the level of engagement and interest in the subject of dementia was much higher. As a result, the team has developed the Somali dementia cafes into a 'mobile' service, taking the cafe to different community venues across the borough to reach more people.

The project recognises that it is crucial that work continues to be undertaken by workers and volunteers from the community, and that it will take time to build relationships and trust between community members, local services and staff. But many people in the Somali community have already acknowledged that there is a need for this work. There is a willingness and desire to learn more about dementia and dementia services within the borough. The Somali Project continues to evaluate and address that need, evolving its Somali-specific services as it learns more about the ways to engage minority ethnic groups in discussions about dementia.

For more information about this work, please contact Towerhamlets@alzheimers.org.uk.

SOUTH ASIAN SINGING FOR THE BRAIN

SUZANNE HUMPHREYS AND ANNA SADLER

Alzheimer's Society Newham received funding to establish a pilot Singing for the Brain group for people with dementia and their family carers from a South Asian background. Singing for the Brain groups are based around the principles of music therapy and singing. The structured sessions use music to encourage communication and participation, and include opportunities to talk to other people. Each session includes a range of activities including vocal warm-up and singing a variety of familiar and new songs. The London Borough of Newham has one of the largest minority ethnic populations in the country. Whilst no one group is in the majority, we have significant numbers of South Asian older people living in the borough. It therefore made sense to offer a pilot service to test the levels of demand for a bespoke service. We worked in close partnership with a local charity for older South Asians. Their volunteers were encouraged to come to the group and to bring their own service users who had memory problems. This aspect was fundamental to the success of the group.

This South Asian Singing for the Brain service met once a week for 18 weeks in 2014 and will continue in 2015.

Service users

As the group developed and service users were recruited, it transpired that the main languages needed were Hindi, Urdu, Punjabi and Gujarati. It had been difficult to establish the language groups before the service was set up, and so planning was quite difficult. Most service users had a diagnosis of dementia and were in the early to mid stages of dementia. The service users with a diagnosis were recruited for the group through their existing contact with memory services. However, there were three to four participants who did not have a diagnosis but who had memory problems and were struggling to make contact with the memory clinic for various reasons. As the pilot proceeded, it became clear that many older South Asian people are living with memory problems but are not presenting to GPs. The Singing group gradually gained more participants who did not have a diagnosis and did not know how to get one. It became clear that the group would have to be open to those people who did not yet have a diagnosis but could be helped to get one, as this situation was more common amongst the South Asian community.

Group leader

We recruited a group leader who is fluent in English, Hindi, Punjabi, Gujarati, Urdu and Bengali. She had previously been a volunteer, is a central figure in the local South Asian women's group, and has acted as a gatekeeper for many of the older South Asian women. She is supported by two volunteers who help to design activities for the start of the session, set up the room and serve refreshments. All participants enjoy the service greatly, and the Alzheimer's Society are helping to guide them towards a diagnosis if they do not already have one. As this is a pilot group, we have taken a very flexible approach. This has included less structured sessions with more general talking and reminiscing, which the participants find helpful.

Our learning

Staff: Getting the right person to lead the group is essential. Language skills must be evidenced at interview, and both the interviewee and the recruiter must be aware of what is required of the role. The applicant also needs good awareness of the cultural background of potential service users and how to engage service users during the group. It is not simply a case of singing songs in another language. On the flip side, it is also important that the staff member is knowledgeable about dementia and local diagnostic pathways. It has also proved useful for the new South Asian Singing group leader to be mentored by an existing leader who has provided advice and guidance regarding structuring a Singing group.

Service users: Due to the low levels of awareness and understanding about dementia in many South Asian communities, we found that levels of diagnosis were disproportionately low. However, there were many people who were aware of continuing memory problems and many who had visited their GP and had been turned away, having been told it was 'normal ageing'. The inclusion of various South Asian communities in one group did work despite different language requirements and varied religious and cultural values. If the numbers and funding permitted, it could be worth aiming to hold specific groups for the different South Asian ethnicities. Although the group participants have enjoying sharing and learning each other's songs, a common thread musically for all, regardless of their language, has been the Hindi songs that many know through Bollywood films, which are very popular in a lot of South Asian communities.

Transport: With other Singing groups the participants either organise their own dial-a-ride or get to the venue themselves. We found that most of our service users for the South Asian group had expected someone to organise the transport for them, and were accustomed to being dropped off and collected (sometimes by family members).

Refreshments: Biscuits and tea were less favourable and were soon replaced with South Asian snacks and fruit squash, reminding us that every detail must be considered and be culturally appropriate for each group.

Conclusion

The group has helped us to reach older members of the South Asian community who are worried about their memories to seek diagnosis and reduce the stigma association with dementia.

One of our key learning points has been close partnership working with an existing South Asian community group that has good links into the community. Establishing trust has been paramount. One service user said:

> I spend most of my time indoors and get very lonely and depressed. I really enjoy coming to this group once a week. I had forgotten how to read Gujarati, but since coming to the group I can now read the song sheets and sing in my language, which I haven't done in many years. I also love meeting the others in the group. It has made me very happy!

For more information on the project please email newham@alzheimers.org.uk.

FULA: FUTURO LATINO AMERICANO

CLAIRE GAULIER

Age UK Lewisham and Southwark's (AUKLS) Access for Black Asian and Minority Ethnic Elders Project (2011–2014) has supported older black and minority ethnic (BME) elders (over-50s) to access mainstream and culturally specific services through individual support provided by a volunteer from a similar cultural or ethnic background. The project reached the most isolated and vulnerable groups such as the Latin American elders, now recognised as a minority ethnic group in some boroughs of London. Referrals coming in were for people from very diverse backgrounds and with a wide range of needs: from socialising more to living better with dementia, or from keeping fit and healthy to looking for a job for the over-60s.

As part of the project, AUKLS worked with community groups and BME organisations. The challenge was to find the right volunteer to match with each BME elder referred in. In 2013, AUKLS and the Latin American Women's Right Service (LAWRS) recruited and trained ten volunteers from a Latin American background as person-centred planners. Six were in their mid-40s and two in their 50s – all were looking to build their skills to increase their employment opportunities.

It is evident that the options for Latin American people to meet others from the same cultural backgrounds and build peer support networks are currently limited. In association with LAWRS and Age UK London, AUKLS organised a bi-monthly meeting for

Latin American over-50s, gathering information on their needs and wishes. Other organisations were invited to give talks on health, social rights, benefits and other topics. At the end of 2013, the group had grown quickly, mixing women from different South American countries and a few men. The group has provided an opportunity for us, as an organisation supporting older people, to understand better the reality and diversity of the needs of older people. It has also been essential to identify at an early stage the most vulnerable people, and to signpost them to adequate services. An example was the daughter of a Latin American woman who was convinced that her mother had dementia and, through our work with LAWRS, we supported her and other women within the group around this issue. We enabled her mother, by providing a volunteer to accompany her on the journey to and from the group, to access services where they could run tests to establish a definite diagnosis.

The desire to meet and socialise was so strong within the group that AUKLS decided to offer a space to meet up weekly, at a local day centre. The meetings organised from January 2014 allowed the group to develop a routine of meeting together, collecting money to buy coffee and biscuits, and organising dinners. AUKLS worked closely with LAWRS to organise the activities they were requesting.

The priority of the group when it was set up was to offer a safe social space. AUKLS opened its doors without charge, in order to reduce the risk of any conflict related to money, which could impact on the attendance of the most vulnerable elders, and in order to give fair access to the activities developed within the group.

The age range was based on a minimum of 50 years. This may seem a relatively young age limit, but it was based on the idea that attendance would help to prevent problems occurring later in life. Our work is focused on activities that will have a positive influence on current and future wellbeing and quality of life.

From the beginning, referrals to the group were mainly from LAWRS, and were for women in their late 50s or mid-60s. Some were still seeking employment, and some were too unwell to keep on working. Most of them had arrived in the UK less than a year earlier and lived in a state of precariousness; others had been brought to the UK by their daughters, to care for their grandchildren. A few referrals came from Mind Care. One such referral enabled a couple, one of whom has dementia, to take part in social activities they would otherwise not have had access to. Otherwise, the members invite acquaintances, promoting the activities through Latin American networks in London. It is a very mixed group.

United St Saviour's – a local charity – recently offered a small financial grant to the group, now called FULA (Futuro Latino Americano – Latin American Future). This grant will mean that AUKLS will be able to sustain and develop activities that will improve how we provide information to the group members as well as to strengthen supportive networks that have been developed, through involving members in decision-making as well as in the delivery of activities and events.

In summary, the Latin American group is a space where people can take part in activities that stimulate them mentally and improve their wellbeing. People with dementia are able to take part in these along with people who do not have dementia. That the activities are provided in a culturally sensitive context, amongst people from a common background, is crucial to the popularity of the project.

If you would like more information about the group, please contact Claire Gaulier at claire.gaulier@ageuklands.org.uk.

A WHOLE COMMUNITY APPROACH TO MEMORY LOSS IN THE IRISH COMMUNITY IN ENGLAND

MARY TILKI AND CHARLOTTE CURRAN

Irish in Britain is an umbrella organisation representing the Irish community in Britain, campaigning on their behalf and working with (Irish) community organisations to provide a range of sustainable social, cultural, health and welfare services. *Cuimhne* (the Irish word for memory, pronounced 'queevna') is one of our major campaigns that adopts a whole community approach to the issue of dementia amongst Irish people. It is an ambitious initiative to involve Irish people, community organisations and businesses in addressing exclusion and improving the quality of life for people with memory loss and their carers. *Cuimhne* is a way of capturing the talents, strengths and energies of the Irish community to address a critical need whilst aspiring to become the first memory loss-friendly minority ethnic community in England.

Background context

The Irish are one of the largest ethnic groups in the UK, with a demographically older age profile than the general population or other black and minority ethnic (BME) groups (APPG on Dementia 2013; Truswell 2013). Calculations based on 2011 Census data suggest that the incidence of dementia among the Irish is the highest of any ethnic group (Truswell 2013). However, these estimates ignore the increased incidence of cardiovascular disease (Harding, Rosato and Teyhan 2008) and other risk factors to which the Irish are predisposed (Tilki *et al.* 2009). Despite this, the needs of the Irish are repeatedly overlooked (APPG on Dementia 2013; Irish in Britain 2014). Being white, they are assumed to have the same socio-cultural needs as the British, and as such, the traditions, cultural practices or life histories that have a profound bearing on people with dementia are neglected (APPG on Dementia 2013; Tilki *et al.* 2011).

Although Irish people have been in England for decades, past experiences of racism and hostility mean that many retain a distance from their local communities (APPG on Dementia 2013; Tilki 2003). Racism and negative stereotyping by health professionals leave many unwilling to seek help, preferring the dignity and expedience of self-help (Tilki 2003). As with other BME groups, the Irish lack awareness of dementia, and fears and misconceptions delay help-seeking. The fear of being 'put in a home' is a major issue for Irish elders. Negative experiences and cultural insensitivity rather than stigma make Irish people reluctant to engage in local activities or access mainstream services, thus precluding support that could help them maintain independence and quality of life (Tilki *et al.* 2011).

Irish voluntary community organisations (VCOs) in England, which emerged over decades to provide services to Irish people, are increasingly dealing with those living with dementia and their carers. They are particularly conscious of older people and carers who 'disappear' because they are embarrassed by memory loss or unusual behaviours. Tilki *et al.* (2011) describe what cultural sensitivity means for Irish people, and highlight examples of good dementia practice within Irish VCOs. Social, cultural and sport-oriented VCOs are keen to become dementia friendly but are often concerned that they lack the skills to support people with memory loss who would use their services (FIS 2010). While individual VCOs can be supported in developing or expanding services, dementia is an issue for the whole community. This requires a multifaceted approach to generate discussion, increase dementia awareness, challenge negativity and engage the whole Irish community in supporting those living with dementia.

Cuimhne: Irish Memory Loss Alliance

Cuimhne is a strategic response to a significant community concern. It is an organic work in progress with the following five strands of activity, some of which are progressing more quickly than others.

BUILDING A COMMUNITY ALLIANCE

We were conscious of the need to raise awareness of dementia, and to break down barriers of ignorance and fear to encourage dialogue across the community. This was achieved in several ways:

- media strategy, community newspapers, radio
- sponsored fun run
- direct approach to businesses
- housing association reminiscence project
- sports project with health focus
- awareness-raising with Irish professional networks
- events hosted by the Embassy of Ireland.

There is much greater awareness across the community as testified by hits to our website, content in community papers, individual communications and donations. We have harnessed the support of several Irish businesses, and some have seen the commercial value of being dementia friendly and have used *Cuimhne* training to ensure their staff are sensitive to people affected by memory loss.

LOBBYING POLICY-MAKERS

Challenging the neglect of the Irish community at policy level is an ongoing task. We continue to do this in different ways:

- presentation of evidence to the All-Party Parliamentary Group (APPG) on Dementia
- presentation of evidence to the APPG on the Irish community in Britain
- presentation of evidence to Public Health England
- raising parliamentary questions
- participating in national consultations and conferences
- presenting a survey of Irish inclusion in Joint Strategic Needs assessments (JSNAs) to JSNA leads, Health and Wellbeing Boards and Healthwatch.

Work needs to be done by VCOs at a local level to ensure that evidence is translated into JSNAs and Joint Health and Wellbeing Strategies (JHWSs).

DEVELOPING AND STRENGTHENING SUPPORTIVE NETWORKS

Cuimhne encourages and assists VCOs to engage with local authorities, mainstream voluntary organisations, voluntary sector councils and churches by providing:

- statistical information and research evidence
- capacity building support
- advice/support on funding
- training staff and volunteers
- links to a local Alzheimer's Society, Age UK etc.

- promoting joint events, for example, Dementia Awareness Week
- initiating a Dementia Action Alliance in Brent

VCOs have begun to expand their offer, linking with a local Alzheimer's Society, church groups or local community activities. Social/cultural VCOs have begun or are planning elders events, luncheon clubs involving local volunteers in community venues, church halls etc.

IMPROVING AWARENESS AND UNDERSTANDING

Cuimhne's major aim was to identify sources of advice and help for people with dementia, carers and community groups. Links were made and enquiries signposted to existing sources of dementia information such as:

- a local Alzheimer's Society
- Alzheimer's Society website, resources, publications
- social Care Institute for Excellence website, resources, publications
- local Irish VCOs, as appropriate
- a local Alzheimer's Society involved in *Cuimhne* training
- research publications relating to the Irish community/older people/dementia.

There is limited information specific to Irish people with dementia. *Cuimhne's* focus has been on training staff and volunteers, but we are in the process of developing culturally sensitive resources, engaging Irish businesses, writers, artists and professionals in producing them.

MEMORY LOSS AWARENESS TRAINING

The terms 'dementia' and 'Alzheimer's' strike fear across the Irish community, so we talk about 'memory loss' where possible.

Cuimhne basic training aims to encourage a different way of thinking by:

- challenging assumptions about people with memory loss
- focusing instead on how *we* think and behave
- understanding the experience of memory loss for the person and carer
- focusing on their abilities, strengths and their personhood
- exploring culturally sensitive ways of connecting, communicating, enabling and supporting people with memory loss.

We have trained over 100 volunteers and staff from Irish VCOs, and evaluations show an increased level of understanding and a 'can do' approach to memory loss. We are recruiting suitably skilled volunteers to cascade basic awareness training within communities while we work with VCOs to develop dementia-friendly environments and expand services for people with dementia.

CUIMHNE: WORK IN PROGRESS AND A LONG WAY TO GO

As an Irish community project, our aim is not to be separatist or to ignore what is happening in the mainstream. It is recognised that many in our community, especially those with memory loss, feel more comfortable in an Irish environment. As the Prime Minister's challenge on dementia acknowledges, dementia is an issue for the whole community. We believe *Cuimhne* is a model that can be adapted for other communities and we are happy to offer our support. For further information visit our website at www.irishinbritain.org/campaigns/cuimhne-irish-memory-loss-alliance.

References

APPG (All-Party Parliamentary Group) on Dementia (2013) *Dementia Does Not Discriminate: The Experiences of Black, Asian and Minority Ethnic Communities*. July. London: Alzheimer's Society. Available at www.alzheimers.org.uk/site/scripts/download_info.php?downloadID=1186, accessed on 11 December 2014.

DH (Department of Health) (2009) *Living Well with Dementia: A National Dementia Strategy*. London: DH.

FIS (Federation of Irish Societies) (2010) *Meeting the Needs of Irish Elders: Findings from the Mapping of Activities of Irish Organisations in England and Wales.* London: FIS.

Harding, S., Rosato, M. and Teyhan, A. (2008) 'Trends for coronary heath disease and stroke mortality among migrants in England and Wales: slow declines for some groups.' *Heart 94*, 463–470.

Irish in Britain (2014) *Degrees of Ethnic Inclusion Revisited: Analysing Irish Inclusion in JSNAs.* London. Irish in Britain. Available at www.irishinbritain.org/cmsfiles/Publications/Reports/JSNA-Report-FINAL-pdf.pdf, accessed on 24 June 2014.

Tilki, M. (2003) 'A study of the health of the Irish-born people in London: the relevance of social and socio-economic factors, health beliefs and behaviour.' Unpublished PhD thesis, Middlesex University. Available at http://eprints.mdx.ac.uk/6724/1/Tilki.phd.pdf, accessed on 24 June 2014.

Tilki, M., Ryan, L., D'Angelo, A. and Sales, R. (2009) *The Forgotten Irish: Report of a Research Project Commissioned by Ireland Fund of Great Britain.* London: Ireland Fund of Great Britain. Available at http://eprints.mdx.ac.uk/6350, accessed on 24 June 2014.

Tilki, M., Mulligan, E., Pratt, E., Halley, E. and Taylor, E. (2011) 'Older Irish people with dementia in England.' *Advances in Mental Health 9*, 3, 221–232.

Truswell, D. (2013) *Black, Asian and Minority Ethnic Communities and Dementia: Where Are We Now? Better Health Briefing 30.* London: Race Equality Foundation.

10

DEMENTIA, ETHNICITY AND CARE HOMES

Alisoun Milne and Jan Smith

Introduction

Increasing policy, practice and research attention is being paid to the importance of ethnicity in, and on, the lives and experiences of older people with dementia in the UK and internationally (Smith 2013). Only very recently has this small but growing body of work begun to incorporate care home residents from black and minority ethnic (BME) communities and their families. As has been identified elsewhere in this book, research on ethnicity, race and ageing and on services for BME populations is a neglected dimension of the burgeoning investment in research and in dementia care practice improvements; this is particularly pronounced in the care home sector.

This chapter has two interlinked aims: to offer an overview of the profile, needs and experiences of care home residents with dementia from BME communities, and to contribute to informing good practice. Most of the evidence from the UK is drawn from work that focuses on one ethnic group often living in one locality (ONS 2011). Studies generally rely on small samples, and typically focus on staff or family members to 'represent' the service users rather than obtaining views from older people with dementia themselves (APPG on Dementia 2013). Also, the majority of research has been done with, and in, the longer established minority ethnic populations, primarily the South Asian or African Caribbean communities (Lawrence *et al.* 2011; Uppal, Bonas and Philpott 2013). Some work is emerging with the Chinese, Middle Eastern, Greek Cypriot and Turkish communities, particularly in Australia, and there is a growing recognition of the need to do research with more recently settled communities such as older people from Eastern Europe and Russia (Mackenzie 2007; Mackenzie and Coates 2003). There is almost no work on people from other Western European countries such as Italy, Greece and France who live in the UK (Botsford, Clarke and Gibb 2011). An overarching factor is that dementia tends to be a hidden and highly stigmatised condition in most minority ethnic communities (Anderson and Brownlie 1997).

It is important to acknowledge a number of intersecting issues that underpin discourse on research on minority ethnic groups in the UK, including that pertaining to care homes (Uppal and Bonas 2014). A primary challenge is that race and ethnicity are contested terms (Adamson 2001; Aspinall 2010). Any narrative that aims to capture 'the story' or 'the experience' of a minority ethnic group or groups will fail to do so; experiences shift temporally, by cohort, by and with generational change, on an intra-group basis, by area, culture, religion, sub-culture, and often depend to a significant degree on history, including migration patterns (Bhopal and Preston 2012; Uppal *et al.* 2013). The incorporation of a number of wider issues such as country of origin and socio-economic status has led to the development of the term 'super diversity'. This describes the enormous variety of factors that influence the meaning of 'ethnicity' and how it impacts on an older person's life, especially when that life is also affected by the experience of having dementia (Vertovec 2007).

Additionally, it is important to acknowledge the role of individual differences and increasing heterogeneity and diversity amongst the older population(s) from minority ethnic groups in the UK. Race and/or ethnicity need to be seen as intersecting with other dimensions of identity and inequality such as gender, age, sexuality and socio-political context, and not as a 'master status' that eclipses all other sources of identity. The evidence reviewed in this chapter needs to be viewed through this multidimensional lens. Although the authors focus primarily on evidence from the UK, where space permits, research from Europe and North America is also included (Milne and Chryssanthopoulou 2005).

Before turning to the chapter's specific focus, the authors offer a brief profile of the care home population and the policy context relating to care home provision for BME groups.

Care home sector in the UK

In the UK, approximately 420,000 older people[1] live in a care home; this represents 6 per cent of the older population. The vast majority of care home residents are women aged 75 or over: most have multiple health problems, particularly in relationship to mobility, mental health and continence (Dening and Milne 2013). It has been estimated that four-fifths of residents have dementia and three-quarters require assistance with mobility (Alzheimer's Society 2007). In fact, dementia, in combination with difficulties in performing activities of daily living, is the strongest health-related determinant for care home admission (DH 2009). Depression is also common – it is estimated to affect between 40–45 per cent of all those entering a care home.

Most people enter a care home because they can no longer live independently as a result of physical and/or mental illness. Over half of the admissions to care homes come from hospital (Bebbington, Darton and Netten 2001); this rises to about two-thirds for nursing home admissions. The biggest single health-related predictor of care home admission is (usually advanced) dementia. In the US a recent study estimated that dementia increased the risk of admission to a nursing home five-fold (Bharucha *et al.* 2004). In 2009 Laing & Buisson (2010) estimated that around 40 per cent of admissions to UK care homes were known to be triggered by dementia, but this is likely to be conservative. Banerjee *et al.* (2003) found that having a co-resident carer had a strongly protective effect – the risk of being

1 Older people are those aged 65 and over.

institutionalised was 20 times higher in people who did *not* have a carer living with them. This must be one of the most striking demonstrations of the importance of family care anywhere in the research literature.

Policy context

The quality of care in care homes is the focus of a number of intersecting policies including the National Dementia Strategy (DH 2009). The importance of culturally appropriate care was first identified in the 'community care reforms' of the 1980s and 1990s. It was built on by a number of policies in the 2000s including the Care Standards Act and the introduction of National Minimum Standards for care homes (DH 2003). The 2006 *Dementia Guidelines* – produced by the National Institute for Health and Care Excellence (NICE) and the Social Care Institute for Excellence (SCIE) – highlighted the importance of recognising the widely diverse experiences of people with dementia and the role played by gender, ethnicity, age, and culture (NICE/SCIE 2006). This was accompanied by a focus on equity of access to services – including long-term care – by minority groups, and a requirement that health and social care agencies ensure that they address the specific and particular needs of minority ethnic groups (CRE 2002; Quince 2013).

Care home residents from BME group populations

Currently, there are relatively few minority ethnic older people in care homes in the UK. In 2001 only 1.2 per cent of those surveyed were from a minority ethnic group (Bebbington *et al.* 2001). Data from the 2001 Census – which is now relatively old – suggests that there are 25,166 'ethnic adults' living in care homes in England and Wales (Mold, Fitzpatrick and Roberts 2005a, 2005b). In the US, figures indicate that higher rates of residential care occur in the majority white population compared with their minority ethnic peers. Whilst this may also be the case in the UK, some work suggests that amongst publicly funded residents, BME elders may be overrepresented

(Bebbington *et al.* 2001). At present, and in general, BME residents are younger, more likely to be male, have higher rates of dementia and incontinence, and are more dependent on admission than their white counterparts.

Specific drivers for admission to long-term care that are more prevalent in BME communities include: later diagnosis of dementia and/or other mental health conditions due (in part) to high levels of stigma linked to mental illness; limited or no language to describe dementia; and reluctance to seek help from, and difficulty accessing, services, especially 'mental health' services (Jutlla 2013; Seabrooke and Milne 2009). BME elders are also more at risk of being placed a distance away from family and community and of an unplanned admission. That family members may be reluctant (or unable) to visit the older person is likely to deepen existing feelings of isolation and alienation. Enhanced exposure to a number of life course inequalities – in particular, poverty, racism and exclusion – amplify these challenges (Milne 2009).

Quality of life: BME older people with dementia living in a care home

Whilst recent work has begun to pay much more attention to the quality of life of care home residents (for example, My Home Life – a national initiative to improve the quality of care in care homes; Owen and the National Care Homes R&D Forum 2006), evidence relating to care home residents with dementia from BME groups is limited in both size and scope.

Language issues are a commonly cited barrier to communicating effectively with care home residents who cannot speak, or who have lost the capacity to speak, English. Criticisms include a lack of sensitivity to accommodating language differences, and limited or no access to staff who can speak the same language (Daker-White *et al.* 2002). Limited or no availability of interpretation services has also been identified; as understanding an older person's needs and wishes are vital for effective assessments of need, mental capacity, and/or dementia, this is a fundamental deficit (Bowes, Avan and Macintosh 2012; Manthorpe *et al.* 2010). Add to this the communication problems that often accompany advanced dementia – and one or more sensory impairments – and the challenge becomes very complex indeed.

The importance of food and providing culturally appropriate meals is widely noted in research with BME older service users (Daker-White *et al.* 2002). Some work from the US suggests that care home residents from a Korean or Japanese background appreciate being offered 'their food' but also enjoy 'American food' too (Machizawa and Lau 2010). Family carers also report that homes offering culturally appropriate foods are a draw for older people from minority ethnic groups (Moon, Lubben and Villa 1998). An Australian study noted inflexibility regarding mealtimes and 'European'-dominated menus as failing to consider the cultural needs of residents from minority ethnic groups (Warburton, Bartlett and Rao 2009). Recent work by Manthorpe *et al.* (2010) in the UK reported evidence of 'ill-disguised racism' amongst staff in some care homes who were negative about family members bringing in food from their own community for residents.

Research has also identified personal hygiene practices as culturally defined, specifically, bathing, hair care and skin care (Daker-White *et al.* 2002). For some religiously observant individuals, washing with particular hands and washing in a certain way after lavatory use are important elements of normative practice. A study in Scotland found that many care homes did not provide water or hoses near toilets, and insisted that service users use toilet paper (Bowes and Wilkinson 2003).

There is some evidence that care home residents from the same minority community prefer to mix with each other; it may offer a sense of security, of 'belonging' and shared identity (Daker-White *et al.* 2002). Not being able to meet regularly with people from the same ethnic background has been cited as a risk factor for isolation and loneliness (Machizawa and Lau 2010). It is important – as with residents from the mainstream population – to acknowledge the role of class, gender, occupational groups, and religion, in informing decisions about social mixing. Recent research with older Chinese service users, for example, reveals that participants were uncomfortable participating in activities with people who shared their ethnic background but who did not share their economic or occupational status (Liu 2003).

Racism and discrimination experienced by older people prior to being admitted to a care home may continue post-admission. This appears to be more prevalent in care homes with small or dispersed minority ethnic populations (Daker-White *et al.* 2002). Older people who migrated to the UK fear that the mainstream population may view them as 'scroungers' or as taking services away from longstanding 'UK citizens' (Manthorpe *et al.* 2010). The role of both intentional and unintentional racism in deepening risks of residents' mistreatment, neglect, loss of dignity, unmet need, and poorer quality of life is profound, and is a key driver for embedding cultural competence (see below) in the care home workforce (Bowes, *et al.* 2012).

In terms of evaluating quality of life of residents from BME groups, the cross-cultural sensitivity of quality of life instruments is a primary issue (Warner, Milne and Peet 2010). Given the importance of culture in influencing and underpinning life experiences, including those relating to ill health, stigma and migration, it is important to acknowledge that instruments developed (mainly) in the West are likely to fail to take account of those dimensions of quality of life that are not shared with mainstream Western culture. This is an issue that needs to be addressed by the research community.

Quality of care: older people with dementia living in a care home

When people are very dependent and live in a care home, quality of life becomes inextricably linked to quality of care. 'Care' includes not only those elements provided within the home, but also external services, such as medical care and social support. Furthermore, good quality care depends on a range of micro-level (satisfied staff) and macro-level (financial stability of the provider) factors and their interaction (Dening and Milne 2011). Before turning specifically to evidence about what constitutes 'good practice' with residents from BME populations, key issues that enhance, or undermine, the quality of care of residents with dementia are briefly reviewed.

A 2008 report from the Commission for Social Care Inspection (CSCI) (the organisation formerly responsible for regulating care homes in England) identified a number of issues as particularly important to enhancing the wellbeing of residents with dementia. Their work included older residents from BME groups. This report noted that the quality of staff communication – both verbal and non-verbal – was significant, as was the nature of interaction. Warm and friendly communication leaves the person with dementia feeling relaxed and happy, whilst interactions that are neutral or negative leave residents feeling withdrawn and distressed (CSCI 2008).

'Being involved' in supportive relationships with staff – and family members – appears to be especially important to helping maintain a sense of wellbeing and bolstering identity, including cultural identity (Bowes *et al.* 2012). Other factors that have been identified as particularly important to enhancing wellbeing are: the reassurance of daily routine; privacy, dignity and choice; opportunities for social interaction; having a role/occupation; contact with family and friends; and the availability of 'pleasurable activities' (Alzheimer's Society 2010; Byrne-Davis, Bennett and Wilcock 2006). Direct attempts to capture the subjective experience of people with dementia in care homes suggest that care home residents experience a mixture of isolation and frustration, employ active efforts to cope with their situation, try to 'make the best of oneself', and strive to maintain an identity (Clare *et al.* 2008; Surr 2006).

Finding out what determines 'a good life' for older people in care homes was the focus of work by the National Development

Team for Inclusion in 2008/09 (2009). Drawing directly on fieldwork with residents with high levels of dependency – some of whom had advanced dementia – the study identified six elements of, or 'keys' to, a good quality of life:

- personal identity and self-esteem
- meaningful relationships
- home and personal surroundings
- meaningful daily and community life
- personalised care and support
- personal control and autonomy.

These findings resonate with the dimensions of the 'Senses Framework' devised by Nolan *et al.* (2006). This framework was developed in work with care home residents with dementia and their paid and family carers, some of whom were from minority communities. They identified six senses that underpin psychological wellbeing: a sense of security, continuity, belonging, purpose, achievement, and significance (Davies and Nolan 2008).

Good practice: BME older people with dementia living in a care home

Pivotal issues that emerge from research as important to delivering good quality care to BME older people with dementia are effective communication and appreciation of the person's individual biography and life history (Milne 2011a). These are core elements of person-centred care (Bhattacharyya and Benbow 2012). To deliver person-centred care, staff need to know what is important to the person, how best to support them, how they communicate, and what their strengths and vulnerabilities are (Kitwood 1997). Understanding of 'need' is culturally situated. In working with a resident who is black or from a minority ethnic group, particular care needs to be taken to take account of – as noted above – linguistic and communication issues, personal care preferences, diet and food, and cultural and social norms including those associated with 'modesty' and dress codes (Mackenzie 2007). 'High quality care is synonymous with respecting individuality' and understanding the person's needs inside their socio-political and historical context and life course (Gibson 2004, p.55).

'Personalisation' – which builds on the person-centred model of care – raises the person-centred bar and aims to ensure all people with dementia are treated with respect and dignity *and* are able to direct their life and support as much as they can (Sanderson and Bailey 2013). This includes choosing when to have meals, what to eat and drink, and when to go out, take a bath and/or watch television. At the heart of personalisation is individualised care. Nowhere is this more important, and more challenging to operationalise, than in a care home. The use of 'talking mats', a low-tech framework comprising a textured mat and visual symbols, allows residents with limited verbal skills to express their views. Early work suggests they can positively influence the quality of interaction between staff and residents, enhance staff's ability to communicate effectively, and involve residents to a greater degree in decisions about their care (Murphy, Oliver and Cox. 2010).

A focus on life stories has rightly been a strong theme in developing person-centred care in services for people with dementia. It is vital that we know and understand a person's life story if we are to deliver nuanced individualised support. It is fundamental to developing relationships and helps us understand what is meaningful to that person in everyday life – what they enjoy and what makes them happy. Life story work aims to deliberately enable the person with dementia to remember, share and record information about their life, helped by relatives and others. It often includes photographs and memorabilia, and can include a 'memory box' (Schweitzer 2005). The benefits of life story work include the following: it is enjoyable for the person and their family and creates a legacy; it enhances self-worth and unique identity; it recalls people's strengths and skills; it identifies past interests, likes and dislikes; and it builds understanding and friendships (NICE/SCIE 2006). It also offers a place to start a discussion or continue a conversation (Stokes 2010).

Crucial to the life stories of many BME residents is the role and meaning of culture, religion, family life, routines, community norms, diet and dress. How these intersect with experiences of living with dementia is largely unexplored (Jutlla and Moreland 2009). Understanding the histories and life courses of residents with dementia from BME communities helps staff to support them to live well. For example, being aware and having an understanding of the origins and 'space' of people who migrated to the UK from the rural Punjab in the 1950s – what that looked like, its smells, community and situation – can help make sense of what the older person may be saying or experiencing. Having appreciation of migration experiences often includes recognition of the role and influence of racism, hostility, marginalisation and discrimination (Mackenzie 2007).

Research on transnational migrants – in particular, Bangladeshis – suggests that they have a 'palpable sense of conflicting desires' whereby they juxtapose the advantages of living in the UK with their disadvantages (Gardner 2002). There is an associated tendency to idealise the country of origin, especially relationships and the availability of informal support. This process is amplified when a relative develops dementia and/or is admitted to a care home (Jutlla 2013). Understanding of this is an important element of providing person-centred care.

Accommodating the religious needs of residents from BME populations is identified as a specific, and key, element of good practice. This includes sensitivity to religious practices, access to religious leaders and opportunities to worship, and recognition of religious festivals including appropriate foods (Evans and Cunningham 1996). Although far from universal, there is an increasing number of good examples. A recent study by Bowes *et al.* (2012) identified that care homes providing support to South Asian elders embedded prayers, singing religious (Hindu) songs, and yoga into their daily routines.

In terms of facilitating visits by relatives, good practice includes providing female relatives with the option of a female driver when being taken on an outing, and providing culturally appropriate food during visits (Ismail and Mackenzie 2003). Another example of good practice is utilising satellite television to offer programmes in languages familiar to residents and their relatives (Manthorpe *et al.* 2009).

Specific issues that impact negatively on quality of care include: poor prescribing patterns, covert administration of medication, and physical restraint. Although electronic tagging has been advocated in certain circumstances to prevent wandering and to facilitate a more open environment, it has been criticised for emphasising technology and control instead of working towards better, more individualised care (see, for example, Hughes and Louw 2002).

Cultural competence

Issues relating to cultural competence are a particularly powerful dimension of good practice in working with older people from a minority ethnic group. For Gallegos, Tindall and Gallegos (2008), cultural competence is 'the process by which individuals and systems respond respectfully and effectively to people of all cultures, languages, classes, races, ethnic backgrounds, religions and other diversity in a manner that recognises, affirms and values the worth of individuals and families and protects and promotes the dignity of each' (p.54). It involves more than having an awareness of cultural norms. It is an approach that values diversity and promotes inclusivity (Jutlla 2013).

Douglas *et al.* (2011) identified the following dimensions of culturally competent nursing care in care homes

- recognition of the impact of culture on attitudes, values, traditions, and behaviours on individual residents
- understanding of health-seeking behaviours of residents, their families, the community and the specific minority population they belong to

- appreciation of language and the nature of communication styles of individuals, families and communities
- understanding of the nature and role of resources (for example, personal/familial, social support networks, religious/spiritual, community) that may have been used or are being used by residents.

There is growing evidence that in services, including care homes, where culturally competent care is practised and supported, the quality of life of minority ethnic residents is enhanced. It is important to note that cultural competency shares much of its value base with the principles and aims of person-centred care (Kitwood 1997). It is also a contested term, largely because it is not (often) conceptualised in a way that can effectively guide practice (Jutlla 2013).

Care home workforce

In 2009/10 the Care Quality Commission (CQC) identified 'chronic difficulties' in the recruitment and retention of care home staff as undermining the development and sustainability of good quality care (CQC 2010). Care homes frequently rely on women working part-time for low wages; many offer limited job security and/or career development (Moriarty 2012). In 2004, only about a third of nursing posts in nursing homes were filled by registered nurses (RCN 2010). This is a common reason for nursing home closures.

Free movement of labour with the European Union (EU) has led to a high proportion of care home staff being from overseas. Homes often employ staff whose first language is not the same as the residents (Wild, Nelson and Szczepura 2010). It has been estimated that about 16 per cent of all social care workers – including care homes – are from overseas; in London the figure is over 50 per cent (Cangiano *et al.* 2009). The vast majority of these workers are from non-European[2]

2 European Economic Area.

countries, most commonly from the Philippines, India, Nigeria, Zimbabwe and South Africa (Hussein and Manthorpe 2005). The dementia care workforce has historically been made up of Asian and British Asian workers, although the picture is now a more mixed one (Hussein and Manthorpe 2012).

The growth of the number of BME older residents with dementia raises the question of whether it is appropriate to target recruitment of staff in order to 'match' culture, language and background. A number of dangers have been identified in taking this course. Such a tactic may result in a single individual being wholly responsible for managing all minority ethnic residents; this assumes that 'culture' is uni-dimensional, that is, that all minority residents share the same heritage, and also ignores the broader need for the whole staff team to become culturally competent (see below). Paradoxically it may actually reinforce stereotypes rather than challenge them. It also denies users a choice, and may undermine the development of person-centred care.

Training issues

There is a strong correlation between the quality and regularity of staff training and development and the wellbeing, quality of life and social engagement levels of residents with dementia (Alzheimer's Society 2007; CQC 2012/2013). Research suggests that training can impact positively on staff attitudes, skills, knowledge and performance; it can also result in increased confidence and higher levels of job satisfaction and retention (Skills for Care and Skills for Health 2011).

Despite these findings and national investment in the 'dementia care workforce', dementia training is often fragmented and ad hoc, even in specialist care homes (DH 2012). Indeed, recent evidence suggests that one-third of dementia care homes provide no dementia training at all (APPG on Dementia 2013). The Health and Social Care Act 2012 has removed the requirement for specific qualification standards in care homes in

England, raising concerns about how training and skills will be promoted nationally.

The need for cultural competency training for those working with people with dementia from minority ethnic populations has been widely reported. In their research briefing on BME older people with dementia and their access to support and services, Moriarty, Sharif and Robinson (2011) identified that whilst workers feel they need more training to both improve their knowledge about dementia and the cultural norms and religious practices of older people from a minority ethnic group, gaining access to it is variable. One of the key barriers to improving cultural competency in care homes is the acute lack of data about the needs of residents from a minority ethnic group, and how these are best met (Dementia Advocacy Network 2009).

'Specialist' vs. integrated care homes

There has long been a tension between the pressure – exerted mainly from existing cohorts of older people from BME groups – to develop specialist separate care homes and the longer-term need to develop good quality care in mainstream care homes that will meet the needs of all residents from all backgrounds (Bhui and Sashidharan 2003). Evidence from service users and their families is mixed. Some evidence, drawn from work with South Asian populations, highlights preferences for integrated services (Dementia Plus 2002), whereas other studies identify preferences for specialist care homes (Daker-White *et al.* 2002). Sometimes specialist services are commissioned when mainstream services fail to provide culturally appropriate care, and some specialist care homes have been developed to address specific cultural and religious needs (Manthorpe *et al.* 2009).

Conclusion

Older people with dementia from BME communities residing in a care home are one of the most marginalised and invisible groups of service users in the UK. They experience multiple disadvantages arising from having a stigmatised condition, living in a setting that may not meet their needs effectively, and that is away from their family, community and social and cultural norms. The number of older people with dementia from minority populations who may need to be admitted to a care home is rapidly growing. This underscores an urgent need to develop culturally competent care and enhance good practice with minority groups across the care home sector.

There are a number of key issues that require attention. There is a primary need to paint an accurate statistical picture of the number and profile of minority ethnic older people in care home settings. There is a related need to extend research beyond locally based studies with well-established minority groups to include more recently arrived minorities and to conduct studies on a national scale. Developing measures, for example, on quality of life, that are cross-culturally valid is also important, as is extending the reach of work that explores 'social care outcomes' in long-term care (Malley and Netten 2009; Netten *et al.* 2012; Smith 2013).

A recent conceptual shift in the dementia care field is that assessment of quality of life is increasingly understood as being rooted in the subjective experience of the person with dementia. It is also now accepted that people with dementia – even those with advanced dementia – are able to communicate meaningfully about their life and experiences (Alzheimer's Society 2010; Clare *et al.* 2008). As there is no doubt that residential care will continue to make a significant contribution to the care of people with advanced dementia in the future, increased emphasis on research that explores the dimensions of quality of life from the perspective of residents is a pivotal component of improving life quality and developing effective care practice (Begum 2006). This work needs to ensure that it foregrounds the experiences and perspectives of BME residents (Milne 2011b). It also needs to inform the national policy commitment to enhancing care practice training and remuneration and systemic improvements inside both individual care homes and across the sector. Whilst there is evidence of excellent practice in some care homes and/or with some minority groups, much work needs to be done before we can be confident that care homes routinely offer good personalised culturally nuanced and respectful care to older people with dementia from BME communities.

References

Adamson, J. (2001) 'Awareness and understanding of dementia in African/Caribbean and South Asian families.' *Health and Social Care in the Community 9*, 6, 391–396.

Alzheimer's Society (2007) *Home from Home: A Report Highlighting Opportunities for Improving Standards of Dementia Care in Care Homes.* London: Alzheimer's Society.

Alzheimer's Society (2010) *My Name is Not Dementia: People with Dementia Discuss Quality of Life Indicators.* London: Alzheimer's Society.

APPG (All-Party Parliamentary Group) on Dementia (2013) *Dementia Does Not Discriminate: The Experiences of Black, Asian and Minority Ethnic Communities.* July. London: Alzheimer's Society. Available at www.alzheimers.org.uk/site/scripts/download_info.php?downloadID=1186, accessed on 11 December 2014.

Anderson, I. and Brownlie, J. (1997) 'A neglected problem: minority ethnic elders with dementia.' In A.M. Bowes and D.F. Sim (eds) *Perspectives on Welfare: The Experience of Minority Ethnic Groups in Scotland.* Aldershot: Ashgate.

Aspinall, P.J. (2010) 'Concepts, terminology and classifications for the "mixed" ethnic or racial group in the United Kingdom.' *Journal of Epidemiology and Community Health 64*, 6, 557–560.

Banerjee, S., Murray, J., Foley, B., Atkins, L., Shneider, J. and Mann, A. (2003) 'Predictors of institutionalisation in people with dementia.' *Journal of Neurology, Neurosurgery and Psychiatry 74*, 1315–1316.

Bebbington, A., Darton, R. and Netten, A. (2001) *Care Homes for Older People, Volume 2: Admissions, Needs and Outcomes.* Canterbury: Personal Social Services Research Unit, University of Kent.

Begum, N. (2006) *Doing It for Themselves: Participation and Black and Minority Ethnic Service Users.* London: Social Care Institute for Excellence/Race Equality Unit.

Bharucha, A.J., Pandav, R., Shen, C., Dodge, H.H and Ganguli, M. (2004) 'Predictors of nursing facility admission: a 12-year epidemiological study in the United States.' *Journal of the American Geriatrics Society 52*, 3, 434–439.

Bhattacharyya, S. and Benbow, S.M. (2012) 'Mental health services for black and minority ethnic elders in the UK: a systematic review of innovative practice with service provision and policy implications.' *International Psychogeriatrics 25*, 3, 359–373.

Bhopal, K. and Preston, J. (eds) (2012) *Intersectionality and 'Race' in Education.* Abingdon: Routledge.

Bhui, K. and Sashidharan, S (2003) 'Should there be separate psychiatric services for ethnic minority groups?' *The British Journal of Psychiatry 182*, 10–12.

Botsford, J., Clarke, C. and Gibb, C. (2011) 'Research and dementia, caring and ethnicity: a review of the literature.' *Journal of Research in Nursing 16*, 5, 437–449.

Bowes, A. and Wilkinson, H. (2003) '"We didn't know it would get that bad": South Asian experiences of dementia and the service response.' *Health and Social Care in the Community 11*, 5, 387–396.

Bowes, A., Avan, G. and Macintosh, S. (2012) *Dignity and Respect in Residential Care: Issues for Black and Minority Ethnic Groups.* London: Department of Health.

Byrne-Davis, L., Bennett, P. and Wilcock, G. (2006) 'How are quality of life ratings made? Towards a model of quality of life in people with dementia.' *Quality of Life Research 15*, 855–865.

Cangiano, A., Shutes, I., Spencer, S. and Leeson, G. (2009) *Migrant Care Workers in Ageing Societies: Research Findings in the United Kingdom.* Oxford: ESRC Centre on Migration.

Clare, L., Rowlands, J., Bruce, E., *et al.* (2008) 'The experience of living with dementia in residential care: an interpretive phenomenological analysis.' *The Gerontologist 48*, 6, 711–720.

CQC (Care Quality Commission) (2012/13) *The State of Health Care and Adult Social Care in England.* London: CQC.

CRE (Commission for Racial Equality) (2002) *Code of Practice on the Duty to Promote Race Equality.* London: CRE.

CSCI (Commission for Social Care Inspection) (2008) *See Me, Not Just My Dementia: Understanding People's Experience of Living in a Care Home.* London: CSCI.

Daker-White, G., Beattie, A., Gilliard, J. and Means, R. (2002) 'Minority ethnic groups in dementia care: a review of service needs, service provision and models of good practice.' *Aging and Mental Health 6*, 2, 101–108.

Davies, S. and Nolan, M. (2008) 'Attending to relationships in dementia care.' In M. Downs and B. Bowers (eds) *Excellence in Dementia Care: Research into Practice.* Buckingham: Open University Press.

Dementia Advocacy Network (2009) *Bringing Dementia out of the Shadows for BME Elders: A Report on the Work of the Ethnic Minorities Advocacy Project.* London: Dementia Advocacy Network.

Dementia Plus (2002) *Twice a Child: Dementia Care for African-Caribbean and Asian Older People in Wolverhampton.* Wolverhampton: Dementia Plus.

Dening, T. and Milne, A. (eds) (2011) *Mental Health and Care Homes.* Oxford: Oxford University Press.

Dening, T. and Milne, A. (2013) 'Mental health in care homes for older people.' in T. Dening and A. Thomas (eds) *The Oxford Textbook of Old Age Psychiatry.* Oxford: Oxford University Press.

DH (Department of Health) (2003) *Care Homes for Older People: National Minimum Standards.* Care Home Regulations. Amended 18 February 2003. London: DH.

DH (2009) *Living Well with Dementia: A National Dementia Strategy.* London: DH.

DH (2012) *Prime Minister's Challenge on Dementia: Delivering Major Improvements in Dementia Care and Research by 2015.* London: DH. Available at www.gov.uk/government/uploads/system/uploads/attachment_data/file/215101/dh_133176.pdf, accessed on 31 January 2015.

Douglas, M.K., Pierce, J.U., Rosenkoetter, M. and Pacquiao, D. (2011) 'Standards of practice for culturally competent nursing care: update.' *Journal of Transcultural Nursing 22*, 4, 317.

Evans, C. and Cunningham, B. (1996) 'Caring for the ethnic elder: even when language is not a barrier, patients may be reluctant to discuss their beliefs and practices for fear of criticism or ridicule.' *Geriatric Nursing 17*, 3, 105–110.

Gallegos, J., Tindall, C. and Gallegos, S. (2008) 'The need for advancement in the conceptualization of cultural competence.' *Advances in Social Work 9*, 1.

Gardner, K. (2002) *Age, Narrative and Migration.* Oxford: Berg.

Gibson, F. (2004) *The Past in the Present: Using Reminiscence in Health and Social Care.* Baltimore, MD: Health Professionals Press.

Hughes, J.C. and Louw, S. (2002) 'Electronic tagging of people who wander.' *British Medical Journal 325*, 847–848.

Hussein, S. and Manthorpe, J. (2005) 'An international review of the long term care workforce.' *Journal of Aging & Social Policy 17*, 4, 75–94.

Hussein, S. and Manthorpe, J. (2012) 'The dementia social care workforce in England: secondary analysis of a national workforce dataset.' *Aging & Mental Health 16*, 1, 110–118.

Ismail, L. and Mackenzie, J. (2003) 'Convening and facilitating support groups for South Asian family carers of people with dementia: experiences and challenges.' *Dementia 2*, 3, 433–438.

Jutlla, K. (2013) 'Ethnicity and cultural diversity in dementia care: a review of the literature.' *The Journal of Dementia Care 21*, 2, 33–39.

Jutlla, K. and Moreland, N. (2009) 'The personalisation of dementia services and existential realities: understanding Sikh carers for an older person with dementia in Wolverhampton.' *Ethnicity and Inequalities in Health and Social Care 2*, 4, 10–21.

Kitwood, T. (1997) *Dementia Reconsidered: The Person Comes First.* Buckingham: Open University Press.

Laing & Buisson (2010) *Care of Elderly People: Market Survey 2010–11*. London: Laing & Buisson.

Lawrence, V., Samsi, K., Banerjee, S., Morgan, C. and Murray, J. (2011) 'Threat to valued elements of life: the experience of dementia across three ethnic groups.' *Gerontologist 51*,1, 39–50.

Liu, Y.L. (2003) 'Aging service need and use among Chinese American seniors: intragroup variations.' *Journal of Cross-Cultural Gerontology 18*, 273–301.

Machizawa, S. and Lau, D. (2010) 'Psychological needs of Japanese Americans: implications for culturally competent interventions.' *Journal of Cross-Cultural Gerontology 25*, 2, 183–197.

Mackenzie, J. (2007) 'Ethnic minority communities and the experience of dementia: a review and implications for practice.' In J. Keady, L.C. Clarke and S. Page (eds) *Partnerships in Community Mental Health Nursing and Dementia Care: Practice Perspectives*. Buckingham: Open University Press.

Mackenzie, J. and Coates, D. (2003) *Understanding and Supporting Eastern European and South Asian Family Carers of People with Dementia.* Bradford: Bradford Dementia Group.

Malley, J. and Netten, A. (2009) 'Measuring outcomes of social care.' *Research, Policy and Planning 27*, 2, 85–96.

Manthorpe, J., Moriarty, J., Stevens, M., Sharif, N. and Hussein, S. (2010) *Supporting Black and Minority Ethnic Older People's Mental Wellbeing: Accounts of Social Care Practice*. London: Social Care Institute for Excellence.

Manthorpe, J., Iliffe, S., Moriarty, J., Cornes, M. *et al.* (2009) '"We are not blaming anyone, but if we don't know about amenities, we cannot seek them out": black and minority older people's views on the quality of local health and personal social services in England.' *Ageing and Society 29*, 1, 93–113.

Milne, A. (2009) 'Mental well being in later life.' In T. Williamson (ed.) *Older People's Mental Health Today: A Handbook.* Brighton: Mental Health Foundation and Pavilion Publishing.

Milne, A. (2011a) 'Living with Dementia in a care home: a review of research evidence.' In T. Dening and A Milne (eds) *Mental Health and Care Homes.* Oxford: Oxford University Press.

Milne, A (2011b) 'Living with dementia in a care home: capturing the experiences of residents.' *Quality in Ageing and Older Adults Special Issue, Dementia Care: A Positive Future 12*, 2, 76–85.

Milne, A. and Chryssanthopoulou, C. (2005) 'Dementia care giving in black and Asian populations: reviewing and refining the research agenda.' *Journal of Community & Applied Social Psychology 15*, 319–337.

Mold, F., Fitzpatrick, J.M. and Roberts, J.D. (2005a) 'Minority ethnic elders in care homes: a review of the literature.' *Age and Ageing 34*, 107–113.

Mold, F., Fitzpatrick, J.M. and Roberts, J.D. (2005b) 'Caring for minority ethnic older people in nursing care homes.' *British Journal of Nursing 14*, 11, 601–606.

Moon, A., Lubben, J.E. and Villa, V. (1998) 'Awareness and utilisation of community long term care services by elderly Korean and non-Hispanic White Americans.' *The Gerontologist 38*, 309–316.

Moriarty, J. (2012) *The Health and Social Care Experiences of Black and Minority Ethnic Older People. Better Health Briefing*, Paper 9. Race Equality Foundation, London.

Moriarty, J., Sharif, N. and Robinson, J. (2011) *Black and Minority Ethnic People with Dementia and their Access to Support and Services. Research Briefing.* London: Social Care Institute for Excellence.

Murphy, J., Oliver, T.M. and Cox, S. (2010) *Talking Mats Help Involve People with Dementia and their Carers in Decision-making*. York: Joseph Rowntree Foundation.

National Development Team for Inclusion (2009) *Finding Out What Determines 'A Good Life' for Older People in Care Homes.* York: Joseph Rowntree Foundation.

NICE (National Institute for Health and Care Excellence)/SCIE (Social Care Institute for Excellence) (2006) *Dementia: Supporting People with Dementia and their Carers.* London: NICE.

Netten, A., Trukeschitz, B., Beadle-Brown, J., Forder, J., Towers, A.-M. and Welch, E. (2012) 'Quality of life outcomes for residents and quality ratings of care homes: is there a relationship?' *Age and Ageing 41*, 512–517.

Nolan, M., Brown, J., Davies, S., *et al.* (2006) *The Senses Framework: Improving Care for Older People through a Relationship Centred Approach.* Getting Research into Practice Series. Sheffield: University of Sheffield.

ONS (Office for National Statistics) (2011) *Ethnicity and National Identity in England and Wales 2011.* Newport: ONS.

Owen, T. and the National Care Homes R&D (Research and Development) Forum (2006) *Quality of Life in Care Homes: A Review of the Literature.* London: Help the Aged.

Quince, C. (2013) *Low Expectations: Attitudes on Choice, Care and Community for People with Dementia in Care Homes.* London: Alzheimer's Society.

RCN (Royal College of Nursing) (2010) *Care Homes Under Pressure*. London: RCN.

Sanderson, H. and Bailey, G. (2013) *Personalisation and Dementia: A Guide for Person-centred Practice.* London: Jessica Kingsley Publishers.

Schweitzer, P. (2005) 'Making memories matter: a project of the European reminiscence network.' *Dementia 4*, 3, 450.

Seabrooke, V. and Milne, A. (2009) 'Facilitating early diagnosis of dementia in an Asian community: lessons from a dementia collaborative project.' *Quality in Ageing 10*, 4, 29–36.

Skills for Care and Skills for Health (2011) *Common Core Principles for Supporting People with Dementia*. Leeds: Skills for Care.

Smith, J.E. (2013. 'Needs, characteristics and experiences from minority ethnic adults with learning disabilities and minority ethnic older people living in care homes across England: an exploratory mixed methods study.' PhD thesis. Tizard Centre, University of Kent.

Stokes, G. (2010) *And Still the Music Plays: Stories of People with Dementia*. London: Hawker Publications.

Surr, C.A. (2006) 'Preservation of self in people with dementia living in residential care: a socio-biographical approach.' *Social Science & Medicine 62*, 1720–1730.

Uppal, G. and Bonas, S. (2014) 'Constructions of dementia in the South Asian community: a systematic literature review.' *Mental Health, Religion & Culture 17*, 2, 143–160.

Uppal, G.K., Bonas, S. and Philpott, H. (2013) 'Understanding and awareness of dementia in the Sikh community.' *Mental Health, Religion & Culture*, 1–16.

Vertovec, S. (2007) 'Super-diversity and its implications.' *Ethnic and Racial Studies 30*, 6, 1024–1054.

Warburton, J., Bartlett, H. and Rao, V. (2009) 'Ageing and cultural diversity: policy and practice issues.' *Australian Social Work 62*, 2, 168–185.

Warner, J., Milne, A. and Peet, J. (2010) *'My Name is not Dementia': Literature Review*. London: Alzheimer's Society.

Wild, D., Nelson, S. and Szczepura, A. (2010) *Residential Care Home Workforce Development: The Rhetoric and Reality of Meeting Older Residents' Future Care Needs*. York: Joseph Rowntree Foundation.

11

END OF LIFE, DEMENTIA, AND BLACK AND MINORITY ETHNIC GROUPS

Karen Harrison Dening

Introduction

People aged 60 years and over make up the most rapidly expanding segment of the population. Between 2000 and 2050, the proportion of the world's population over 60 will more than treble, from 605 million to 2 billion (WHO 2012). Not only are more people surviving to old age, but once there, they are also tending to live longer. Over the next 50 years global life expectancy at age 60 is expected to increase from 18.8 years in 2000–2005 to 22.2 years in 2050 (WHO, National Institute on Aging and National Institutes of Health 2011). In the UK alone, the percentage of older people (aged 65 and over) increased from 13 per cent of the total population in 1971 to 16 per cent in 2005 (ONS 2005), the numbers of the oldest ages increasing the fastest. In 2008 there were 1.3 million people in the UK aged 85 and over, with the number expected to increase to 1.8 million by 2018, and to 3.3 million by 2033 (ONS 2009).

Population censuses in the UK have shown an incremental rise in numbers and diversity of ethnic groups (ONS 2012), representing one-fifth of the population in 2011. Data for England showed that in 2009, whilst 9 out of 10 people over the age of 65 were white British, there had been substantial increases in the number of black and minority ethnic (BME) groups when comparing data from the 2001 Census. Population projections suggest that both the numbers and proportions of people from

BME groups will increase in the UK, and they will represent a larger portion of older people; estimates are that there will be over 1.3 million people aged 65 and over (compared to over half a million in 2001) (ONS 2012).

Dementia

It is estimated that there are currently 44.4 million people worldwide with dementia, and (if mortality, prevention and treatment remain the same) this number will increase to an estimated 75.6 million in 2030, and 135.5 million in 2050 (ADI 2013). Ferri *et al.* (2005) conducted a Delphi consensus study, which aimed to provide dementia estimates separately, for each world region. Twelve international experts were provided with a systematic review of the available data and asked to calculate prevalence estimates for each five-year age band in 14 regions, based on a combination of geography and patterns of mortality. The group response for each region was then summarised as a 'mean prevalence estimate'. According to their findings, over 24 million people had dementia worldwide, and they predicted that this was likely to double every 20 years, to over 81 million in 2040. Stephan and Brayne (2008) indicate that age-specific estimates of dementia are consistent worldwide, with a predicted exponential rise in dementia with age.

In the UK it has been estimated that as many as 25 million people (42 per cent of the UK population) are affected through knowing a close friend or family member (Alzheimer's Research Trust 2010). Exact figures for people with dementia are hard to obtain, but the 2010 dementia report (Luengo-Fernandez, Leal and Gray 2010) estimates that the number of people in the UK with dementia (both diagnosed and undiagnosed) is currently around 820,000. This figure equates to 1.3 per cent of the entire UK population. Although these statistics have been challenged (Norton, Matthews and Brayne 2013), we know that increasing age appears to be the strongest risk factor for developing dementia, and that these numbers are forecast to rise (ADI 2013). Estimates from the UK Medical Research Council

Cognitive Function and Ageing Studies (MRC-CFAS) project, a large multicentre population cohort study looking at the health and cognitive function of 13,000 older people, suggest that 1 in 3 people over the age of 65 will die whilst suffering from dementia (Brayne *et al.* 2006).

Knapp and Prince (2007) detailed the prevalence and cost of dementia in the report, *Dementia 2007*, commissioned by the Alzheimer's Society. Although not a government report, it provided a comprehensive summary of dementia in the UK, and gave projections and estimated financial costs for the future. They were unable to calculate the projected increases in absolute numbers, but they were able to predict, with confidence, a significant increase in the proportion of older people with dementia from BME groups compared to the general population. This is because the large numbers of people who migrated to the UK from the Caribbean, Indian subcontinent and China in the 1950s, 1960s and 1970s are now entering old age, and are therefore at increased risk of developing dementia.

Multiple morbidity, frailty and dementia

Health promotion and prevention approaches are having some success, such as in cardiovascular disease and its treatment, and the survival rates of some cancers are improving, so more people are living longer into old age. This has led to an increase in the numbers of people living long enough to develop the multiple morbidities associated with old age, in particular, neurodegenerative diseases such as dementia. Multiple morbidities will have a cumulative effect on function, quality of life and care needs. Added to this is the risk of superimposed acute physical illness. In the UK and other developed countries there will be a steady increase in the number of deaths, and in the proportion of those who die over the age of 85 (Gomes and Higginson 2008). Despite the fact that the vast majority of deaths occur in adults over the age of 65, there is widespread evidence that older people have inequitable access to good end-of-life care, and that people with dementia experience further barriers (Davies and Higginson 2004; Sampson *et al.* 2006). Frailty becomes more common with increasing age; by the age of 90, 32 per cent will be frail (Gavrilov and Gavrilova 2001). Frailty has been defined as:

> An aggregate expression of risk resulting from age- or disease-associated physiologic accumulation of subthreshold decrements affecting multiple physiologic systems resulting in adverse health outcomes. (Abellan van Kan *et al.* 2008, p.71)

Frailty and dementia are multifactorial in origin, and share some common aetiological pathways, such as smoking, obesity, lack of physical activity and depression, and have been linked to the development of both frailty and dementia (Hamer and Chida 2009; Ownby *et al.* 2006; Peters *et al.* 2008). Thus, frailty and dementia have been conceptualised as final common pathways resulting from cumulative factors over a number of years (Neale *et al.* 2014).

Both dementia and frailty have an adverse impact on a range of outcomes. People with dementia are at higher risk of acute hospital admission (Mukadam and Sampson 2011), falls (Myers *et al.* 1991), and of being placed in a care home; these are crisis or transition points at which the diagnosis is often made for the first time. Frailty also increases the risk of emergency hospital admission, overnight hospital stays (Wagner *et al.* 2006), falls (Fried *et al.* 2001), and institutionalisation.

Despite the impact that dementia and frailty have on older people and their families, they have not traditionally been conceptualised as 'terminal' or 'life-limiting' syndromes. Care home medical and nursing staff seem to consistently overestimate prognosis in advanced dementia. In one study of nursing home staff and physicians, at admission only 1.1 per cent of residents were perceived to have life expectancy of less than six months; however, 71 per cent died within that period (Mitchell, Kiely and Hamel 2004).

In recent years there has been a significant increase in policy and guidance, across many countries, which directly affects the influence and organisation of palliative and end-of-life care for non-malignant life-limiting conditions. In the UK the provision of palliative care services, irrespective of diagnosis or age, has been supported by a number of government reports (DH 2001, 2003, 2008a), and more recently to include dementia (DH 2008b, 2009, 2012).

Palliative and end-of-life care in BME groups

The core aim of the *End of Life Strategy in England* (DH 2008a), and its equivalents in the devolved countries, was to tackle the vast variability in provision of high-quality palliative and end-of-life care (see Box 11.1). The National Dementia Strategy (DH 2009) has an overarching aim of improving access to 'hard-to-reach groups', including BME and religious groups, supporting end-of-life care for people with dementia and their families through a specific objective (DH 2009, No. 12, p.61).

Box 11.1: Definition of palliative care

The World Health Organization (2011) defines palliative care as: 'an approach that improves the quality of life of patients and their families facing the problems associated with life threatening illness, through the prevention and relief of suffering by means of early identification and impeccable assessment and treatment of pain and other problems, physical, psychosocial and spiritual.'

However, the call to improve end-of-life care for all, irrespective of disease or population group, is particularly tempered for BME groups by persistent evidence of low use of palliative care services. However, to add to this, there is increasing evidence to suggest that ethnic and cultural differences continue to influence patterns of advanced disease, and illness experiences, and affect health care-seeking behaviours and service usage (Calanzani, Koffman and Higginson 2013). Calanzani *et al.* (2013) reported on 45 literature reviews that described disparities in palliative and end-of-life care provision for BME groups, such as in access and receipt of care. The National Council for Palliative Care (NCPC 2013) report also highlighted that belonging to a BME group is recognised as an important barrier to accessing optimum end-of-life care.

Access to services

A common theme running through studies on BME issues in palliative and end-of-life care is in respect of low uptake of such services. Several authors have suggested possible explanations for this. Among these are lack of self-referrals or professional referrals, poor knowledge of services or knowledge about what palliative care involves, as religious and family traditions might conflict with palliative and hospice care philosophies (Ahmed *et al.* 2004; Johnson 2001; Koffman *et al.* 2007; Werth, Gordon and Johnson 2002a).

Older people with dementia generally have poor access to optimum end-of-life care and palliative care and hospice services (Robinson *et al.* 2006). Although there is a belief that BME populations are less likely to access hospice care at the end of life, this is not supported in the literature (Connolly, Sampson and Purandare 2012). Connolly *et al.* included 20 studies in a systematic review of end-of-life care for people with dementia from BME groups. In respect of access to services, they suggested that although poor access to hospice services is considered a concern in dementia, BME populations may be equally or more likely to receive hospice care in some circumstances. However, caution must be expressed as the majority of studies included in their systematic review were American, and may not be representative of the situation in the UK. Connolly *et al.* (2012) conclude that overall, disparities in end-of-life care for people with dementia from minority groups appear to exist, and they suggest that these may be due to the double disadvantage of having dementia and minority ethnic status.

Language and communication problems can often be a barrier for BME groups in their access to palliative and end-of-life care services (Firth 2001). However, this could include a broad area of issues such as lack of sensitivity to culture and religion, or a lack of translation resources.

Accessible assessment and delivery of timely interventions is dependent on high-quality communication (Calanzani *et al.* 2013). Poor-quality communication can generate much misunderstanding amongst BME families (Koffman and Higginson 2001). Guidance from the NCPC (2013) suggests that the use of sensitive and appropriately translated materials and interpreters who have the correct language and dialect of the person with dementia is essential in order to avoid relying on family members to act as interpreters. The use of professional interpreters is essential to provide independence to the voice of the person with dementia, and to reduce the extra burden and stress placed on family members (see Chapter 8). I would add that, in situations where decisions are sought, the translator would ideally have knowledge of capacity assessments to ensure information gained is based on informed choice and deliberation (HMSO 2005).

Some studies report that communication can be further hampered when the cultural background of the health care staff or provider of social care differ (Cox *et al.* 2006). This can affect people with dementia receiving care, whether domiciliary care delivered in their own homes or within care homes that are specifically aimed at care for a specific culture. This may lead to heavy reliance on other family members to translate or deliver more direct care than should be expected. It is acknowledged that little is known about the numbers of people from BME groups resident in care homes, or the extent to which their end-of-life care needs are addressed in line with their specific requirements. However, if care staff fail to understand the language or culture of a person, this can result in dissatisfaction and stress, leading them to hold negative feelings, and to perhaps distance themselves from the person they are to care for (Badger *et al.* 2006).

End-of-life care decisions and interventions

Wishes and preferences for future care are assumed to be based on the principles of autonomy, whereby a person expects to retain personal control in making decisions. However, there is often a desire in older adults to consider family ties, and the collective process of family decision may be of equal importance (Roberto 1999; Whitlatch, Piiparinen and Friss Feinberg 2009). However, most of the literature that explores decision-making for end-of-life care within BME populations is American, and largely about African Americans, and considers the broader population rather than dementia. Advance care planning (see Box 11.2) in dementia is a little-researched field compared to the broader older population (Dening, Jones and Sampson 2011); however, what evidence there is shows that BME groups are less likely to be involved in advance care planning or to complete an advance directive to refuse treatment.

Box 11.2: Advance care planning

Advance care planning (ACP) has been defined as a process of discussing and recording wishes, values and preferences for future care and treatment held between an individual and their care provider(s) (Froggatt *et al.* 2008; Henry and Seymour 2007) that takes effect when the person loses capacity. ACP differs from general care planning in that it is usually used in the context of progressive illness and anticipated deterioration.

ACP is a voluntary process of discussion and review to help an individual who has capacity to anticipate how their condition may affect them in the future. If they wish, they can set on record choices about their care and treatment and/or an advance decision to refuse a treatment in specific circumstances, so that these can be referred to by those responsible for their care or treatment (whether professional staff or family carers) in the event that they lose capacity to decide once their illness progresses.

Under the terms of the Mental Capacity Act 2005, formalised outcomes of ACP might include one or more of the following:

- advance statements to inform subsequent best interests decisions
- advance decisions to refuse treatment, which are legally binding if valid and applicable to the circumstances at hand
- appointment of Lasting Powers of Attorney ('health and welfare' and/or 'property and affairs').

It is proposed that advance care planning enables a person to indicate their wishes and preferences for future care, at a time when, due to illness, they lack the capacity to make such decisions (DH 2008a). Given all that has been discussed thus far in respect of BME populations and access to palliative and end-of-life care services, do we know enough about the wishes and preferences of BME communities that would influence end-of-life care decisions? Drawing from focus groups held with African Americans and Caucasians, Modi, Velde and Gessert (2010) found that there were more similarities than differences in how decisions were made, and included elements such as following the wishes of the person with dementia, being true to their faith and religion, and concerns about physicians overriding these. Although, again, most literature is American and may not represent UK BME groups, the influence of religion and principles of faith provides us with valuable insights that can support optimum care at the end of life.

Braun *et al.* (2008) conducted a retrospective cohort study to test whether the use of common life-sustaining treatments differed significantly by race/ethnicity in patients with cancer, non-cancer or dementia. They found higher rates of interventions for life-sustaining treatments in BME groups with dementia, so these have a greater likelihood of receiving blood transfusions, resuscitation and mechanical ventilation. However, there is a very small UK literature base that examines interventions at end of life for BME groups, with the majority literature being American, which is largely driven by the financial implications of their health insurance system (The Economist Intelligence Unit 2010).

A review by Connolly *et al.* (2012) examined seven studies that explored differences in artificial nutrition between BME groups and majority groups. They reported that all found higher rates of artificial nutrition and hydration in the BME groups, to varying levels, with African Americans having the highest rate when compared to Caucasians. Although evidence is limited, BME caregivers (of people with dementia) are more likely to make a decision to provide more aggressive care at the end of life of their family member.

Reasons for such differences in receiving end-of-life health care interventions are complex, with results of studies sometimes contradictory. The most commonly highlighted issue proposed by those surveyed was a general mistrust of medical decision-making and the health care system (Dening, Jones and Sampson 2013; Werth *et al.* 2002b), the importance of religion (Johnson, Elbert-Avila and Tulsky 2005), and perhaps difficulties in trying to apply a Western model of autonomy on different cultures (Payne *et al.* 2005). However, such mistrust is thought to be influenced by the legacy of centuries of abuse and discrimination that results in a fear of being prematurely deprived of life or of receiving suboptimal care. This is perhaps not an unreasonable assumption to make, as often the assessment and treatment of symptoms, such as pain, in people with advanced dementia is common and is often under-detected and under-treated (Scherder *et al.* 2009).

Western values tend to underpin and dominate the processes and direction of decision-making in end-of-life care (Baker 2002), with the idea of autonomy and individual control over dying not shared by all parts of the world and its cultures. Autonomy is an important concept in relation to the philosophy of the self and with regard to decision-making. However, whilst Western society also tends to regard cognitive attributes as being of the highest order (Post 2006), people with dementia lose autonomy and come to rely more and more on others to support their decision-making as their capacity declines. The literature, whilst limited, shows there are differences in decision-making for end of life for people with dementia across BME groups, particularly in respect of whether to withhold treatments or not, and that they are less likely to have an advance directive in place.

Religion also has a significant influence on the wishes and preferences for end-of-life care in BME groups (Johnson *et al.* 2005). Care should be taken in clinical and care settings that due attention is paid to how this influences or determines care towards the end of life and after death. In some religions the belief may be held that God is the only one with the power to decide life and death, the one capable of making a miracle.

There are very wide variations in the degree of adherence to religious practice and in the nature of that practice. There are also many variations in attitudes within most of the major religions as a person approaches death and after death (see Table 11.1) – for example, the difference between Orthodox and Reformed Judaism, or within Sikhism, or different Christian denominations.

TABLE 11.1: RELIGIOUS OBSERVANCES, BOTH OF THE DYING PERSON AND AFTER DEATH

Baha'i	• No rituals before death. • Always buried, never cremated. • Place of internment within one hour's journey of place of death. • Prayers and observations arranged by family or local Baha'i community.
Buddhism	• Resuscitation is acceptable. • Like full information about imminent death to make preparation. • May not want sedatives and painkillers near to death. • Buddhist priest to be informed as soon as possible after death.
Christianity	• Differing views within the different denominations of Christian religion, e.g. Roman Catholic, Church of England, Free churches. • Roman Catholic – visit by priest to receive Holy Communion and/or Sacrament of the Sick (formerly known as Last Rites). • African-Caribbean people may want to have singing and special prayers near to death. • Many of the Travelling community are Roman Catholic or Christian.
Christian Science	• Relies on God for healing, so may not wish to have drug treatments. • Church enables people to make their own choices about the treatments they will accept or decline. • No last rites.
Hinduism	• Prefer to die at home, as death in hospital can cause distress. • Readings from the Bhagavad Gita (Holy Book). • May wish to lie on the floor, near to death, to symbolise the closeness to Mother Earth. • Holy Rites, including a thread tied around the wrist or neck. • Eldest son to be present before, during and after death. • After death, non-Hindus should not touch the body unless wearing gloves. • All adult Hindus are cremated.
Jainism	• Family to be present near to and after death.

Judaism	• Orthodox (conservative) or Progressive (liberal) – needs will vary. • Jewish law forbids euthanasia as all human life is sacred. • Psalms and prayers are read near to death. • Rabbi to visit and someone is to be with the dying person at all times. • As little intervention as possible from staff. • Last offices are usually given by the Jewish Burial Society. • A 'watcher' is to stay with the body until burial.
Islam	• Resuscitation is allowed, so is a matter of choice. • Suicide and euthanasia are considered to be major sins. • Muslims may wish to lie or sit facing Mecca if near to death. • Readings from the Qur'an/Koran (Holy Book) may be recited. • If possible, non-Muslims should not touch the body after death, but if necessary, then gloves should be worn. • Burial, never cremation. • People from Pakistan may be sent back for burial.
Rastafarianism	• Unwillingness to receive any treatment which will contaminate the body. • Preference for alternative therapies, herbalism or acupuncture. • Visit in groups, with praying at the bedside. • Burial is preferred.
Sikhism	• Wearing of the five symbols of Sikhism – these should not be removed unless absolutely necessary, even after death. • Reciting of readings from the Sikh Holy Book – Guru Granth Sahib. • After death, the family may wish to wash and lay out the body. • Always a cremation.

SOURCE: MOOTOO (2005)

Johnson *et al.* (2005) assert that life-limiting interventions may be seen as hastening death and in defiance of the law of God. The challenge for health and social care in such a multicultural society is for health and social care practitioners to have a greater awareness of faith and cultural practices to enable better care to the dying person and beyond in caring for their body after death (al-Shahri and al-Khenaizan 2005; Mootoo 2005; Prosser, Korman and Feinstein 2012). Many health and social care organisations have developed policies and guidance for their staff to deliver care that is sensitive to the many faith and cultural backgrounds of people in their care. It is important therefore to consult closely with the individual or family concerned, as part of planning and delivering care.

Conclusion

The numbers of people with dementia who will need end-of-life care is set to increase rapidly over the next ten years. BME population projections suggest that both the numbers and proportions of people with dementia from BME groups will increase in the UK. Although there has been a growing interest in research and policy in the field of dementia and end of life, there are many gaps, particularly with regard to identifying the issues for people with advanced dementia from BME communities who will benefit from palliative care and how best to provide services to them and their carers.

References

Abellan van Kan, G., Rolland, Y.M., Morley, J.E. and Vellas, B. (2008) 'Frailty: toward a clinical definition.' *Journal of American Medical Directors Association 9*, 2, 71–72.

ADI (Alzheimer's Disease International) (2013) *Dementia Statistics*. London: ADI.

Ahmed, N., Bestell, J.C., Ahmedzai, S.H., Payne, S.A., Clark, D. and Noble, B. (2004) 'Systematic review of the problems and issues of accessing specialist palliative care by patients, carers and health and social care professionals.' *Palliative Medicine 18*, 6, 525–542.

al-Shahri, M.Z. and al-Khenaizan, A. (2005) 'Palliative care for Muslim patients.' *The Journal of Supportive Oncology 3*, 432–436.

Alzheimer's Research Trust (2010) *Dementia Statistics*. London: Alzheimer's Research Trust.

Badger, F., Pumphrey, R., Clarke, L., Clifford, C. *et al* (2006) 'The role of ethnicity in end-of-life care in care homes for older people in the UK: a literature review.' *Diversity in Health and Care 6*, 1, 23–29.

Baker, M.E. (2002) 'Economic, political and ethnic influences on end-of-life decision-making: a decade in review.' *Journal of Health and Social Policy 14*, 27–39.

Braun, U.K., McCullough, L.B., Betyth, R.J., Wray, N.P., Kunik, M.E. and Morgan, R.O. (2008) 'Racial and ethnic differences in the treatment of seriously ill patients: a comparison of African Americans, Caucasians and Hispanic veterans.' *Journal of the National Medical Association 100*, 9, 1041–1051.

Brayne, C., Gao, L., Dewey, M. and Matthews, F.E. (2006) 'Dementia before death in ageing societies – the promise of prevention and the reality.' *PLOS Medicine 3*, 10, e397.

Calanzani, N., Koffman, J. and Higginson, I.J. (2013) *Palliative and End of Life Care for Black, Asian and Minority Ethnic Groups in the UK.* London: Marie Curie.

Connolly, A., Sampson, E.L. and Purandare, N. (2012) 'End of life care for people with dementia from ethnic minority groups: a systematic review.' *Journal of the American Geriatrics Society 60*, 351–360.

Cox, C., Cole, E., Reynolds, T., Wandrag, M., Breckenridge, S. and Dingle, M. (2006) 'Implications of cultural diversity in Do Not Attempt Resuscitation (DNAR) decision making.' *Journal of Multicultural Nursing 12*, 1, 20–28.

Davies, E. and Higginson, I.J. (2004) *Better Palliative Care for Older People.* Geneva: World Health Organization Europe.

Dening, K.H., Jones, L. and Sampson, E.L. (2011) 'Advance care planning for people with dementia: a review.' *International Psychogeriatrics* 23, 10, 1535–1551.

Dening, K.H., Jones, L. and Sampson, E.L. (2013) 'Preferences for end-of-life care: a nominal group study of people with dementia and their family carers.' *Palliative Medicine 27*, 5, 409–417.

DH (Department of Health) (2001) *National Service Framework for Older People.* London: DH.

DH (2003) *'Building on the Best Choice': Responsiveness and Equity in the NHS.* Norwich: The Stationery Office.

DH (2008a) *End of Life Care Strategy.* London: DH.

DH (2008b) *Transforming the Quality of Dementia Care: Consultation on a National Dementia Strategy.* London: DH.

DH (2009) *Living Well with Dementia: A National Dementia Strategy.* London: DH.

DH (2012) *Prime Minister's Challenge on Dementia: Delivering Major Improvements in Dementia Care and Research by 2015.* London: DH.

Ferri, C.P., Prince, M., Brayne, C., Brodaty, H. and Fratiglioni, L. (2005) 'Global prevalence of dementia: a Delphi consensus study.' *Lancet 366*, 2112–2117.

Firth, S. (2001) *Wider Horizons: Care of the Dying in a Multicultural Society.* London: National Council for Hospice and Specialist Palliative Care Services.

Fried, L.P., Tangen, C.M., Walston, J., Newman, A.B. et al. (2001) 'Frailty in older adults: evidence for a phenotype.' *Journals of Gerontology Series A: Biological Sciences and Medical Sciences 56*, M 146–156.

Froggatt, K., Vaughn, S., Bernard, C. and Wild, D. (2008) *Advance Planning in Care Homes for Older People: A Survey of Current Practice.* Lancaster: International Observatory on End of Life, University of Lancaster.

Gavrilov, L.A. and Gavrilova, N.S. (2001) 'The reliability theory of aging and longevity.' *Journal of Theoretical Biology 213*, 527–45.

Gomes, B. and Higginson, I.J. (2008) 'Where people die (1974–2030): past trends, future projections and implications for care.' *Palliative Medicine 22*, 1, 33–41.

Hamer, M. and Chida, Y. (2009) 'Physical activity and risk of neurodegenerative disease: a systematic review of prospective evidence.' *Psychological Medicine 39*, 1, 3–11.

Henry, C. and Seymour, J. (2007) *Advance Care Planning: A Guide for Health and Social Care Staff.* London: Department of Health, End of Life Care Programme.

Johnson, K.S., Elbert-Avila, K.I. and Tulsky, J.A. (2005) 'The influence of spritual beliefs and practices on the treatment preferences of African Americans: a review of the literature.' *Journal of the American Geriatrics Society 53*, 711–719.

Johnson, M. (2001) *Palliative Care, Cancer and Minority Ethnic Comminities: A Literature Review.* Leicester: Mary Seacole Research Institute, De Montfort University.

Knapp, M. and Prince, M. (2007) *Dementia UK – The Full Report.* London: London School of Economics and King's College London.

Koffman, J. and Higginson, I.J. (2001) 'Accounts of carers' satisfaction with health care at the end of life: a comparison of first generation Black Caribbeans and white patients with advanced disease.' *Palliative Medicine 15*, 337–345.

Koffman, J., Burke, G., Dias, A., Raval, B., Byrne, J. *et al* (2007) 'Demographic factors and awareness of palliative care and related services.' *Palliative Medicine 21*, 2, 145–153.

Luengo-Fernandez, R., Leal, J. and Gray, A. (2010) *Dementia 2010: The Economic Burden of Dementia and Associated Research Funding in the United Kingdom.* London: Alzheimer's Research Trust.

Mitchell, S.L., Kiely, D.K. and Hamel, M.B. (2004) 'Dying with advanced dementia in the nursing home.' *Archives of Internal Medicine 164*, 3, 321–326.

Modi, S., Velde, B. and Gessert, C.E. (2010) 'Perspectives of community members regarding tube feeding in patients with end stage dementia: findings from African American and Caucasian focus groups.' *Omega 62*, 77–91.

Mootoo, J.S. (2005) *A guide to cultural and spiritual awareness.* London: RCN Publications.

Mukadam, N. and Sampson, E.L. (2011) 'A systematic review of the prevalence, associations and outcomes of dementia in older general hospital inpatients.' *International Psychogeriatrics 23*, 344–355.

Myers, A.H., Robinson, E.G., Van Natta, M.L., Michelson, J.D., Collins, K. and Baker, S.P. (1991) 'Hip fractures among the elderly: factors associated with in-hospital mortality.' *American Journal of Epidemiology 134*, 1128–1137.

NCPC (National Council for Palliative Care) (2013) *Reaching the Whole Community? End of Life Care for All Who Need It.* London: NCPC.

Neale, R., Brayne, C., Johnson, A.L. and Medical Research Council Cognitive Function and Ageing Study Writting Committee (2014) 'Cognition and survival: an exploration in a large multicentre study of the population aged 65 years and over.' *International Journal of Epidemiology 30*, 6, 1383–1388.

Norton, S., Matthews, F.E. and Brayne, C. (2013) 'A commentary on studies presenting projections of the future prevalence of dementia.' *BMC Public Health 2*, 13, 1.

ONS (Office for National Statistics) (2005) *Focus on Older People.* London: The Stationery Office.

ONS (2009) *Statistical Bulletin: National Population Projections, 2008-based.* Newport: ONS.

ONS (2012) *2011 Census: Key Statistics for England and Wales, March 2011. Statistical Bulletin.* Newport: ONS.

Ownby, R.L., Crocco, E., Acevedo, A., John, V. and Lowenstein, D. (2006) 'Depression and risk for Alzheimer disease: systematic review, meta-analysis, and metaregression analysis.' *Archives of General Psychiatry 63*, 5, 530–538.

Payne, S., Chapman, A., Holloway, M., Seymour, J.E. and Chau, R. (2005) 'Chinese community views: promoting cultural competence in palliative care.' *Journal of Palliative Care 21*, 2, 111–116.

Peters, R., Poulter, R., Warner, J., Beckett, N., Burch, L. and Bulpitt, C. (2008) 'Smoking, dementia and cognitive decline in the elderly, a systematic review.' *BMC Geriatrics 23*, 8, 36.

Post, S. (2006) 'Respectare: Moral Respect for the Lives of the Deeply Forgetful.' In J.C. Hughes, S.J. Louw and S.R. Sabat (eds) *Dementia: Mind, Meaning and the Person.* Oxford: Oxford University Press.

Prosser, R., Korman, D. and Feinstein, A. (2012) 'An Orthodox perspective of the Jewish end of life experience.' *Home Healthcare Nurse 3*, 10, 579–585.

Roberto, K.A. (1999) 'Making critical health care decisions for older adults: consensus among family memberss.' *Family Relations 48*, 167–175.

Robinson, L., Hughes, J., Daley, S., Keady, J., Ballard, C. and Volicer, L. (2006) 'End-of-life care in dementia.' *Review in Clinical Gerontology 15*, 2, 135–148.

Sampson, E.L., Gould, V., Lee, D. and Blanchard, M.R. (2006) 'Differences in care received by patients with and without dementia who died during acute hospital admission: a retrospective case note study.' *Age and Ageing 35*, 2, 187–189.

Scherder, E., Herr, K., Pickering, G., Gibson, S., Benedetti, F. and Lautenbacher, S. (2009) 'Pain in dementia.' *Pain 145*, 3, 276–278.

Stephan, B. and Brayne, C. (2008) 'Prevalence and Projections of Dementia.' In M. Downs and B. Bowers (eds) *Excellence in Dementia Care: Research into Practice*. Maidenhead: McGraw Hill.

The Economist Intelligence Unit (2010) *The Quality of Death: Ranking End-of-Life Care Across the World*. London: The Economist Intelligence Unit.

Wagner, J.T, Bachmann, L.M., Boult, C., Harari, D. et al. (2006) 'Predicting the risk of hospital admission in older persons – validation of a brief self-administered questionnaire in three European Countries. *Journal of the American Geriatrics Society 54*, 1271–1276.

Werth, J.L., Gordon, J.R. and Johnson, R.R. (2002a) 'Psychosocial issues near the end of life.' *Ageing and Mental Health 6*, 4, 402–412.

Werth, J., Blevins, D., Touissant, K. and Durham, M. (2002b) 'The influence of cultural diversity on end-of-life care and decisions.' *American Journal Of Behavioral Science 46*, 2, 204–219.

Whitlatch, C.J., Piiparinen, R. and Friss Feinberg, L. (2009) 'How well do family caregivers know their relatives' care values and preferences?' *Dementia 8*, 2, 223–243.

WHO (World Health Organization) (2011) *WHO Definition of Palliative Care*. Geneva: WHO.

WHO (2012) *About Ageing and Life-Course*. 28 March. Geneva: WHO. Available at www.who.int/ageing/about/ageing_life_course/en/, accessed on 31 January 2015.

WHO, National Institute on Aging and National Institutes of Health (2011) *Global Health and Aging*. Available at www.who.int/ageing/publications/global_health.pdf, accessed on 31 January 2015.

Section Three

PERSPECTIVES OF FAMILIES LIVING WITH DEMENTIA

12

TELLING IT AS IT IS

PERSONAL EXPERIENCES OF ETHNICITY AND DEMENTIA

Joy Watkins and Shemain Wahab

Introduction

These are stories from a group of family carers who were members of Uniting Carers Dementia UK. They come from a variety of backgrounds and cultures, and have experienced not only the stress, loss and pain that dementia can bring, but also the sometimes unforeseen healing.

Most carers, irrespective of their ethnic or cultural background, can feel stressed and under-appreciated at times. The following stories powerfully illustrate how people who are 'different' can find themselves isolated and alone. Perhaps most importantly, and a thread that runs through many of the contributions, is how carers (and indeed many of us in life) may unwittingly compound a sense of isolation by finding it hard to accept the need for support.

Thinking about the impact of people's culture and ethnicity in relation to dementia is still new for many people, yet it goes to the heart of our identity, of who we are and what matters to us as individuals. These stories illustrate how people from different backgrounds have experienced dementia.

Many of the stories share both the internal and external pressures that can impact on people's experiences of dementia. Family carers give so much yet often feel isolated and that they have to battle to be heard. These carers are openly and intimately sharing their experiences in the sincere hope that, whoever you are and whatever your role, you will be able to learn from them.

Each in their different way reminds us how important it is to see beyond superficial stereotypes about culture and ethnicity, and to connect with the unique and complex individual. We need to see beyond the obvious to ensure there is real equal access to support and services. I hope that you will be moved and perhaps find something unexpected that will enrich you on your journey with dementia.

DANISH, POLISH, MEXICAN, BRITISH, DEMENTIA, UGANDAN AND INDIAN?

GILLIAN LASOCKI

GILLIAN AND HER MOTHER, GUNVOR

I am 51 and an only child caring for my extremely elderly parents. I am British, adopted by my Danish mother and Polish father as a baby. For the last seven years we have lived together in the house that was my childhood home. We live with my daughter, born and brought up in Mexico and now at university in London. My son still lives in Mexico. I am a full-time carer and everything else takes second place including my career, which is now part time. We are, according to my father, his worst nightmare – three generations of women of the same family living under one roof. To me we are four family members, born in four different countries, with four different first languages.

My daughter has started bandying about the phrase 'mixed race' to describe herself. Technically I suppose she is. On ethnic monitoring forms she is constantly frustrated by there being no reference to Latin Americans, much less to an English/Mexican mix, of which she is. Then again, by using the phrase 'mixed race' we all imagine someone with at least a '*café au lait*' hue to her skin and dark hair; and if the adverts for holidays in Mexico are to be believed, she was born with a sombrero and a bottle of tequila in one hand and the Union Jack in the other. In actual fact she passes for English very easily on the outside. The bane of her Mexican childhood was people calling her '*guera*' or blondie as a form of endearment. My father speaks excellent English, albeit with a thick accent he has never been able to lose, and my mother had no discernable accent at all. I can never decide if I should put White British/White European on forms. So, to us, stereotypes are really not very helpful!

We, as a family, believe that it is the empathy and feeling we have for another person which counts most. In our family we would not expect to be sent a professional carer who has experience of our particular cultural mix. That would be ridiculous, if not impossible. But we would expect to have a carer who is willing to listen, observe and learn all they can about the person with dementia and our family set-up – in short, someone with an open mind.

I would argue that no matter what culture you come from, all general traditions are personalised by each family. For example, in our family, 3 out of 4 of our cultures celebrate Christmas on Christmas Eve, so we do that, but we also eat turkey on Christmas Day. We try to encompass a little of each culture to make up our own 'family culture'.

To start at the beginning…my mother, who is the person with dementia in our family, was a physiotherapist for 35 years. Hers was a caring profession, and she was a sociable and caring person. She chose to practise this profession amongst people who were 'culturally' very different to her – us Brits! She had a talent for languages in her native Denmark and excelled at school in English, German, Swedish, Norwegian and French as well as Danish.

She arrived in the UK in 1949 and later met and married my father, a Pole, who also coincidentally spoke several languages.

My father used his language skills to take up a second job translating technical papers from Russian into English in the evenings after finishing a full day as an engineer. When they both retired, he and my mother joined the University of the Third Age where he took up Ancient Hebrew and Ancient Greek. I did wonder at the time of his learning Hebrew if he wasn't going through a conversion – he was brought up a Roman Catholic. I found him on several occasions early in the morning chanting in Ancient Hebrew whilst swaying backwards and forwards as I had seen Orthodox Jews do, but he dismissed this as just a practical measure to keep his rhythm in the chanting of the ancient texts of the Torah. He was very pleased to tell us that his teacher was proud of his progress – he was the only non-Jew in the class.

My mother was a deeply spiritual person. She was brought up a Lutheran but converted to Catholicism after about 20 years of being married to my father. She always said that it was his influence that made her consider this conversion, which seemed strange to me since although he was brought up a Catholic, he neither practised nor believed. Since being bedridden, my mother has twice given us the fear that her end was near, and on the second occasion I brought in a priest to administer 'The Last Sacrament'. I knew that this would have been her wish if she could have expressed it. I naturally told my father what I was planning, and his response was that he hoped I wouldn't do any such thing for him when his time came!

Maybe now you can see why our particular peculiar cultural combination cannot be replicated with all the very best will in the world. And we certainly wouldn't expect it to be.

When we initially asked for a carer to help we were sent a Polish carer by the care agency that thought that the Polish surname must mean that my mother was Polish. I had, of course, told them that my mother was Danish. However, my mother had taken Polish lessons for many years, so when she heard the carer's accent, she immediately smiled and said '*Dzien Dobre!*' ('Good day' in Polish) and continued to respond like that whilst this carer remained with us. The carer was extremely shocked and swore that she had never ever said anything in Polish to my mother.

We do not have any extended family living in the UK, and there is no close family in Denmark anymore. My father has one sister living in Warsaw, Poland, and a nephew and his family. My mother's two most constant visitors in recent years are two Polish friends. Sadly, her oldest Danish friend cut off all contact with my mother more than ten years ago when my mother became too forgetful and dithering. She explained to my father rather matter of factly that 'there really didn't seem to be much point in maintaining contact anymore because my mother wouldn't gain anything from it, much less remember it'.

This is a shocking but unfortunately also typical response to a crippling illness. People's opinions of dementia vary; friends do seem to become fewer. My father certainly said that he wanted to go out less and less with my mother because he was embarrassed by her behaviour, but with both in their early 90s, there are fewer friends around as a natural course of life.

My mother had a gift for languages and spoke English well. She enjoyed trying to communicate with the locals on foreign holidays, much to my embarrassment. Only now do I appreciate what a gift she had to intuitively try and make contact with people, whether she knew their language or not. So it is because of this that in the later stages of dementia, when she was reduced to not being able to express herself, that questions about her ever having been able to speak English were particularly offensive. Not all immigrants are uneducated and ignorant. This is also why my admiration for the professional carers who have attended my mother since she became bedridden grows daily. They do not have my insider knowledge of her likes and dislikes: we don't have a life story book. Her spoken communication has gone, yet they seem to draw on hidden skills unlisted on their job applications. Is it intuition or fine-tuning to a person's needs? Whatever it is, I am perfectly confident in leaving them alone with my mother, knowing no one can do better for her welfare.

When I resigned from my post as a lecturer in Mexico, all who heard I was going home to care for my mother said, 'You're more like us than we thought!' When I came home to the UK, however, I felt more like an immigrant. My daughter and I had no contacts – we had to make new friends and life was isolating for a long time. Luckily for us an Admiral Nurse came soon after our arrival to help and support me, so that I, in turn, could give the best care for my mother.

My lovely, wonderful, previously active mother in the later stages of dementia became bedridden in November 2012 after a bout of pneumonia nearly killed her. She still smiled at us but said little. She used her right hand to pull hands towards her mouth so she could kiss them to acknowledge how much she liked the person. She didn't do this indiscriminately, but she regularly did it to me and my daughter and her professional carers… No, they are not Danish and never have been! They are (in the order in which she sees them in a day) Ugandan, Indian, English and Polish. She has the same carers daily at the same time and she recognises them and is pleased to see them and responds to them as they have always done to her.

As a postscript to the above, my mother died on 28 February 2014, aged 91, a week to the day after a cedar tree she had planted in the back garden 40 years previously came down in high winds. Twenty years of living with dementia, being looked after by my father Adam, seven-and-a-half years of being cared for by me and by many carers of many nationalities and cultural backgrounds came to an end. I am quite sure that my mother would not have lived as long or as well without the love and care she received from all of the carers. And although dementia is a horrible illness and many friends expressed the idea that my mother's suffering was finally over, I cannot really, honestly, feel that her last 20 years were so horrible. She seemed to have had many enjoyable moments, and even in the last 15 months of her life she smiled whilst she was conscious and seemed to know how much she was loved by all.

At Gunvor's end, our Indian and English carers were both there – we cried and hugged each other when we lost her. It might be because we are a similar age, but I like to believe it is a shared experience of the last year of life of another human being that has meant that we possess a new understanding of each other's 'inner spirit', which we would not have had if we had met under other circumstances. The two ladies continue with us, caring for my 93-year-old father who does not have dementia but is bedridden. We regularly swap food and other cultural snippets and remember my mother.

MIGRATION AND CULTURE: A TRINI'S JOURNEY WITH HER MUM IN LONDON TOWN

MARYLYN DUNCAN

MARYLYN WITH A PICTURE OF HERSELF, HER MOTHER AND SON

I was barely in my 20s when I left my mum behind in Trinidad to come over to England. She came here after my father died in the 1980s, and at that time was much younger and was able to go out, to go shopping, and take my son to the park. There was a bench between my home and the park, and she would sit there and talk to people. She was always out and about, and was socially and physically mobile.

She never wanted to live here, but the fact is that I am an only child, hence when mum became unwell with the early signs of dementia I had to uproot her from the family home permanently to live with me. There are many effects of migration, especially for the elderly, including loss of extended family, loss of independence and stability. Even though my mum was one of four sisters, my aunt in Trinidad told me that my mum was my responsibility, so I had to look after her. Mum would have wanted to stay in her home and be supported there, but that couldn't happen. She had to give up everything she felt dear to, to come over to a foreign land where everything was alien to her. Being in her 80s, she couldn't easily adapt to the culture she was brought into.

My mum lived in a village where everyone knew everyone else. They assisted each other if anything happened. People could be called on at whatever time – day or night. My mum always said that she didn't want to live here because she felt you never saw your neighbours from one day to the next and there was a sense of social isolation. She always found it strange the way we interact with each other, that people didn't just drop in on other people, that you either had to phone or be invited.

I am sure, had my mother remained in Trinidad, she would have been able to go out shopping because her long-term memory was there. Had my aunt been able to support her, mum would have been able to live in her own home. She wouldn't have had to attend a day centre with her neighbours around. Coming over here she had to adjust; she didn't have her creature comforts around her, which initially served to make her disorientation worse. Because of all this, I made sure I took my mum to Trinidad every year. For the first few days when we arrived she was really disorientated, but it was surprising how, when she looked around, she was in her home. She sat out on her veranda, the neighbours passed by and came to visit. But would her dementia have been acknowledged/understood in Trinidad? I don't know.

I felt really awful having to bring her here rather than returning to Trinidad to look after her. That's something I have to live with, but I always tried to make sure that all her needs were met.

My mother was a very private, independent person. She received Attendance Allowance but as far as she was concerned, you should be able to look after yourself. If she didn't have dementia she would have been mortified to know she had to rely on other people. She wasn't happy having to rely on me to look after her personal needs (physically she was riddled with arthritis), but she still tried to hold on to her independence. There was always that pride.

Physical

The care of my mum's skin and hair was really important. With our skin, it's quite dry and needs to be creamed. As mum's dementia progressed, she needed prompting to cream her skin. It was something she used to do automatically, but whenever she went into respite, her skin became dry and flaky. So I took cream in and always did a profile about mum, and highlighted the things that I identified as being important. In order to comb her hair because our hair is natural, you need to cream it.

My mum was old school. She never went out without a bra or stockings – no matter how hot it was she would wear pop socks. My mum was in respite, and because of this I couldn't take her to an appointment at the hospital – a carer had to, and I met them there. My mum turned up looking ever so dishevelled. Her hair wasn't combed, her skin wasn't creamed, she didn't have on a bra or her stockings – she looked worse than an orphan. I couldn't believe that she was my mother. This is despite telling the staff how my mum dresses.

Spiritual

My mum was old Anglican, very much into the Bible, and quoted scripture like nobody's business. Whether it was relevant or not, she would pick out bits and sometimes it was so apt that it was upsetting. She had this deep spirituality. Lots of people say they have faith or a religious spirituality and ideology, but my mum's was really deep-seated. It got her into trouble, and one example was when she was an inpatient. I always informed those caring for her that she had never been a good sleeper. When she couldn't sleep she prayed and sang hymns, which apparently did not go down very well with the staff on night duty, but at least one other patient sang along with her. At one point they gave her a tranquilliser and knocked her out completely. It was documented that she refused to take it and told the nurse to take it herself! One of the ancillary staff expressed her concern to me as my mum couldn't eat breakfast or lunch because she couldn't wake up. However, there was a Filipino nurse on night duty at the time, and he told me that because of the way he grew up, he found it refreshing to hear my mum pray and sing, and that he joined her during his shift. He couldn't understand why the others got upset as she was in a bay with people like herself. He knew people had complained from the handover, but he found it quite calming and refreshing.

There's always a melting pot of staff, but the one who had the greatest affinity with my mum was that one Filipino nurse.

Ethnicity

Because of ethnicity, people get lumped into a category. So if you're black you are either Nigerian or Jamaican. You just get put into this box. Cultures are different. We might all come from the same realms but we are not the same. My mum was from Tobago and there can be significant differences, even if people have the same skin tone and type of hair.

We talk about having culturally sensitive services. I needed help from a social worker, as mum was not settling into her first day centre. She said she could get her referred to an Afro-Caribbean day centre that had spirituality as its ethos. This centre had a religious service, but the pastor was a woman. My mum was old school, and in her upbringing, women did not lead service, so that didn't go down well at that stage of her dementia. The service wasn't dementia-sensitive. So there was a dichotomy between trying to meet the needs of someone from a whatever-it-is black background, but at the same time there were anomalies.

Food

My mum never ate much but she expected to see her plate adequately filled, so she refused to hand over her dinner money, her argument being that the portions were small. And then there was the matter of food preparation – she's from a background where food is well seasoned with lots of spices. And my mum was an excellent cook. She couldn't cope with the bland meals, and when she went into respite there were times when she wouldn't eat because she said the food tasted like medicine. It's about finding out more and diving into people's deep-seated culture. I know it's not always easy to do, but we are living in an increasingly mixed society, and it is so important that this is on the agenda of those providing services.

Language

My mum didn't grow up and didn't live in this country for a long period of time, so language was something that was different. Even though she spoke English, the words people used were different, and my mum at times found it difficult to understand. It's not to say she was dumb and stupid – it's just that things need to be phrased differently. Many a time I had to intervene to interpret, decipher or ask people to use different words so that she would understand. Initially she would say, 'I don't understand, can you explain it', but as her dementia progressed, she would stay quiet and just look at you and you might think she was away with the fairies. At the same time, if you made the effort to break words down and to try and meet her where she was at, it made a real difference.

Racism

During my nurse training in England racism was rife. Patients didn't want us to touch them because we were black. That was psychologically painful. They would also say they didn't want to speak to us because we didn't speak or understand English. The senior staff allocated us the worse jobs – the bedpan rounds and cleaning up the sluice. I remember there were times when the doctors used to give lectures on the wards and we weren't allowed to go. No explanations were given as to why.

All of these experiences made us bolder and made us challenge everything. We got support from each other, but we were always on the defensive. That's why I was really protective of my mother, knowing that she didn't have the 'life experience' of living in this country. Racism is more covert than overt.

I cannot say that I experienced overt racism during the time spent caring for my mum, although there was discrimination due to her dementia and age. I think probably because I am the person that I am, I was always quite direct in my approach to people and in fighting my mum's corner, so they would have been wary. However, when she was assessed for community physiotherapy, I remember during her assessment the person took one look at her and decided that she wouldn't be able to understand, and because of that, she wouldn't be able to walk (which she eventually did). Was that overt racism or discrimination?

Assumptions, stigma and ignorance

Whenever we went anywhere people addressed me rather than my mum. I always said if you speak clearly, slowly and use simple words, my mum will respond, so speak to her. Once, while being admitted into respite, a staff member brought the menu to me to complete with my mum. I asked my mum to read it and said I'd explain (as there would be food items she wasn't familiar with). The staff member was absolutely gobsmacked when my mum began to read it herself. Mum smiled and said, 'I don't understand what this is about but I'm reading it anyway.' The assumption being, she was black and elderly – I can't blame her dementia as I don't know whether the staff were aware she had dementia – I go by the fact that she was black, old and appeared illiterate.

Our borough offered me a sitting service. Initially it was through an agency that sent a young person who was a different culture to my mum, and there was no interaction. My mum eventually refused to have her, describing her as 'a living dead'. I was then approached by another service that provides a sitting service for different nationalities. They sent someone to sit with my mum. She said they would find someone closer to my mother's age who was religious. It turned out to be this elderly Asian lady who didn't have a clue about my mother's culture or her dementia. It was like chalk and cheese. In the end, that, too, fell apart. I didn't have anyone subsequently as I found that the stress of the carer was worse than the stress of looking after my mother.

People didn't understand dementia here or in Trinidad. Family members are no different. Whenever people visited, mainly those who really knew her from the very beginning, there was always the shock when she said something, or disagreed with something.

Family members visited. They spent time but no one offered to take my mum overnight, or offered to stay with her so I could have time out. I believe this embraces all cultures because lots of carers say the same thing – it is often 'one person' who carries the burden. Others would come and make a fuss of her and talk about the past, but then they went and that was it until the next visit.

My advice to professionals is, be sensitive to all without making assumptions. Our outward appearance may be the same, but our cultural needs may be different. Assess and treat each person you meet as individuals in their own right.

YESTERDAY'S MENUS, YESTERDAY'S TUNES

DAPHNE ZACKON

BARNEY AND DAPHNE

When, in 1966, both aged 38, my lawyer husband and I arrived in England from South Africa with our three children to start a new life here, there were no particular distinguishing features of dress or general appearance to indicate to an onlooker that we were different.

There were, however, two threads of difference between us and our new neighbours: we were Jewish (although this was not indicated by a wig on my part, or a beard, side locks, black hat, or fringed garments on his), and we were South African (although we were not carrying the popular South African snack of biltong – dried springbok meat – or even a bouquet of proteas, the South African floral emblem!).

In fact, these two strands of influence ran remarkably deep in both of our backgrounds. First, the Jewish aspect. Neither of us were especially strict in our observance of the religious rules, but nor were we of the section of Jewry that ignored religion and our culture entirely.

My husband, Barney, had had what I would call the average middle-of-the road Jewish upbringing of a South African Jewish boy – attending Hebrew School on Sunday mornings, preparing for his Bar Mitzvah, attending Synagogue pretty regularly with his parents and friends, and so on. We had married in Synagogue as well, but after our marriage we did not stick to a very rigid observance of all the laws of Judaism, although I still lit the Sabbath candles on Friday nights, and he sang the Kiddush blessing over the Sabbath glass of wine in his lovely tenor voice. As for Synagogue attendance, it tended now to be more of a 'three-times-a-year affair', on the major Holy Days rather than every Sabbath.

But we always felt entirely Jewish and enjoyed Jewish jokes, literature, keeping up with what was going on in the Jewish community and in Israel in particular, etc. His parents still spoke Yiddish quite a lot, and I learned it to a lesser extent from them, and enjoyed it. We both (but Barney especially) had a great liking for the Hebrew liturgical and Cantorial music, and Barney could actually sing along some of it when we played our recorded versions by some of the great Cantors.

As for the South African strand: it would have been easy for someone who didn't know us to jump to the conclusion (once they heard that we were South African – and Barney in particular had quite a strong South African accent, having grown up in an area where there was a great deal of Afrikaans spoken) that we had the prevailing white South African views of the time, that white supremacy was okay and to be desired. However, nothing could be further from the truth.

Both of us were heavily involved in anti-apartheid activities. In his law practice, Barney was one of the very very few who had black articled clerks (one of whom, incidentally, was the son-in-law of Chief Luthuli, who was Nelson Mandela's predecessor as leader of the African National Congress). Barney was also one of the few white lawyers who were prepared to take cases defending people charged with political offences, and he was consistently vocal and indeed vociferous in opposing all aspects of the oppressive apartheid regime. He was not afraid to make speeches in public, and inevitably attracted the government's attention. This eventually led to his being served with a punitive banning order, imposing severe restrictions, which limited the normal family life of the children and myself. In the end there was nothing we could achieve politically on the scene (he could not even be quoted, for instance, let alone speak to any other banned person or attend any 'gathering'), and it resulted in us emigrating to the UK in 1966.

In any event, we were able to build a new life for ourselves in this country. Barney got on well with people. He never liked pompousness but preferred people to be natural and easy-going, and he had a good sense of humour and easy laugh, and could pretty well always call on a reserve of optimism when the going got tough.

Of course, no one had any idea of the troubles that lay ahead in the form of the vascular dementia that he developed in the 1990s. The actual diagnosis was not until 1996, because until then, I had, I suppose, been in denial, and had put off actually getting the bad news spelled out, as it were.

Once we were unmistakably aware of the situation and at last recognised that we needed help, it was natural to turn to Jewish Care, which is the largest provider of welfare services in the London Jewish community. The local day centre was excellent. Barney clearly felt at home with the feeling of familiarity he experienced there, with Jewish dishes, Jewish songs and music (some Israeli), and of course it was good that neither he nor I had to wonder if the meals might include forbidden foods such as pork, bacon and shellfish. Although not ultra-Orthodox in his practice of Judaism, he would have been very uncomfortable finding such foods on his plate. Also, the whole experience was enriched by the Jewish holidays being marked with songs, appropriate pictures on the walls, and special foods.

When his condition became so advanced that he needed to enter a home for long-term care, it was a conscious and deliberate decision to choose a Jewish home. I felt sure that his quality of life would be immeasurably enhanced by the input of a warm, positive Jewish atmosphere.

We did have to wait a couple of months for a vacancy, but in the end it turned out to be the right decision when he was able to settle in to his new home. Here, too, the Kosher food was an important part of the provision, and the residents were served the traditional foods appropriate for particular Jewish festivals (cheesecake and dairy foods on Shavuot, the harvest festival, apple with honey for a blessing for a sweet New Year on Rosh Hashanah, doughnuts and fried potato fritters on Chanukah, in remembrance of the special miracle believed to have occurred when the precious oil in the Temple menorah lasted eight days longer than it normally would, until replacements could be brought after the Romans had desecrated the Temple!). And of course, at Passover, the first two nights were marked by beautifully arranged Seder meals, and Barney greatly enjoyed not only the special foods, but also the Hebrew songs which he had always sung at home with such gusto when he had presided over our family Seders, and I am sure it also brought back memories of the Seders in his childhood years.

Jewish Care made sure that their care staff of whatever origin (Philippine, Caribbean, Indian, African) had specific training sessions in the aspects of Judaism and Jewish customs that were relevant. This was invaluable.

Another provision in the home that was of tremendous value was the little Synagogue on the ground floor, with regular services conducted by a dedicated, warm-hearted team of volunteers. I cannot stress too highly the value this gave, not only to Barney (who clearly came to life on entering the Synagogue and being greeted by these men and women who became his true and familiar friends), but also to me and the whole family. Throughout the eight-and-a-half years of Barney's life in the home, and to this day (five years after his death), we have been made to feel part of the little community they have created, and always feel at home there, giving and receiving affection.

On one occasion Barney had been ill and was too frail to be taken downstairs in his wheelchair as usual to the Rosh Hashanah service, and thus had not had the opportunity to hear the Shofar (sacred Ram's Horn) blown on that special Holy Day. He was visited in his bedroom by two senior volunteers who were able to give him this experience after all. I was with him, and I will never forget the look on his face of pure delight, and I think it was a spiritual moment for him, although he was not able to articulate his feelings and thank them verbally, as he heard the haunting tones of the Shofar and the appropriate blessings.

As an example of another very welcome gesture from a Synagogue, this time our local Synagogue, of which he was still officially a member although no longer able to attend, the Rabbi, a lovely man with a very engaging smile, used to visit Barney in the care home, and bring his guitar and sing to him. The staff would make sure that we had a quiet room available for this private family visit, and it always did Barney so much good!

After Barney's death, it was even made possible for us to arrange a traditional prayer session for family and friends during the Shiva week of mourning.

To return to the South African aspect of our heritage, another thing he enjoyed was when I played some of the old Afrikaans songs we used to know from childhood. He would clearly respond. Sometimes the other residents and even staff members would join in, even though they wouldn't know the words but could just sing the tunes, so a good time was had by all.

One thing I used to do when the occasion arose was when I was helping him with his lunch in the dining room. If there was a newish staff member at the table helping another resident with their meal, and if this staff member was from Africa, I would start a conversation to try and build a connection between this new staff member and Barney, asking him/her what part of Africa they were from and adding we were also from Africa, from Cape Town, and if the conversation proceeded sufficiently, I could even go on to include a little of Barney's political anti-apartheid past; this usually resulted in the beginnings of a good relationship, which I would hope helped Barney in any future interaction with the staff member. Barney by now had no verbal ability and could only communicate by gestures and facial expression. I used to feel that one of my roles as a family carer for Barney in his dementia was to interpret the world to him and him to the world, and I suppose the example I have just given illustrates this to some extent.

The strands of culture and ethnicity are not always obvious on the surface; they can also be misleading because of their complexity. But they do run deep and have far-reaching consequences. In dementia care they need consideration. It is surely a subject to be included in training programmes for care staff, social workers, and all who are involved with the care of people living with dementia.

BRIDGING THE GAP

ANON

My mother has been living with Alzheimer's probably for about four years, but was only diagnosed last year. I am the youngest of four daughters, living closest to my mum. I have mixed heritage, my mother is Chinese/Cantonese-speaking, and all of us only speak English. My mother is 86 and still lives alone.

Although still living in assisted living accommodation, every day is a struggle. My mother is the only Chinese resident and only a handful of residents are not white English. There is no support provided to meet her ethnic and cultural needs. Many of the residents feel that my mother has never bothered to learn to speak English, but in fact she was fluent before her dementia. My mum is very isolated where she lives and there are no services within the area to support people specifically with dementia, let alone any for Chinese people with dementia. There is certainly little knowledge or support for family carers in my situation.

There has also been a constant battle to get a diagnosis and get direct payment to employ a carer to support my mum. There is a lack of trained bilingual Chinese carers which means communication between the carer, our family and my mother is difficult. There is also a stigma within the Chinese community around mental health issues, and people who were friends of my mum suddenly no longer want to speak to her.

Being the closest in distance and the youngest child of the family I have always felt a lot of emotional and practical pressure to care and ensure that my mum is okay. Also, because of my profession in the social care field I have also, like so many of my peers, believed that I should be able to cope without help. However, just like everyone else, I have emotions and get stressed in extreme situations.

The pressure of caring has caused much tension between family members. There are four of us and up until recently I always felt I had to fight for the support I needed. Recently, one of my siblings stepped up to take on a major coordination role, helping me to coordinate our mother's care. This has finally taken a lot of pressure off me.

I know that the travelling distance for my family doesn't make the situation any easier; however, so many tasks could be completed by using the internet, email and mobiles. Simple offers to take on medical appointments, making calls, filling out forms could and should be shared, but too often it is not until the main carer can't cope and is on the edge of collapse that this happens.

Being the main carer and witnessing the deterioration of someone who is close to you, on a daily basis, is so painful that it is difficult to put into words the way you feel. At the same time as doing practical tasks such as cleaning, prompting and cooking, you are also dealing with the feeling of endless loss over a protracted period of time. It's a constant reminder that someone close to you, and in this case, my mother, is terminally ill. It's also a reminder of your own mortality.

Another difficulty for all of us in our family is the fact that my mother is finding it more difficult to communicate in English, and we know probably deep down there may come a time when we will no longer be able to speak to her in English. So we won't be able to understand each other anymore!

All of these things make me feel that every spare minute I have I should try spending it making things better for her. For me there is a constant feeling of whether I should be having some time to myself or be doing things with my mum. Very hard not to feel guilty and end up exhausted.

I try to keep focused on other things such as work, so my mind is not constantly preoccupied with worry. But it means often my mind drifts and I, too, have become forgetful. I also wonder and fear that I will inherit or develop dementia. I guess this is something that many of us fear who care for someone with the disease. Here's hoping very soon a cure will be found.

THE BATH

VIVIANA FAIN-BINDA

VIVIANA AS A CHILD, WITH HER MOTHER, HORTENCIA

My mother, Hortencia, was born in Argentina. So was I. My paternal grandparents were English and that made me British. My mother was a '*criolla*', a descendant of Spanish colonials born in the Americas, and also British by virtue of having married my father.

I arrived in London in 1970. In 1974 Mamá visited me for two months in my attic in Belsize Park. One morning we went to the hardware store to buy light bulbs. As the man was packing them Mamá said, 'Could you test them first, please?' They worked. In our culture we mistrust everyone – shopkeepers, taxi drivers, officials. We fear being tricked. We only trust our family and our doctor.

This was Hortencia's first time in England. She cherished everything – gardens, museums, even the weather. When the two months were up, she extended her ticket. Her second marriage had collapsed in Argentina and she wasn't ready to return just yet. Her English, though, was inadequate. She was a chartered accountant so decided to work as one in Britain: 'using numbers,' she'd say, 'my poor English doesn't show!' Going to the theatre, reading and making friends, her language rapidly improved. Fiercely independent, she soon had a place of her own. Twenty-five years later she was still in London having become a successful Spanish tutor.

In the early 1990s, while teaching, Hortencia's mind went blank. Some weeks later it happened again. Alarmed, she gave up her job. I felt it was over-emotional but could not dissuade her. After Ronald Reagan declared he had Alzheimer's, my mother, while driving, said, 'I wonder if I have the same?' I dismissed it out of hand as being melodramatic.

Months later, I telephoned her saying I was in Waitrose and would it help if I bought the ingredients for the following day's supper? It was my husband's birthday and Mamá had offered to cook. 'Nobody told me about it!' she said furiously and put the phone down. Something was amiss and I didn't know what.

Once she gave up work Mamá changed. She became anxious, refused to see anyone, made a mountain out of a molehill and fell out with people. The latter was not unusual. She loved her friends until she didn't, and then turned them into monsters. Now this was more frequent and with people she had always been close to.

Suddenly, Hortencia went into hospital for an emergency operation. After surgery her behaviour is stranger than ever. She wants to smoke in the ward and is abusive to me for stopping her. I see in her the look of a demented being. She stares at me with hatred. I go home shaken.

They want to discharge her. I insist she stays put until assessed by a geriatrician. They relent. Days pass. Weeks pass. A month passes. No sign of a professional. I remind them daily.

I take time off work and storm into the ward saying, 'A Harley Street doctor in a Rolls-Royce would've been cheaper than Mamá blocking a bed.' Next day a geriatrician descends from the seventh floor.

He enters the cubicle where my mother is sitting. After some minutes he exits declaring: 'She's fine, a bit confused for being so long in a strange environment, but otherwise fit.' I'm incredulous. 'It's no longer a strange environment,' I say, 'she cannot remember her own apartment.' I beg him to return shortly. He looks at me annoyed, as if saying 'I'm the doctor here.' I remind him we have waited for him for a month, therefore a few more minutes doesn't seem extravagant.

Half an hour later we go in together. Mamá, coquettishly, (she loved men) says, 'We've met before, your face looks so familiar.' He is dumbfounded. She had said that earlier. Outside he exclaims, 'She's the best window-dresser I've seen – has no short-term memory.' His description still resonates. A window-dresser indeed!

'Martin Fierro' is Argentina's epic poem. In it a cynical old man offers this advice: '*Hacéte amigo del juez; no le des de qué quejarse*' – 'Get pally with the judge; don't give him motives to complain about you.' Befriend the powerful; they'll protect you in your hour of need. Even in her confusion, my mother's instincts warn her not to show intellectual inferiority in front of such an influential person as a doctor. A physical illness – fine, a mental one – humiliating.

I am beginning to feel like my mother at the hardware store, except that now the light bulbs don't work. The community psychiatric nurse says my mother is sound, only I have nefarious intentions. The GP thinks my mother is fine because she can add, forgetting she's an accountant. The geriatrician is coaxed into coming again, only then realising my mother has no short-term memory.

My trust in the medical world is crumbling fast. I speak six languages and interview people for a living, yet whoever I ask for a professional opinion about my mother's condition patronises me and fobs me off.

Hortencia is accepted at a day centre specialising in caring for someone with dementia. Here, at last, I feel understood. She's motivated and valued, and so am I. I'm happy for the first time in ages.

When the condition finally steals my mother's mind, she enters a home. There the real nightmare begins. She no longer speaks

English but understands it and responds in Spanish. Many members of staff in London's care homes are newcomers to Britain, with poor English themselves. They decide my mother talks gibberish and progressively ignore her. As these are not well-paid jobs, staff turnover is high. I explain my mother's predicament to one lot, only to repeat it incessantly because employees change relentlessly. Continuity is non-existent. My mother deteriorates fast.

We visit her daily to translate her problems. I notice her wrists are bruised. I ask why. They say my mother refuses to have a bath. 'And we don't understand what she's saying.' 'Why didn't you call me?' I enquire, 'My mother hates baths, she only takes showers. It's hot in Latin America and showers are refreshing. She feared you were drowning her.'

Hortencia died some time ago.

I wondered why during this sorry saga only the day centre had understood the impact of Alzheimer's on me, the carer, holding my hand judiciously.

You see, Alzheimer's spawns two victims: the person with the condition and the family carer. It is an unequal distribution. While the abilities of one diminish, the burden on the other increases exponentially, until it is total and overwhelming. The day centre understood this, which made all the difference. They reassuringly said: 'We cannot love your mother as much as you do, but we can care for her as well as you can.'

I noticed there were no booklets or videos giving advice and support to family carers from the carer's perspective. As a filmmaker, in 2004, I made such a film. It is called *Life with Two Hats*. The message was, 'Don't suffer stoically. Don't feel guilty. Ask for Help!' I hope I succeeded.

NILAR AND FATE

U. HLA HTAY

HTAY AND MINNIE TOGETHER

We were both born in Myanmar – Minnie (Nilar) a Eurasian, and I, a pure Myanmar. Minnie spent a few years in India as a Second World War evacuee with her family, and then moved to Belfast where she had bad experiences with the Catholic nuns and lost her faith. We met in London in 1967 and got married in 1971 three times – at the Marylebone Registry Office, Myanmar Embassy and at home with Buddhist blessings by Thai monks. When I explained to Minnie that the bad experiences she had encountered were from individuals with frailties, not according to the true teachings of her faith, Minnie accepted it wholeheartedly. I am a practising Buddhist, and at 15 my father took me to a Vipassana meditation centre; I have continued to practise ever since. Minnie, who was not religious when we met, would help me with my religious duties – attending sermons, joining religious celebrations at the monasteries and at charity events.

Minnie was diagnosed with an early onset dementia type of Alzheimer's. In Myanmar, dementia means reverting to second childhood, as distinct from mental illness or madness. However, some Myanmar believe that such suffering is due to bad *kamma* committed during this or previous lives, or as a result of a curse. One close friend of mine apologetically suggested I seek the help of someone with mystic powers; I told him I did not believe in it, and it would not help Minnie. Instead I made humble requests to the

Sayadaws (chief monks) in the UK and in Myanmar to bless Minnie with their *metta* (loving kindness) for a comfortable and happy life and ultimate cessation of her sufferings in this life and beyond.

Around that time I completed my tutelage to practise maritime arbitration after gaining professional qualifications and experience. It had good prospects for earning very well, but it required attending meetings at home or abroad, at short notice. Instead I decided to care for Minnie, as I didn't want her left in a care home with strangers. I told our three sons about her dementia from the first day of her diagnosis, and later shared this news with her siblings. We received unflinching support from our sons and their families throughout the caring journey.

Minnie and I used to go to cafes and restaurants in the West End in the early stages. Minnie, with her European looks, hint of Oriental charm and mystery, was often interesting to people. She joined me at the workshops I attended. Ladies helped her into the toilet while I waited at the door. When I first took Minnie to female public toilets, the ladies screamed at me, so I then took Minnie with me to the gents. I received funny looks but I could handle it better.

Minnie's behaviour markedly changed, with increased wandering and the use of more colourful language. She had never used rough, rude or derogatory words before. When we went shopping or strolling in parks, people openly said she should not be in a public place as she was mad. One of our neighbours called social services, attempting to put Minnie into institutional care. When I explained to people that Minnie's behaviour was due to dementia, some listened, but the majority repeated their views, demonstrating their ignorance and prejudice. Strangers often believed that Minnie's behaviours were directed at them and were unable to understand it was the dementia, even when I explained. I just gave up explaining in the end. I knew it was more through ignorance and fear of the unknown that people reacted, rather than malice, but it was hard to deal with.

It seems to me that the embarrassing behaviour of dementia patients in public adversely affects the family carer most, hence, perhaps, the tendency to keep them out of sight. Our family decided it was important to enjoy sharing nature's beauty and life's offerings to the full together with Minnie as long as we could.

By accepting her condition we could look for suitable medicines and access services and support. I used all available means to administer medicine, short of forcing Minnie to take them, which would have conflicted with my ethics. I also never demanded conjugal rights when Minnie was not able to consent anymore. Buddha taught me tolerance, equanimity, respect to self and others with loving kindness. This helped me develop the mental capacity to turn around adverse events in our life. By practising Vipassana meditation as a Buddhist one escapes from attachments, miseries and ultimately attains Nirvana. Armed with these concepts, when I learnt the devastating dementia diagnosis, I felt no stigma in seeking professional support for the long journey we would undertake together with the Three Musketeers, our three sons. Whenever I took Minnie out for a walk or to the Centre, I said prayers for her happiness and for her fellow sufferers. I also encouraged Minnie to say a single Buddhist prayer word, which only lasted with her for a short time, but she liked it.

When Minnie received care at home and in the respite home, our request that personal care was delivered only by female carers was respected. But when we accessed domiciliary care services and respite care regularly, the horrible stories that happen to other families came true for us as well. One carer shaved Minnie's eyebrows and pubic hair, claiming that it was the local custom in her Far East Catholic country. Upon complaining, the female Centre manager told us that it was bikini shaving for elderly women who never sunbathe! As male and female en-suite bedrooms were on the same floor, sexual transgressions did occur due to staff shortages or staff not recognising the vulnerability of their patients. One male, who was doped with medicine for wandering, was found in Minnie's bed. Another man was described as 'a frisky naval officer' with a history of groping, and was moved to another floor after his transgression on Minnie, despite vehement protests from his family. This was very upsetting for us. Battles became part of my life caring for Minnie.

Initially Minnie would not let any 'coloured' home carers look after her, which wasn't like her. Later we had a Somali carer who got on really well with Minnie, and from then on she didn't mind 'coloured' carers. I think Minnie's response may have been due to her bad experience in India. The Somali carer helped feed lunch to Minnie and got upset every time uneaten food was thrown away. I invited her to join us for lunch, and from then on M&S chicken was out and it was in with halal chicken and everyone was happy. One day I cooked pork for us, and without knowing what the fragrant aroma coming from the pot was, she wanted to taste it. I wanted to say 'yes' as a tease, but knew that it is forbidden food for her, and I must respect her religious dietary requirements.

When paid carers treated Minnie with a genuine sense of care, then that was good enough for Minnie and me – their origins or language became secondary. If the carers and professionals looking after Minnie had empathy, knowledge and experience of person-centred dementia care, it made such a difference. But many had no clue about dementia care, which was very stressful, and meant we had many difficult times and changes in staff.

As Minnie's spoken language deteriorated and she became aggressive and often rude, it could be very difficult. At the monastery she would say all kinds of inappropriate things, which made me not want to take her back, but I also wanted her to be with me in such a tranquil and peaceful environment.

My Buddhist religious guidance and continued meditation helped to make my caring journey easier and more enjoyable, and helped me tackle the daily variety of challenges.

Minnie has now died and I am forever grateful to her for giving me the chance and opportunity to care for her. I did my best with her best interests in mind, and couldn't have done it without the regular support from the families of the Three Musketeers. Whenever Minnie gave us a faint smile in response to something we did, it was worth all the hard work. Such appreciating gestures of Minnie never ceased and lasted to the end.

FRIENDSHIP ACROSS THE MILES

BETH BRITTON

BETH AND HER DAD

Dementia poses huge challenges for any family. Most of us never consider what having a loved one with dementia will really mean, how life will change, and how you will be constantly tested by the disease and the circumstances it puts you in.

For an intensely private man like my father, dementia was arguably the worst possible disease he could have developed. His 19 years with vascular dementia reduced him to immobility and the need for round-the-clock specialised care, including, of course, very personal care. My dad had hardly ever been unwell in his earlier life. Indeed, when he had a bout of the flu during a particular winter in my childhood, being confined to bed infuriated him, and he was extremely reluctant to allow the doctor to even listen to his chest when my mother called her in for a home visit.

Prior to his dementia, dad was fit and active, very self-reliant and someone who looked after his family, rather than needing care himself. He had grown up in rural East Anglia and spent the majority of his working life devoted to the countryside and farming. He never travelled abroad, very much out of choice, and wasn't a social butterfly or someone who had lots of friends, generally preferring the company of his beloved cattle and, of course, the privacy and security of his family home.

Having retired, begun to develop dementia and gone ten years without a diagnosis, dad would eventually join – not by his choice or ours as his family – the thousands of older people who live in residential care. His symptoms at that time were such that he wasn't allowed to return home – his life of peaceful tranquillity and familiarity in a small, very classically English village ended by dementia.

By this point in his life, he had little understanding of the realities of moving into a care home, aside from knowing on day one that it wasn't home and that he wanted very much to go home. As his family we were understandably anxious, but felt very reassured by the staff we met whose outlook and kindness had been a major factor in choosing where dad would live.

Like many UK care homes, all three of the homes my dad would live in during the last nine years of his life were staffed mainly by foreign care workers, generally either from the Philippines or Eastern Europe. For them English was not a first language, and many of the cultural nuances specific to England, for example, English cuisine, were alien to them and not covered by the standard training they undertook.

Given that my dad was never a globetrotter and had lived a relatively sheltered rural life, moving to an environment where everyone was a stranger to him and where the people providing his care were obviously visually and audibly foreign, we anticipated having difficulties trying to settle dad into this new way of living. He wasn't familiar with other cultures and accents, and coming from a generation that grew up during the Second World War, he had been exposed at a young age to some of the negative viewpoints of other countries and cultures that existed during those years.

Yet far from shunning this new environment and becoming aggressive or difficult to care for, over time my dad formed a bond with his carers that unmistakably turned to a deep friendship. Cultural divides and language barriers didn't prove an obstacle for dad when he found himself surrounded by friendship, fun, smiles and love.

Whilst many foreign care workers have been the subject of negative coverage of their work in the UK, our experiences could not have been more positive. We found the Filipino carers who looked after my dad some of the most caring and loving people we had ever met. They were hard working, honest, loyal and, coming from a very family-orientated culture, often more caring than their English counterparts.

Nothing was ever too much trouble; they had a very sunny outlook and took a personal interest in dad, wanting to learn about his life and then talking to him about it. They were wonderfully observant and quick to pick up on his mood changes, physical needs or when potential health problems were brewing. They managed to make dad's care home a real home-from-home, not just for him, but also for us as his family, and it was a welcoming atmosphere that became priceless to us all.

The Filipino staff also understood the importance of religious faith in everyday life. Although coming from a strong Catholic background, they were very supportive in helping dad to continue to practise his Church of England faith, joining in hymn singing, ensuring he attended church services in the home and that he received communion from the visiting vicar in the privacy of his room. They never imposed their religious beliefs on dad, but I think having their individual faiths helped to engender a mutual respect between dad and those who were caring for him.

Of course there were differences. The Filipino carers couldn't grasp that we have cranberry sauce with our Christmas turkey and applesauce with roast pork, preferring to serve the fruit sauces with custard or cream for dessert. Perhaps more fundamentally, their written and spoken English wasn't always easy to understand, but their ability to care, listen and love was there for all to see, and as a result they made what was a time of huge change for dad and for us as his family a much easier period.

When dad left the nursing home that he had spent around eight years in and moved, via a spell in hospital, to another care home, his Filipino carers remained great friends to us all. We kept in touch via social media, his keyworker came to visit dad in hospital and again, in the last days of his life, in the new care home, and many of his carers came to his funeral. Since then we have attended dad's keyworker's grandson's christening, and we will always be lifelong friends. There are no words to thank his carers for the love and devotion that they showed dad – from many miles away, and some might argue a world apart, we found friendship in the mutual human instincts of love and care.

MY SAINTED AUNT

GLENNIS SCADDING

PORTRAIT OF SISTER FELICITAS

When we first met I was about two-and-a-half and cross with her, since she had displaced me from my bed and bedroom, back into the cot in my parents' room. That crossness did not last long, and my memories of that Christmas are a blur of happiness.

Her next furlough occurred several years later, and I began to realise that this person was different: she had a habit, not a kind of repetitive behaviour, but the sort worn by nuns for centuries – black and thick in winter, thin and blue in summer. She was thin, very thin, but full of life, with twinkling eyes and a quick smile. Her life was governed by ritual: waking in the dark early hours to pray and repeating this several times a day. One could not disturb her then, but at other times she was available for fun and games, and would sometimes champion me against the demands of my parents. Her love of nature was profound, and we always had to make sure the cat was fussed over and the birds fed, somehow keeping the second away from the first. It was sad when she left to make the long voyage back to Africa.

When she next arrived back in the UK I was in my teens and was able to understand more about her life and to marvel at the stories of the wild life, horrified by the black mamba which she had found sharing the latrine with her. I also questioned her about why she became a nun. She told me that at 14, the fourth happy child of a soldier's family fallen on hard times after his early death, she realised that she had a religious vocation, but her mother was not happy about this and persuaded her to try nursing. This she did – including a stint as a midwife in the East End of London where the filth and poverty appalled her – but she did not veer from her intentions, and became a member of one of the few Anglican orders of nuns. Their original convent was a leper colony in Essex where sufferers who had contracted leprosy (then an untreatable disease) abroad were housed and looked after, and this is where she began her work, later transferring to Africa.

A highlight of my life was my first trip to Africa when I was able to take time to visit her, travelling by train across the equator, then by local bus, sharing my seat with, in turn, a baby, then a baby goat. She met me, a boiled lobster in my crimplene dress, looking her usual calm, elegant self, totally at ease in the chaos of Tanga bus station, chatting to locals. This was where she was really at home. The convent was also calm, cool, with the stewed, immediately available tea I have learnt to associate with convents everywhere. My aunt did not live there but was up in an outpost at the top of a steep hill, just reachable by Land Rover straining up the track in first gear. She was in her element there, loving the land, its animals and its people. She took me to meet her friends, the totos had not seen anyone with long blonde hair before and marvelled, stroking it gently. One place my aunt showed me was the hillside where she wanted to be buried when the time came. Sadly this was not to be: the Order withdrew its mission from Africa and my aunt returned to live in damp, grey England, initially as an Essex girl, in a medieval chapter house in Ipswich, later moving to a Lutyens house in Surrey. She was sad about leaving Africa, but did what her vocation demanded, and obeyed, helping locally as she was now too old for the nursing for which she was trained.

I remember the first time that she told me something was wrong with her mind: 'I'm losing words, Glen.'

Stupidly (for this was my first experience with dementia), I reassured her, but when her next letter to me was so poor compared with previous ones, I alerted Mother Superior who had her seen and tested at the local hospital. No treatable cause was found, and my lovely aunt gradually lost the ability to understand and to converse, and became horribly anxious and sad. She was lovingly cared for by her Sisters until they could no longer cope with her wanderings; then she was transferred to a care home. This was always locked and I found it hard at first to see her there, but amazingly, she settled in well. She proudly showed me her room, as she had in Africa, though this one was larger and more ornate than any previous one. Her few possessions did not fill it. We would always go into the garden together to see the birds, flowers and fish. The staff were mostly young Afro Caribbeans, and their broad smiles and friendly ways suited my aunt, who, I think, thought that she was back in Africa.

On my first visit I asked somewhat tentatively for my aunt by her family name, though she had given this up years before to become Sister Felicitas. The beautiful young woman who had opened the door smiled and said, 'Oh you mean Sister', and led me to her.

My aunt, still wearing her habit and pectoral cross, was delighted to see me and to introduce me, managing to remember my nickname. The warmth and affection between her and her carers was obvious, with much smiling and reassuring patting on both sides. Somewhat less stewed tea soon appeared for us both, together with chocolate biscuits.

This ease was not present in some of the other inhabitants, mostly white, elderly, middle-class, suburban individuals, who were worried by their carers because of the lack of common ground – with age, culture, race all being different, they were unsure of what to expect. The carers were louder, more demonstrative and some of the residents found it hard to adapt. Would my aunt have managed so well without her African experience? I suspect not, but like to think that she would have adapted to her circumstances in time, as she did throughout her life.

I learnt to take her chocolate, which, like me, she loved, and a family photo album. We would talk about the various people shown as though they were still alive (I made the awful mistake at first of telling her of my mother's death, which had taken place some years before, but which she had forgotten, only to see her so distressed that it was hard to comfort her, and never did that again), and I would give her greetings from all of them. In fact, it struck me that her life in the home was similar to that which she had been accustomed to for years: institutional, with only a small space of her very own, surrounded by Africans whom she loved and with family distant. She was, I think, as happy as she could be there; she seemed to have reached the sunlit uplands of her dementia when she had no further insight and therefore no anxieties. She died there and was buried, after a beautiful service, close to the south coast of England in a rural setting, not quite where she desired, but I know that she would have settled for it as she was always adaptable, loving God and all His creations and being a genuine world citizen without worrying about barriers of race or creed.

A LITTLE OLD IRISH LADY CALLED MARY

MIKE MCCARTHY

MIKE AND MARY AT LOURDES

My name is Mike. I am a 53-year-old male looking after my 85-year-old mother Mary, who suffers from vascular dementia and Alzheimer's. I have been a full-time carer since my mother was first diagnosed. I am also studying for a BA Honour's degree with the Open University, in Health and Social Care. Although she has been diagnosed for three years, all the warning signs were there a long time before. Due to my mother's age and cultural beliefs – 'You only go to a doctor if it is serious so as not to be wasting the doctor's time!' – the diagnosis took longer than we would have liked.

The family did eventually manage to talk her round to visiting her GP, and that's where the road to treatment took off. When the diagnosis was confirmed, it was at that point when the 'label' of Alzheimer's was given to Mary that family attitudes changed. Different perspectives and stereotyped expectations attached to Alzheimer's from family members was another hurdle I would have to overcome. I come from a large family of eight siblings. Some are deceased and some have moved away. Coming from a large Irish family used to have many advantages; however, as time goes by, it also has its drawbacks – no communication between each other and dealing with family conflict has pretty much left me unsupported and sometimes quite isolated.

As a full-time carer I have come across a number of barriers, both within the family and also when dealing with health care professionals – from consultants to health care providers. The 'joined-up' approach within the health service seems to be harder when advocating for someone who speaks Irish and suffers from dementia, and also when dealing with some health care professionals' own linguistic barriers. I usually spend my time translating on her behalf, then being told that they need to hear it from the patient herself, which then causes more frustration and confusion for us both. They then ask to speak to me again on my own! Sometimes we took many backwards steps to go forward.

My mother is Irish Catholic with very strong and deep-rooted views on family matters. For example, all personal affairs should be kept indoors and dealt with internally, and we most certainly do not accept any help from outside agencies or 'strangers'. She does not believe in taking medication, seeing a doctor, or allowing people to 'do things for her' such as personal care and meal preparation – we still struggle with that one. The 'shame' and stigma of having those people (carers) in the house would just not be entertained or considered.

Giving us the option to buy our own care package through the individual budget scheme was a massive help, or so we thought. Personalisation allowed me to interview potential care assistants to help out on a one-to-one basis with personal care and to provide continuity. We were looking for someone who had previously looked after a 'little old Irish Catholic lady', but none of the people we interviewed had any experience of this.

Most of the care assistants we interviewed had their own stereotyped expectations and assumptions of what my mother would be like without even having met her.

I interviewed a number of carers and finally arrived at one quietly spoken English lady who had all the qualifications needed for the job, albeit on paper, but not so much with life experience when dealing with a 'little old Irish Catholic lady'. We did not anticipate the language barrier she would have with my mother right from the start.

Not being able to understand Mary's dialect, colloquialisms and accent proved difficult; also the speed at which my mother spoke was difficult for anyone to understand, let alone the care assistant. In all fairness to her I don't think she had come across anyone like my mother before in her life! Repeatedly being asked what was she doing in her house and why was she wasting her time coming when all she does is drink tea all day? Mary still thinks carers are for old people!

Something that we look back on, smile and shake our heads from side to side is when the care assistant took my mother to Mass for the first and last time. At the interview I asked whether the care assistant would have a problem taking my mother to Mass, as her religious and spiritual beliefs are an important part of her cultural upbringing and overall wellbeing. 'No' was the answer, 'I always attend Mass on a Sunday.' On coming home from Mass my mother described how the priest had chased the care assistant out of the church because she had put the communion host in her pocket. Whilst getting ready to go for communion my mother had said to her, 'It's best if you go to communion and take it home with you', thinking she would know what this meant. The care assistant explained that she hadn't a clue what my mother was talking about, and it was a while since she had been to Mass! We were all mortified by that experience, and I immediately apologised to the priest – fortunately enough, he was very understanding! The care assistant didn't last long after that; the language barrier was proving to be more difficult than we anticipated.

I find it easier now to take my mother to Mass most days of the week. We find that routine is an essential ingredient when dealing with dementia. Doing this has also helped me to renew my faith; I stopped practising my religion some time ago.

I volunteer with Age Concern and visit the day centre quite often. After a lengthy interview with the manager, I was assured that they could meet my mother's cultural and ethnic needs, that they could adopt a person-centred approach to her care, assuring me they would respect her privacy and autonomy.

We now have Age Concern coming in daily and attending to personal care, and preparing a light snack that Mary likes, one morning and one evening call. Her dietary needs are very important to us, and it's not very often we get an Irish service provider who can make a good pot of stew or a dish of what the Irish call a 'coddle' (boiled bacon, sausage and potatoes etc.), so it's important for us to make sure her diet consists of familiar food that she was brought up on.

Everybody has their own unique identity, and trying to make sure my mother's cultural preferences are maintained is very important to us both.

Living a short distance away is very advantageous for me as a carer. As I don't live with my mother, it helps me to 'come away' from the daily struggles and frustrations of living with dementia, and it also helps me to make sure I look after my own general health and wellbeing. The wandering sensor we had fitted on Mary's front door can keep me awake night after night; equally it gives me a very early morning alarm call while she is looking for Patch, our Jack Russell, until she realises that Patch is in my house! I have since bought a couple of canaries and left them downstairs where she can see them so that she doesn't have to open the front door and set the alarm off (yet!)!

Studying with the Open University has helped us to overcome some of the professional jargon and some of the language used by health care professionals. It has also given me an insight into the ethical principles of being a caregiver, especially when it comes to a son looking after his mother.

Caring has had an impact on my life. Sometimes it does leave me socially isolated; long nights and many a broken night's sleep; early mornings and ever-changing mood swings can sometimes be very demanding. Financial insecurity and living with the stigma of being on benefits can be very frustrating; Carer's Allowance does not go anywhere. Somehow you just learn to keep it in the day and get on with it. It does have its benefits – this year I will be doing a two-mile outdoor swim and raising money for the Alzheimer's Society. When Mary is off to the day centre, I toddle off to the swimming baths to keep my own sanity! Caring can be hectic one minute and leave you twiddling your thumbs the next. Organising and prioritising is the key and you learn to adapt.

Now that I have everything 'ticking over' (just for today!), it's a joy to be a full-time carer for my mother in her old age. I would now say that all Mary's cultural needs are being met as well as they possibly can be. Her dietary needs are being met, personal care is being looked after, and she attends day care twice a week. The 'strangers' have now become a welcome sight and a refreshing change where they can have a cup of tea and a good old gossip. Having me to orchestrate the care package and introduce the 'outsiders' into her own home and into her own little world of dementia has all been a worthwhile slog, one that I can look back on and say, 'Yes, I did my best'.

DON'T YOU ASIANS TAKE CARE OF YOUR OWN?

MANJIT KAUR NIJJAR

MANJIT WITH HER DAD AND BROTHER

My parents came to England in the 1960s. My dad came here having served in the British Indian Army as many Sikhs had done. Like many children of immigrants, my brother and I grew up in a hybrid world, being both Indian and British at the same time.

Dad and I had an incredibly close relationship. When I was 15 or 16 years old my friends were all getting engaged. Instead of encouraging me to follow suit, dad pulled me to one side and said: 'Manji, I think it's about time you ran away from home!'

So like any good girl I did what my dad told me! When I wanted to go to university, dad encouraged me. He begged me to pick a course that meant living away from Wolverhampton and living abroad. One of the words of wisdom he gave me to cope with being homesick was to 'take my heart with me wherever I went'; that way, the people I loved would go with me too, and I would never be lonely.

When I was 25 years old I came back home. My brother had married and moved to Canada. I suppose, looking back now, dad had already started to show signs of dementia. He was forgetful but would cover up by saying he was being silly or more often blaming us for confusing him.

By 2004 it was obvious something was seriously wrong. He was behaving differently, becoming very suspicious of me, and what I might be doing, and insisted on escorting me to work and back. When my dad became afraid of the dark, he started sleeping downstairs and couldn't bear to be alone, so for a while, mum, dad and I were all sleeping in the living room.

2005 followed in the same vein. I encouraged mum to take dad to our GP. In February mum was diagnosed with terminal cancer and given less than six months to live. In May dad was given a preliminary diagnosis of Alzheimer's. In June mum died.

My dad's behaviour became increasingly erratic. He wasn't sleeping, he was wandering and he never settled. He stopped being the dad I knew. I was totally unprepared for this. I had no idea what was going on. I understood he was ill, but his decline was so rapid I didn't get it. What was going on? Was it because mum had died?

If I didn't get it, dad's friends certainly didn't – they couldn't understand how a man who had worked hard, raised a family, gotten his son married and settled in Canada was behaving so strangely. There was, of course, only one answer. Dad had been cursed and had bad karma. And the cause was obvious – me. I wasn't married and, compared to my friends, I had been given far too much freedom. I had failed to behave the way I ought to have done, and this was the price that dad had to pay for my actions.

So they avoided him. They didn't want to be associated with a madman, or even risk the possibility of being contaminated. I tried to explain that he was unwell. One thing I learnt very quickly was that there is no hard-and-fast dividing line between superstition and knowledge.

The fact that he had been an active member of the community for over 40 years became irrelevant. The support he needed after mum's death never appeared. Some of the kinder people would say that dad had gone mad after mum's death, and I made it worse by not being married, which added to his burden.

The one good thing about a curse is that there is a cure. Remedies included rubbing his head with almond oil or turmeric, putting almond oil in his tea, and turmeric in warm milk for him to drink. Of course, the best cure was for me to get married to a man from India.

One of the principles of Sikhism is seva – selfless service to the community, which includes helping the congregation, feeding the homeless, visiting the sick. With one distinct exception – if you have dementia. Then you have to repent your sins. So against all logic I paid to have special prayers said for him both in India and in a local Gurudwara [Sikh Temple], partly in hope of a cure and partly because of our faith. He was dad and I needed him, especially as mum had just died. He was all I had.

Dad had always been a religious man so I would take him to our local Gurudwara. The one and only time we stayed to have langar (the food served after the service) we were told to sit behind a column so the congregation didn't have to look at us. In the blink of an eye we had become invisible.

Part of the problem is that the priests are not from the UK. They come from India and it is a job. If you are lucky, spirituality is a by-product. Some speak English and others don't. They do not understand dementia, or what the pressures are for those of us who have been born and raised here. I kept hearing comments like 'Children born in this country are stupid and know nothing of our values'. The community look to these priests to set the standard. There is an expectation that you will honour your parents by caring for them – asking for help is dishonourable, shameful and disrespectful. Above all, you must do your duty.

Everyone – I mean everyone from the professionals to my friends and family, the community as a whole – thought caring was a natural thing. I didn't even have a pet growing up; I had never cared for anything. All of a sudden, I was an expert! I was ashamed that I found it so hard. This was the man I loved above all others – it shouldn't have been so hard.

Some Asian professionals we met judged and gave us very little or no help. This was made more difficult as my brother wasn't here, and as a woman my thoughts and opinions did not carry the gravitas needed. It wasn't until my brother came to visit us in 2006 that the psychiatrist revealed that dad had a dual diagnosis of vascular dementia and Alzheimer's. So this would explain the rapid decline.

Prior to my mum dying, we had no involvement with social workers. We never asked for help from the authorities – the shame of asking for help; can you imagine not being able to take care of your family? Only people from bad families did that, and we were better than that. So, when we had a social worker, I was horrified. In a two-and-a-half year period we had seven social workers. One of the social workers was Asian, so we felt we could ask her more forthright questions.

- How long did dad have? The answer – how long is a piece of string?
- Would we have to put dad into a home? The answer – I would never put my parents into a home.

So I was no further forward and just felt stupid for asking those questions.

When my mum was dying of cancer at the same time, we were involved at every stage:

- What treatment was available?
- Where mum would go before she came home.
- How and where mum wanted to die.

I just assumed that the same would happen for dad; after all, there was no cure for dementia. So I assumed we would get the same level of care and support.

I later had to become on speaking terms with the local drug dealers and prostitutes in the area where we lived so they left dad alone. Unfortunately, I hadn't banked on the kids who mugged and beat him up for fun. I couldn't protect him whilst I was at work, so I needed day care.

Trying to access day care services for dad brought its own problems. After all, 'Don't you Asians take care of your own?' There is a perception amongst statutory bodies that Asian communities don't use services because of extended family networks. For some families that is true, but not for all of us.

So in that sense, how are we any different than any other community living in the UK?

To compound the issue, when dad was finally allocated day care, I was asked 'Why have you thrown your father away?' by members of the Asian community who knew him. Even though dad has now gone, I am being told this is the worst way in which I failed him. There is one woman who spits at me when she sees me because of what I did.

Day care came with its own set of challenges. It wasn't what I had expected. I decided against complaining when I saw dad eating beef sandwiches. One of the highlights, however, was my dad making friends and learning the names of the Zimbabwean staff. They were a blessing and treated him with respect and kindness.

My relationship with dad had totally changed. He talked about India and I simply couldn't relate. I had never been to our village; I didn't know what it looks like. I didn't know the people who lived there. I never met any of my grandparents so I couldn't bridge that gap. It was an aspect of his life I knew nothing about. The only people who understood were the taxi drivers who were from India. They talked to dad about places and things I still don't understand.

I felt that I was failing no matter how hard I tried. It was just unrelenting and remorseless. I was being condemned by the perceptions of the Asian community and the statutory bodies. There was no one on my side when I needed it most. It was a very dark and lonely place to be. I confess I am envious of my friends here who have had support through their Admiral Nurses or have had a similar service to hold their hands, listen to their worries and concerns, help plan for the future as they travel on their dementia journey.

Despite all the struggles we went through, I didn't have to worry about what my husband or in-laws were going to say or do. I didn't have to ask permission to care for my dad. Or worry about the impact dementia would have on my children's marriage prospects. I didn't have the extended family meddling and causing me untold headaches. I did have access to services and managed working and caring for dad.

The one thing I did know was that I wanted to make a difference – dad and I couldn't have gone through all this for nothing! Dad said the true values of being a Sikh were to fight injustice, to make things better so that no one else had to suffer needlessly. So I decided that working with Asian families living with dementia for a charity in Wolverhampton would be the best way forward. I have offered support, listened, given the information they desperately needed. Everything we didn't have. I understand the shame and the fear. I have tried to break down barriers by empowering carers and people with dementia to do what is right for them and not to worry about what others think and say. To stand up, speak out and improve the services that they are receiving in Wolverhampton.

This involves:

- raising awareness of dementia
- helping people living with dementia and their carers, by providing support and advice in a culturally appropriate manner
- working with statutory services to promote greater understanding of services and offering alternatives to day care settings where appropriate through the use of direct payments.

There is no place for judgements, recriminations or false cures. What I am doing is not rocket science; there are pockets of good work going on across the country.

In this day and age most of us would be horrified to be discriminated against on the basis of the colour of our skin, our religion, our sexuality, our likes and dislikes. Yet discrimination against people with dementia and their carers is very present and readily accepted.

As someone who was born and raised as a British Indian Sikh, I had a rude awakening when it came to the cultural aspects of living with dementia. I had no idea of all the double standards and nuances. These assumptions and expectations I had, as well as our experiences, caused me to internalise my fears and frustrations. The impact of this affected both my mental and physical health.

My dad finally succumbed to pneumonia, leaving me alone. For a long time I stood at the edge of a precipice, not knowing what to make of it all. I mean, this had been my life for nine-and-a-half years. I had lost myself, who I was, and what I wanted from life. All my friends had gotten married and had families – what was I supposed to do?

My deepest regret is that dad didn't get all that he needed when he needed it – he deserved so much better. I wouldn't wish that on anyone else. I am now finally finding my way again after a long and difficult journey.

HOLDING ON TO GOD

KAUSER AHMED

BAYJEE AND HER DAUGHTER, DR ZAIB DAVIDS

When my mother-in-law became ill in the summer of 2000, her illness blindsided us. We were shocked by the unexpected affliction of mental illness and its repercussions on our family.

Bayjee ('mother' in Punjabi, and the name by which my mother-in-law is affectionately known to family and friends alike) had a reserved and dignified nature with immense inner strength. She was born in a small hilly village in the state of Punjab in Pakistan, some 86–87 years ago, where villagers rarely registered the births or deaths of family members. Doing so involved an arduous and hazardous journey to the city, at the end of which they would have been mocked, as who could possibly care about life and death in the poverty-stricken backwaters of the Punjab?

Bayjee was the eldest of nine siblings, of whom only two survived. Her early life was full of poverty and tragedy. Poverty always brings painful privations, but also cruelty, and Bayjee's family were stigmatised for their bad luck.

Her father, a potter and subsistence farmer, had very poor health and struggled to make a living. The misfortunes of his family deeply traumatised both him and his wife. Bayjee witnessed her parents' suffering and how their faith in God gave them strength to endure and carry on. When she was 18, Bayjee's father suddenly died, leaving her, her mother and brother without an adult male protector in a predatory society where that was essential. Bayjee's stoicism in the face of cruelty, unhappiness and hardship was forged into her from a very early age.

At the core of Bayjee's being is her relationship with God, her faith a source of strength and solace, throughout the adversity and challenges of her life. The unchanging rituals and prayers of Islam provided her with an anchor in the uncertainties of her world.

Bayjee brought up her family with rigorous values of faith, hard work and probity. She arrived in England in 1966, hiding her sense of displacement and loneliness under her introvert and serious nature, diligent in domestic and familial responsibilities.

Bayjee had a passion for education. She bitterly regretted that she had never been to school because of her gender and her family's poverty. She secretly taught herself to read and write Urdu, and with the help of an English tutor, learnt basic English, spelling words letter by letter. With Bayjee's support and encouragement her children became doctors and scientists. As her daughter-in-law, she extended that support towards me, caring for my son whilst I went to university.

When Bayjee suffered her 'breakdown', we were living in Devon – my husband and me, our two boys and Bayjee; the rest of our extended family was in London. As a Muslim family of Pakistani heritage we were a minority living in a rural English area, but saw ourselves as well adapted to British life and culture. (The Census figures for 1991 showed a non-white population in Devon of less than 2 per cent.)

Bayjee busied herself by helping to care for her grandsons, travelling into Exeter city centre, attending English language lessons and socialising with English friends and neighbours. At weekends we visited the beaches and moors, enjoying the natural beauty of Devon. Bayjee loved her garden, planting flowers and vegetables; she was energetic and happy. This idyllic existence made her illness all the more shocking.

During Bayjee's breakdown, paranoia was the chief symptom. Her terror was directed at us. She refused all food, saying it was poisoned and we wanted to kill her. Bayjee wouldn't leave her bedroom, didn't wash, dress, and more worryingly, perform the Muslim Salaat, or prayers which she never missed, even if seriously ill.

The dread and fright emanating from Bayjee was so powerful that my husband and I began to feel guilty, as well as panicked and distressed. My memory of that awful time is that we were all in the grip of a terrible nightmare.

Bayjee's breakdown met with differing responses from the extended family – some felt we were making too much of her paranoia and that she was just 'unwell'; others saw this as a fatal collapse of body and mind.

It took over six months for Bayjee to recover. Thankfully, she had early medical intervention, as we were persistent in seeking help. Bayjee was seen by a consultant psychiatrist from the local psychiatric team at home as an emergency. The drugs to control her paranoia started to take effect within days, and to witness the change from the fearful person back to someone who was able to tentatively smile was an immeasurable relief. It had been a frightening and bewildering experience for us all, but we were confident that this was an isolated incident and that she would recover completely.

As Bayjee slowly regained her confidence and started to take part in her usual activities, we noticed that she could no longer converse in English. She seemed completely unaware of this, and would chat away in Punjabi to her friend Eileen. We teased her about this and Bayjee laughed at herself, but we were all unsettled by it.

At home she wore loose Salawar Kameez, the traditional clothes of the Indian subcontinent, stitching this herself on her sewing machine. Bayjee loved to buy bits of fabric in the local market and then cut out designs to stitch together. She started having problems working out how to cut and bring the pieces together. Her innate sewing skills seemed to desert her. Years later, I found carrier bags full of material that had been spoiled during cutting that Bayjee had hidden at the back of her wardrobe, too embarrassed to tell anyone.

Other problems started to appear. Bayjee lost her confidence as she realised that her English language was now down to a few words. Despite encouragement from everyone to carry on conversing, she became more reserved, no longer engaging in banter with English friends. She stopped going in to town by bus, staying home.

When Bayjee forgot the burglar alarm code, we put that down to a 'senior moment' and made the code easier. These senior moments became more frequent. Bayjee began to forget people's names and faces; she 'forgot' visitors as soon as they left. It began to worry us when we repeated the same thing for the umpteenth time, that her forgetfulness was more than just the ageing process. Familiar objects, such as can openers, confused and bewildered her as if she was encountering them for the very first time.

As much as Bayjee was at a loss to make sense of events, actions and things around her, we were unnerved by witnessing her struggles. One day Bayjee found herself stuck in the porch because she had forgotten to unlock the outside door but had closed the inner door and she did not have her keys to unlock either door. When I found her she was sat on the floor amongst the shoes, tearful, distraught and reciting prayers. The floor was wet and it was a struggle to lift her off the floor, sitting hunched in the porch left her in agony, unable to straighten up. She was too distressed to say how long she had been there. There was no point in saying, 'Why didn't you put your keys in your hand before you closed the door?'

Already feeling vulnerable and confused, this was a huge blow to her self-confidence. After that, Bayjee refused to go out alone, and the humiliation of having to relieve herself in the porch made her fearful of being caught out again.

Five years from her 'mental breakdown', Bayjee changed from a happy, confident, sociable and busy individual to someone who had retreated into herself, only intermittingly interacting with her family. Matters were made worse by the fact that our sons only speak English, so Bayjee no longer conversed with them. My husband and I spoke to one another in English; we only spoke in Punjabi to Bayjee. There were no other Punjabi speakers we knew who could supplement her meagre social interactions. Bayjee started to sleep in the afternoon for up to two or three hours a day, her waking times out of sync with everyone else's. She was losing touch with what was happening in the household, let alone the outside world. Her world had contracted to her bedroom where she would stay sleeping, praying and reading the Qur'an.

Always conscientious in carrying out her religious duties, Bayjee became even more absorbed in her faith. As well as the five regular prayers, she would wake up in the early hours to make supplementary prayers. On Mondays and Thursdays she would fast. Her day was punctuated and synchronised by prayers and Qur'an reading. Bayjee got up at 3am, to read the Qur'an, went to sleep at 9 and woke at 11 when everyone was out at work or school, becoming isolated from the rest of the family.

Eventually Bayjee could no longer read the time. Prayers would be made at whatever time it popped into her head to make them, and as she didn't remember if she had prayed or not, she often read the same prayer numerous times. There are five compulsory prayers a day, and if she repeated any or all, her total tally could be 15 prayers, so including time making ablution, her day was totally absorbed.

Bayjee refused suggestions to go for walks to the beach or town with us. She didn't want to miss her prayers. Once my husband demanded that she come out with us, saying she was being unreasonable. Throughout the trip Bayjee was silent, obviously unhappy and anxious. After an hour she implored, 'Please can I go home?' Her son was devastated, realising her distress. Bayjee was no longer the confident mother who would previously have resisted being bullied into doing something that she didn't want to do.

As her dementia progressed, it became harder to engage Bayjee in conversation. Once we watched the news and discussed world events. Now, if we talked about anything outside of her immediate concerns, her gaze shifted and attention wandered. She responded with bland generalisations such as 'Allah knows best, we can only pray.' Even a comment about the weather would be met with 'Allah is the creator, he does what he wants, good or bad.' A query about her health would elicit, 'I have pain but Allah will give me patience to bear with this'. Such answers cut dead further conversation; she was increasingly isolated from everyone.

By 2006, we could no longer ignore Bayjee's mental deterioration and knew we were failing her if we didn't act. Nobody used the dread word 'Alzheimer's', but she was slipping further away from us, emotionally and mentally. In that year, we moved to Hertfordshire, hoping that increased contact with her extended family would stimulate and invigorate Bayjee. Our new GP referred her to the local memory clinic, where she was diagnosed with Alzheimer's disease. We were optimistic when she was prescribed the new wonder drug, Aricept, that there would be an improvement in Bayjee's condition. It was not to be.

Conversations with Bayjee became difficult, as her mind was preoccupied with the past. Every recollection ended with an invocation to Allah, for forgiveness and mercy. As we encouraged her to talk about her parents and siblings, the depth of her relationship to God became clear; the unwavering faith, which had sustained her throughout her life, was her only preoccupation.

Bayjee went into hospital for a knee replacement. As the anaesthetic wore off, her first thoughts were of her prayers. She struggled to the bathroom to make ablution. As she tried to lift her leg to wash her foot in the sink, she fell. Bayjee had completely forgotten her knee operation a few hours previously. Everyone put her distress down to her fall, but it was the realisation that she couldn't do her prayers. Bayjee's normality was through her relationship with God.

Knowledge of Bayjee's early life allowed us to understand some of her behaviour as her dementia progressed. When she spat out her grape seeds, she was seeing not carpet, but the mud floors of her earlier homes. She would walk towards the windows when she needed the toilet, because she wanted to go out into the fields and grasslands, where in the village everyone went to answer the call of nature.

Our local park became the setting for her childhood village. The copse of ancient trees was 'the jungle' which lay just outside the inhabited area. The few corrugated buildings dotting the park were houses of her family. That one, her father built, the other, her uncle, who'd died in the war. She relived her childhood traumas. The only way to cope was to pray fervently for God's help.

Bayjee's decline was discernible by her circular thoughts and short attention span; but when she lost her ability to perform her prayers, we realised that our Bayjee, who had been the strength of the family, had disappeared. Bayjee had long stopped knowing the times of prayers. Now she forgot the actual rituals of standing, sitting and prostrating, and for ablution, she would remain in one position, her eyes darting around the room, her body and mind disengaged.

Should Bayjee become paranoid, we could divert her by reading the Qur'an. Although she couldn't read the words, Bayjee would trace the words with her fingers, getting solace from the physical contact. The Qur'an should only be touched by someone who has performed ablution and is 'clean', but we know God understands.

Bayjee no longer comprehends what we say to her. However, certain phrases will trigger an instinctive response, such as '*Allah Khair*' (God protects), '*Bismillah*' (in Allah's name), or '*Inshalla*' (if God wills). When the indignities of toileting or personal care make Bayjee angry or distressed, her carers have been taught to say, '*Bismillah*', or '*Allah Khair*', and she is reassured.

When Bayjee sits in her chair, looking lost, her hands flutter restlessly, searching for something to hold on to. We give her the Tasbih or rosary and her fingers move instinctively along the familiar beads. At night, her son will recite familiar prayers so Bayjee can sleep. Bayjee may not remember the names of the family she nurtured and raised, but her mind still reverberates at the mention of God.

Section Four

THE WAY FORWARD

13

STRATEGY AND POLICY

Jill Manthorpe

'Public bodies cannot meet the full range of needs which exist for their services unless they recognize, value, and address the diversity of the society which they serve' (NAO 2004, p.3). There are many accounts of the difficulties faced by black and minority ethnic (BME) people with dementia in the UK of trying to access culturally appropriate health and social care services of satisfactory quality (Moriarty 2008). The relevance of this statement from the National Audit Office is now discussed in relation to dementia policy and strategies, in addition to the practice areas covered elsewhere in this book. While there is a widespread need and obligation to develop culturally sensitive, fair and responsive services for the increasingly diverse communities of people with dementia and their carers in the UK, the spread of good practice has been slow. One reason for this may be that however much individuals attempt to respect culture and diversity, the policies and cultures of their workplaces do not support this. Furthermore, in the current climate of austerity and cutbacks, sufficient resources may not accompany overarching policies.

Policy-making at different levels and in different spheres has addressed some of the challenges identified by BME people with dementia themselves, by carers and family members supporting BME people with dementia, and by practitioners and campaigners committed to equality. This chapter takes four perspectives: age-related policies and strategies; dementia-specific policies and strategies; equality-focused policies and strategies; and practitioner-related policies. It aims to set out policy or strategic ambitions and their connections, and also to consider implementation challenges.

Policies are not confined to central government but feature in local government and among service providers. Professional bodies, too, may have policies as well as regulators and employers. Policy-making is not generally as simple as the development of a plan, or policy document, or even a piece of legislation, followed by implementation (Manthorpe and Stevens 2014). Although this chapter cannot address all policies, it aims to point out that many people working in services will be at the receiving end of policies – they also write them, evaluate them and modify them. As an example of this, while there is a National Dementia Strategy (DH 2009) in England, almost every NHS commissioning body has produced its own local strategy, and so, too, have many service providers and local authorities. There are well over 100 local strategies, and many of these bodies will also have carers' strategies, strategies for older people, and strategies for mental health services and public health. Within services or within multi-agency arrangements, other policies will be relevant to the wellbeing of BME people with dementia, such as safeguarding policies, community safety policies and social care policies. There would seem to be no shortage of policies.

Overall, policies are not generally an easy or interesting read. The Department of Health (2014) itself acknowledged that many of its policies are not understood, are greeted with cynicism, and are thought to be boring or irrelevant. Can the same be said of policies at local level or policies written by managers and practitioners in any of the wide range of groups and organisations working with people with dementia? One key theme of this chapter is that policy-making is not only confined to the government – many more of us write them, read them and interpret them. It is up to us to ensure that they are not hard to understand, dull or seem peripheral.

Age-related policies and strategies

This section starts by revisiting the National Service Framework (NSF) for Older People (DH 2001). This is one policy where there is specific mention of the diversity of older people. Improving access to culturally appropriate services and enhancing responses to the needs of older people from BME backgrounds featured among its aims. This policy did not see separate services as the answer to problems of lack of take-up of services. Instead, it is possible to map each NSF for Older People standard to BME or ethnic diversity considerations (see Table 13.1). In the national evaluation of the NSF, consultations with BME older people seemed to confirm this approach as a way of addressing multiple needs and challenges. General levels of satisfaction with health and care services amongst BME older people consulted were higher than had been anticipated, and possibly even more than the NSF had suggested. Where they had concerns, they were more about the incomplete recognition of the culturally specific needs of older people from BME groups by mainstream services than concerns about the separate development of services for BME older people (Manthorpe *et al.* 2009).

TABLE 13.1: COMPONENTS OF THE NATIONAL SERVICE FRAMEWORK FOR OLDER PEOPLE RELATED TO BME OLDER PEOPLE

Introduction
• Acknowledgement of growing proportions of older people from black and minority ethnic (BME) groups (para. 10) • Recognition of greater prevalence of some long-term conditions among minority ethnic groups (para. 11) • Call for services to be culturally appropriate (para. 12)
Standard 1: Rooting out age discrimination
• Recognition of increased risk of disadvantage among older people from BME groups (para. 1.5) • Identification of BME groups' greater disadvantage in accessing services (para. 1.7)

Standard 2: Person-centred care
• Requirement to recognise individual differences and specific needs such as cultural and religious differences (para. 2.1) • Call for greater availability of interpreting and translation services • Call for information to be made available in a range of languages (para. 2.15) • Call for good assessment not be culturally biased, and for staff to make sense of the ways in which race, culture, religion may affect a person's needs and may impact upon each other (para. 2.31)
Standard 7: Mental health service specialisation and improvement
• Recognition that mental health services for people from minority ethnic communities should be accessible and appropriate (para. 7.3) • Demand that mental health services should enhance trust by not being culturally biased, and that information should not just be available in translation (para. 7.3)
Standard 8: Health promotion
• Call for health promotion activity to acknowledge differences in lifestyles and the impact of cultural/religious beliefs • Call for health promotion services to be devised in conjunction with local BME communities (para. 8.3)

SOURCE: DH (2001)

The standards highlighted in the NSF for Older People were not particularly new aspirations. In the 1970s there had been attempts to identify the health and social care needs of older people from BME groups. In 2003, Better Government for Older People (Manthorpe, Harris and Lakey 2008) commissioned a survey of local government strategies for BME older people. The survey identified that a third of responding local authorities had approaches underway; another third were considering or initiating strategies; but approximately one-third of local authorities had no plans to produce a strategic document to reflect their plans in meeting the needs of their BME older communities. Interestingly this report considered that older people's groups often raised the importance of being inclusive, and many had undertaken outreach activities to address increasingly diverse communities, or had built up links with BME communities.

The Audit Commission also highlighted problems such as institutional barriers, including the low priority given to race equality, the belief that it was not an issue affecting every local community, and difficulties in engaging with older people from BME groups (Audit Commission 2004). At another level, the Healthcare Commission (the regulator succeeded by the Care Quality Commission) concluded that many of the longstanding negative experiences of NHS care experienced by older people from BME groups could 'mean that staff in the NHS are not taking account of cultural differences and sensitivities when they are treating patients' (Healthcare Commission 2006, p.21). However, there is increasing recognition of the diversity among Britain's older BME groups and of the variations within as well as between them (Moriarty 2008) – also described as 'within group' differences. These may create changing and quite different patterns of need between different localities requiring fine-tuning of strategies and policies. A further challenge is to take more of a life course perspective – and to see patterns of advantage as well as disadvantage as being cumulative. One way to assess the ways in which local older people's strategies address diversity is to investigate them – not only what they say, but which older people have been consulted about them, whether what they say is reflected as a result, and if they address strengths as well as problems.

Dementia-specific policies and strategies

In February 2008 the government produced the policy document *Living Well with Dementia: A National Dementia Strategy* (DH 2009). The five-year plan set out 17 recommendations for the NHS, local authorities and others to improve dementia care services. The recommendations focused on three key themes: raising awareness and understanding; early diagnosis and support; and living well with dementia. Truswell (2013) has suggested that BME groups are likely to find themselves 'late to the table' in contributing to such strategic and commissioning discussions where clinical and academic institutional interests are already embedded.

The National Dementia Strategy prompted many local commissioners (in the NHS and local authorities) to evaluate their dementia services and to give dementia services greater priority (see Box 13.1).

Box 13.1: Example of strategic work at regional level

NHS East Midlands held regional workshops on the National Dementia Strategy, but had limited representation from the BME communities.

Nottingham Health Care team believed that BME community elders within Nottinghamshire were not accessing dementia services in proportion to the expected incidence. However, there was very little local evidence to support a strong business case. So, the community development worker and the General Manager of the Mental Health Strategy for Older People worked together to gather evidence with support of other committed individuals. They conducted head counting in wards to show occupancy by ethnicity, creating basic evidence to support their observations. They supported their findings by extrapolating national level statistics to estimate dementia locally by ethnicity. NHS East Midlands Development Centre was able to offer match-funding to support efforts to increase the proportion of BME community elders accessing dementia services in Nottingham.

The team worked in close collaboration with the BME community and other partners to develop two linked strategies: raising awareness of dementia services in collaboration with 20 community organisations, and training local Community Development Champions. The aim was to raise awareness of dementia among ethnic minority communities in Nottingham.

SOURCE: EEIC (2012)

This joint working in Nottinghamshire was also facilitated by a shared commitment among local commissioning bodies to reducing ethnic health inequalities and a wish to 'dovetail' two national strategies – Delivering Race Equality and the National Dementia Strategy – as well as a wish to foster good relationships between different organisations at community level. However, fears were expressed that forthcoming reorganisations locally might undo this work or destabilise activity. Writing of the dementia navigator pilots, Clarke *et al.* (2013, p.298) noted that these risks are pertinent to many such initiatives:

> Innovation, creativity and the embedding of new services are compromised by short timescales and a 'project' like approach to their development. Greater attention should be given to securing commitment to sustainability before commencing so that unexpected changes in policy do not result in undue distraction from service delivery.

In his review of the progress of the National Dementia Strategy from a race equality perspective, Truswell (2013) first argued that existing policy guidance relating to BME communities was overlooked in the roll-out of the National Dementia Strategy, and that a more targeted approach was essential. He advocated the use of 'community dementia navigators' as an innovative pathway. In his view, paid befrienders would be able to help individuals with dementia and their carers receive day-to-day support and assist them in finding their ways around the health and social care system. While the evidence about dementia care navigation is equivocal (Clarke *et al.* 2013), these suggestions about what should be commissioning priorities illustrate a powerful sense that dementia care pathways are not clear or well communicated.

Secondly, Truswell (2013) argued for improvements in training in cultural competency among care professionals so that individuals are better supported, and suggested that improvements in such training for professionals across the care pathway were linked to desired outcomes, such as the reduction of late diagnosis of dementia among BME communities, and ensuring that individuals are better supported throughout their treatment (care and support). This proposal is also optimistically presented as an 'invest to save' opportunity for the NHS, by leading to reductions of expensive unscheduled hospital admissions and/or moves to care homes. Similarly, Truswell suggested that adopting a community dementia navigator model would 'likely' lead to savings, indicating the apparent necessity for any policy suggestion to be able to claim a potential for cost-effectiveness.

'Dementia doesn't care about the person. We should.' was the title of a video produced by the Runnymede Trust (2013). The term 'double discrimination' was used to argue that current systems do not address the 'unique issues' faced by BME people with dementia – the double discrimination covering race/ethnicity as well as dementia. This line of argument is longstanding, and some have argued that there is actually a triple jeopardy (race, age and poverty), while others have referred to multiple jeopardy or intersectionality (Koehn *et al.* 2013), and reject double or triple jeopardy as over-simplification of differences and similarities. Regardless of such terminological debates, such arguments call on individuals and organisations to make changes in their own lives, workplaces and communities to tackle racism, but also on policy-makers to respond to problems of access, acceptance and attitudes. Research that deliberately focused on areas in England with comparatively few BME people found that policies should be respectful of staff and not assume a 'deficit model'. This means more than giving staff information or telling them what they are doing is not right, because a strong theme among the care practitioners interviewed in this study was how unskilled they felt, and how they feared 'saying the wrong thing' (Moriarty, Sharif and Robinson 2011).

The All-Party Parliamentary Group's (APPG) recent report, *Dementia Does Not Discriminate* (2013), sought evidence about the experiences of people from black, Asian and minority ethnic communities (in this chapter, the term 'BME' is used). As a result of this inquiry, seven recommendations were presented to help people with dementia and their families from BME communities to live well, echoing the overarching aspirations of the National Dementia Strategy. Some of these might be construed as 'policy-related', such as the call for government to fund a public campaign to raise awareness of dementia among BME groups (recommendation 1), but many of them are related to NHS activity and linkages, such as targeting work on modifying risk factors (recommendation 2). In terms of policy, the APPG is an intriguing example of policy influence and the ways in which the politics of dementia is being 'performed' by the interweaving of exhortation and appeals. The APPG, whose administrative support is provided by the Alzheimer's Society, stands in the interesting position of potentially being able to comment on policy, but in this instance its recommendations feature words such as 'encouragement' and 'share' more than calls for legislative reform or policy revision.

Elements of these approaches have already been adopted in some localities and will be important to evaluate. Box 13.2 illustrates one of these – the local authority and (then) the NHS commissioning joint strategy in the northern town of Bury.

Box 13.2: Dementia, ethnicity and culture

The Strategy will look at how we engage with BME [black and minority ethnic] communities when developing dementia services with the aim of increasing cultural awareness within mainstream services. Bury's largest BME groups are the Jewish and Muslim communities. The Bury Dementia Advisor pilot provides a hub and spoke model with a BME focus. We hope to identify through this pilot the most effective ways of communicating and providing tailored information in order to break down some of the barriers and stigma associated with dementia within these communities. Further awareness-raising campaigns will be planned using the preferred language to describe dementia and the symptoms. We hope these methods will empower people to come forward for earlier diagnosis and enable Social Care and Health to assess the extent and nature of need amongst ethnic communities in order to plan services. (Team Bury 2010)

New structures also have to develop dementia-related strategies, such as NHS England (which is targeted in recommendation 1 of the APPG report, see above). In many ways there are no new themes emerging, but new organisations tend to have to revisit, refresh and reiterate previous work, or others suggest that they should. As one example of this, a recent 'summit' event at regional level involving stakeholders from NHS England, the Regional Clinical Network and Senate (NHS England 2013) seemed to discuss many familiar items, but the event presented an opportunity to introduce these new bodies to existing dementia interest groups and to place on record their interest in this subject. Generally, while no new policies or strategies emerge from such events, they potentially have a 'soft' impact in policy implementation and adaptation. Truswell's (2013) observations about who gets to be 'at the table' in such events will be a useful indicator of whether the policy aspirations for BME community involvement are being realised.

There is now a sharper focus on health-related risk factors specific to British BME groups, as other chapters in this book have outlined. However, there is evidence that ethnic inequalities in health are largely a consequence of socio-economic differentials to which racism and the perception of living in a racist society may contribute (Nazroo and Williams 2005). In the next section we explore not only policies and strategies related to older BME people with dementia, but also the wider policy world affecting those who work with them in dementia services.

Practitioner-related policies

It is easy to think that policies and strategies only relate to patient and user groups, or as the focus of this book suggests, BME people with dementia and their carers. Dementia care, however, is an area of practice where employment and professional policies have the potential to ignore or to respond to matters of ethnicity, culture and equalities. According to the sector skills body, Skills for Care (2014), of registered managers of care homes in England whose details are recorded on the National Minimum Data Set for Social Care (NMDS-SC), 87 per cent are British, 84 per cent are female and 80 per cent are white. With one-fifth of care home managers being from BME groups, this means that many of the people who have profound influence on the management of quality of care and care home cultures as managers are themselves likely to be familiar with BME communities, and had experiences of racism and discrimination. This applies even more to care staff in frontline positions, many of whom are from BME backgrounds or are migrants. It is estimated that the profile of the dementia care workforce resembles the rest of the highly diverse care workforce, except that it contains relatively more Asian or Asian British workers and more women (Hussein and Manthorpe 2012).

Some research has identified problems of racism in dementia care settings – against BME or migrant staff. Employers need to have strategies and policies on how to address this. Clearly policies are no good if they remain unobserved, but they can be helpful in supporting staff to raise their concerns and to seek solutions. From interviews with care staff, Stevens, Hussein and Manthorpe's (2012) research highlighted the importance of open styles of management, where workers feel able to report problems in the expectation of being taken seriously. Balanced approaches to supporting workers are also to be promoted, combining help with managing situations and assistance for staff in developing cultural and language skills they can use in direct interactions with other staff, care users and family members. Similar findings and recommendations emerged from a study of CALD (culturally and linguistically diverse) dementia care workers in Australia (Nichols *et al.* 2013), where guidelines for practice to improve outcomes for the multicultural workforce were strongly advocated as a way of building 'culturally connected' work practices in dementia care. Nichols *et al.* (2013) specifically recommended:

- strengthening policies on non-discrimination and cultural inclusivity and translating into practice
- building cultural competence through education
- recognising and translating the nuances of local culture: language, colloquialism, practices
- embedding policies and practices in orientation, education and performance review.

One of the few studies that has taken the perspectives of staff in care homes, BME residents and families, and explored the policy implications of their findings about care perceptions and practices was that by Bowes, Avan and Macintosh (2011). Overall, they found that the perspectives of residents and family members were less positive than those of staff. Managing relationships well in care homes may help prevent mistreatment, neglect and abuse. In multicultural contexts and possibly emotionally charged dementia care settings, racism, misunderstandings about cultural differences and problematic attitudes are additional issues that can negatively affect people with dementia and also frontline staff.

Bowes *et al.* (2011) suggested that for BME residents, being able to use one's own language is fundamental to identity and therefore dignity, suggesting that policies on race and racism might also usefully be related to policies about dignity and safeguarding. This may help to foster workplaces in which culturally competent care or practice is influenced by knowledge and understanding of cultural diversity, and thereby helps deliver good care. Rather than waiting for incidents or complaints or high staff stress and turnover, the helpfulness of workplace policies and strategies could be included in audit, peer review, supervision and training. And, as Smith *et al.* (2007) suggested, valuing and recognising the talents of a diverse health care workforce is a further approach that may need to be better reflected in care settings.

Bowes *et al.* (2011) undertook their research as part of a programme of work related to elder abuse and neglect, and so their findings are also relevant to policies related to safeguarding from elder abuse and neglect. BME residents and family members may be inhibited from complaining about poor care more than other people. Low expectations and possible feelings of guilt amongst residents and their families may sustain poor care. Complaint and compliment policies are unlikely on their own to change matters, but how they are written, displayed and communicated can be addressed with cultural competence.

Equality-focused policies and strategies

This section ends with observations about the role of equalities through a policy perspective. These include the adoption of policy by commissioning and other public sector activities. The Equality Act 2010 is then considered, which can be seen as the culmination of policy campaigns promoting equal opportunities. Policy-making is often seen as the most important of stages, but as has been noted elsewhere, metaphors of the policy-making process are not always applicable – it is rarely linear and not particularly cyclical (Manthorpe and Stevens 2014). Implementation is a complex matter and may be affected by ambivalence or other competing priorities.

The Evidence and Ethnicity in Commissioning (EEiC) project described typical elements of commissioning work and the actions that might be taken to improve health care commissioning for multi-ethnic populations. Two earlier Better Health Briefing Papers (Salway *et al.* 2013a, 2013b) had presented the case for why health care commissioning needed to make race equality a central concern. In the NHS, both provider organisations and Public Health England have a legal duty to address inequalities, and for the latter, each of its priorities is subject to a health inequalities assessment. The new emphasis on public health and prevention in England means that it, too, must be visible in meeting the high-level policy imperatives on dementia (DH 2012). For example, Public Health England's declared priorities for 2013–2014 include its aims to:

> Reduce the incidence and impact of dementia, through implementing the Prime Minister's challenge on dementia. We will work with partners across the NHS, local government and voluntary and community sectors to develop a co-ordinated national approach to preventing dementia, maximising the contribution of NHS Healthchecks, and we will focus on reducing the burden and stigma of dementia on families by supporting Dementia Friendly Communities. (Public Health England 2012)

Health care commissioning has the potential to reduce inequalities in access and to improve experiences and outcomes between ethnic groups. This is a global aspiration, as other countries' policy-making experiences reveal, such as commitments in Canada to 'continue to work with French and Aboriginal populations to enable equitable access to services in their communities' (Fried 2012, p.10). However, organisational cultures and structures may not pay attention to ethnic diversity and inequality amidst a plethora of policy imperatives, while individual commissioners often do not recognise their responsibility, or lack the skills and confidence to engage in this work.

The Equality Act 2010 simplified the law relating to equalities by combining a large range of legislation into one Act (Government Equalities Office 2013). (The Act applies to Great Britain (England, Scotland and Wales), but additional legislation is planned in Northern Ireland to harmonise equality law across the UK.) The Act extended legal provisions in regard to diversity and equality, protecting individuals from unfair treatment, and promoting a more equal society. It applies to what are termed 'protected characteristics', the grounds on which discrimination is unlawful. These are:

- age
- disability
- gender reassignment
- marriage and civil partnership
- pregnancy and maternity
- race, religion or belief
- sex, and
- sexual orientation.

As can be seen, many of these are potentially applicable to people with dementia, and more so to BME people with dementia. In broad terms, all public sector (e.g. as local councils and NHS trusts) and voluntary organisations have to comply with the law. However, they may make exceptions if they can 'objectively justify' the reasons for their actions (for details of the implications of this for different forms of social care, see Moriarty and Manthorpe 2012).

This Act placed a 'public sector equality duty' on public bodies to have due regard to the need to eliminate discrimination, advance equality of opportunity, and foster good relations between different people when carrying out their activities. Thus, one impact of the Act and earlier equalities legislation is that public bodies increasingly ask for information on the characteristics of service users and carers (Manthorpe and Moriarty 2013). This should help in being more specific about usage of dementia services or other community services that might be more accessible to BME people with dementia. Similarly, policy-makers may be better able to analyse information to see whether there are differential unmet needs or uptake among different sections of the community according to their protected characteristics. In a context of unequal access to dementia services and community facilities, the Act may present opportunities to be mindful of all strands of equalities and the need to avoid compounding social exclusion. This chapter ends with some final observations from this necessarily brief consideration of policy and strategy in which the role of practitioners as instigators, implementers and recipients of these plans and directives has been highlighted.

Final thoughts

One important development in policy-making over the past decade or so has been the engagement of people with dementia in policy-making spheres, as perceptively summarised by Williamson (2012), who observed that ethnicity and diversity feature as important threads in charting the emergence of this potentially powerful group in policy-making processes. Their engagement and that of their carers is likely to increase in influence, but it may also serve to highlight conflict and disagreements. One interesting feature of dementia policy shaping and making has been a sense of consensus. Many of the same media outlets and opinion leaders that have highlighted immigration as a political problem demand that more is done for dementia 'sufferers' and carers. Many of the same groups that call for austerity in public spending call for increases in services for people with dementia. These contradictions may move centre stage as policy-making in dementia evolves – from recognition and claims making – to address wider social problems and values.

Acknowledgements and disclaimer

This work was undertaken as part of the Department of Health's Policy Research Programme of support for the work of the Social Care Workforce Research Unit. Thanks to Jo Moriarty and Steve Iliffe for their assistance with this chapter. The views expressed are those of the author alone, and should not be interpreted as representing the views of the Department of Health, the National Institute for Health Research or the NHS.

References

APPG (All-Party Parliamentary Group) on Dementia (2013) *Dementia Does Not Discriminate: The Experiences of Black, Asian and Minority Ethnic Communities.* July. London: Alzheimer's Society. Available at www.alzheimers.org.uk/site/scripts/download_info.php?downloadID=1186, accessed on 11 December 2014.

Audit Commission (2004) *The Journey to Race Equality: Delivering Improved Services to Local Communities.* London: Audit Commission Publications.

Bowes, A., Avan, G. and Macintosh, S. (2011) *Dignity and Respect in Residential Care: Issues for Black and Minority Ethnic Groups.* London: Department of Health. Available at www.panicoa.org.uk/sites/assets/dignity_and_respect_in_residential_care.pdf, accessed on 1 February 2015.

Clarke, C.L., Keyes, S.E., Wilkinson, H., Alexjuk, J. *et al.* (2013) *The National Evaluation of Peer Support Networks and Dementia Advisers in Implementation of the National Dementia Strategy for England.* London: DH.

DH (Department of Health) (2001) *National Service Framework for Older People.* London: DH.

DH (2009) *Living Well with Dementia: A National Dementia Strategy.* London: DH.

DH (2012) *Prime Minister's Challenge on Dementia: Delivering Major Improvements in Dementia Care and Research by 2015.* London: DH. Available at www.gov.uk/government/uploads/system/uploads/attachment_data/file/215101/dh_133176.pdf, accessed on 1 February 2015.

DH (2014) *Policy Improvement Plan 2014/15.* London: DH.

EEiC (Evidence and Ethnicity in Commissioning) (2012) *Where There Is No Data: BME Dementia Project in Nottingham.* Sheffield: Sheffield Hallam University. Available at http://research.shu.ac.uk/eeic//mcs/dementia/, accessed on 1 February 2015.

Fried, L. (2012) *The Impact of Dementia on the Strategic Priorities with Ideas and Solutions on How to Constructively Address Those Impacts: Response to the Central LHIN Integrated Health Service Plan 2013–2016 Strategic Framework.* Ontario, Canada: Alzheimer Society York Region. Available at www.alzheimer.ca/kw/~/media/Files/chapters-on/york/CLHIN%20Presentations/Evidence_Brief_feedback_to_IHSP_2013-2016_sm.ashx, accessed on 1 February 2015.

Government Equalities Office (2013) *Information and Guidance on the Equality Act 2010, Including Age Discrimination and Public Sector Equality Duty.* London: HM Government. Available at www.gov.uk/equality-act-2010-guidance, accessed on 1 February 2015.

Healthcare Commission (2006) *Variations in the Experiences of Patients Using the NHS Services in England.* London: Commission for Healthcare Audit and Inspection.

Hussein, S. and Manthorpe, J. (2012) 'The dementia social care workforce in England: secondary analysis of a national workforce dataset.' *Aging and Mental Health 16*, 1, 110–118.

Koehn, S., Neysmith, S., Kobayashi, K. and Khamisa, H. (2013) 'Revealing the shape of knowledge using an intersectionality lens: results of a scoping review on the health and health care of ethnocultural minority older adults.' *Ageing and Society 33*, 3, 437–464.

Manthorpe, J. and Moriarty, J. (2013) 'Examining day centre provision for older people in the UK using the Equality Act 2010: findings of a scoping review.' *Health & Social Care in the Community.* Available at http://dx.doi.org/10.1111/hsc.12065, accessed on 1 February 2015.

Manthorpe, J. and Stevens, M. (2014) 'Adult safeguarding policy and law: a thematic chronology relevant to care homes and hospitals.' *Social Policy and Society 14*, 2, 203–16.

Manthorpe, J., Harris, J. and Lakey, S. (2008) *Strategic Approaches for Older People from Black and Minority Ethnic Groups: A Report for Better Government for Older People.* London: Social Care Workforce Research Unit, King's College London.

Manthorpe, J., Iliffe, S., Moriarty, J., Cornes, M. *et al* (2009) '"We are not blaming anyone, but if we don't know about amenities, we cannot seek them out": black and minority older people's views on the quality of local health and personal social services in England.' *Ageing and Society 29*, 1, 93–113.

Moriarty, J. (2008) *The Health and Social Care Experiences of Black and Minority Ethnic Older People.* Better Health Briefing 9. London: REU, Communities and Local Government.

Moriarty, J. and Manthorpe J. (2012) *Diversity in Older People and Access to Services: An Evidence Review.* London: Age UK. Available at www.ageuk.org.uk/Documents/EN-GB/For-professionals/Research/Equalities_Evidence_Review_Moriarty_2012.pdf?dtrk=true, accessed on 1 February 2015.

Moriarty, J., Sharif, N. and Robinson, J. (2011) *Black and Minority Ethnic People with Dementia and their Access to Support and Services.* SCIE Research Briefing 35. London: Social Care Institute for Excellence.

NAO (National Audit Office) (2004) *Delivering Public Services to a Diverse Society.* London: The Stationery Office.

NHS England (2013) *Mental Health, Dementia, Neurological Conditions Summit: Report with Recommendations.* Manchester, Lancashire and South Cumbria: NHS England, Strategic Clinical Networks and Senate.

Nazroo, J.Y. and Williams, D.R. (2005) 'The social determination of ethnic/racial inequalities in health.' In M. Marmot and R. Wilkinson (eds) *Social Determinants of Health.* Oxford: Oxford University Press.

Nichols, P., Horner, B., Fyfe, K. and Freegard, H. (2013) *Toward Building a Multicultural Workforce in Residential Dementia Care.* Perth, Western Australia. Available at www.fightdementia.org.au/common/files/NAT/1600-Nichols.pdf, accessed on 1 February 2015.

Public Health England (2012) *Strategic Priorities for 2013–14.* London: Public Health England.

Runnymede Trust (2013) *Dementia doesn't care about the person. We should.* Available at www.youtube.com/watch?v=FKjtO4WiPvM&list=UU9TriyK6-HhGJCD7MqXtRVw&index=6, accessed on 1 February 2015.

Salway, S., Turner, D., Mir, G., Carter, L. *et al* (2013a) *High Quality Healthcare Commissioning: Why Race Equality Must Be at its Heart.* Better Health Briefing Paper 27. London: Race Equality Foundation. Available at www.better-health.org.uk/briefings/high-quality-healthcare-commissioning-why-race-equality-must-be-its-heart-0, accessed on 1 February 2015.

Salway, S., Turner, D., Mir, G., Carter, L. *et al* (2013b) *High Quality Healthcare Commissioning: Obstacles and Opportunities for Progress on Race Equality.* Better Health Briefing Paper 28. London: Race Equality Foundation. Available at www.better-health.org.uk/briefings/high-quality-healthcare-commissioning-obstacles-and-opportunities-progress-race-equality, accessed on 1 February 2015.

Skills for Care (2014) *Open Access National Minimum Dataset for Social Care Dashboards.* Leeds: Skills for Care. Available at www.nmds-sc-online.org.uk/reportengine/dashboard.aspx, accessed on 1 February 2015.

Smith, P., Alla, H., Henry, L., Larsen, J. and Mackintosh, M. (2007) *Valuing and Recognising the Talents of a Diverse Healthcare Workforce.* London: Royal College of Nursing.

Stevens, M., Hussein, S. and Manthorpe, J. (2012) 'Experiences of racism and discrimination among migrant care workers in England: findings from a mixed-methods research project.' *Ethnic and Racial Studies 35*, 2, 259–280.

Team Bury (2010) *Joint Commissioning Strategy for People with Dementia and their Carers in Bury 2010–2015.* Bury. Available at www.bury.gov.uk/CHttpHandler.ashx?id=8541&p=0, accessed on 1 February 2015.

Truswell, D. (2013) *Black and Minority Ethnic Communities and Dementia: Where Are We Now?* Better Health Briefing. London: Race Equality Foundation.

Williamson, T. (2012) *A Stronger Collective Voice for People with Dementia*. York: Joseph Rowntree Foundation. Available at www.jrf.org.uk/sites/files/jrf/dementia-groups-influence-policy-full.pdf, accessed on 1 February 2015.

ABOUT THE EDITORS AND AUTHORS

Editors

Julia Botsford is Research and Evaluation Admiral Nurse at Dementia UK. After a degree in History and Philosophy, Julia trained as a general and mental health nurse. Early on in her career she made a decision to work within dementia care. Since then she has held a number of different posts, both in clinical practice and education. Until April 2015 she was Senior Admiral Nurse at Barnet, Enfield and Haringey NHS Trust. She completed a PhD at Northumbia University in 2011 and is currently visiting Clinical Associate Professor (Mental Health with a focus on dementia) at Middlesex University.

Karen Harrison Dening is Director of Admiral Nursing at Dementia UK. Her key interests are palliative and end-of-life care in dementia, advance care planning and specialist and advanced nurse practice. She has recently completed her doctorate at University College London in the Marie Curie Palliative Care Research Department researching advance care planning in dementia. Karen is a member of both the National Council for Palliative Care Dementia Working Group and the Royal Society of Medicine Palliative Care Council and is an honorary Senior Lecturer at the University of Nottingham.

Authors

Vincent Goodorally was born in Mauritius, and started his nursing career in the UK at an early age. He has a particular interest in issues of culture, ethnicity and access to dementia care services. He has won local and national awards for his work as an Admiral Nurse. In 2013 he completed a project funded by Dementia UK and the Foundation of Nursing Studies to 'improve the assessment experience of people affected by dementia through the adaption and pilot of a culturally sensitive tool, the Culturagram'.

Karan Jutlla graduated from the University of Salford with a first-class honours degree in Health Sciences in 2006. Her interest in ethnicity and dementia led to her doctoral study at Keele University where she researched how personal histories and migration experiences influence experiences of caring for a person with dementia for Sikhs living in Wolverhampton. As a result of her research, Karan brings a depth of knowledge about the experiences and challenges for those living with dementia in minority ethnic communities.

Omar Khan is Director of the Runnymede Trust. Omar sits on the Department for Work and Pensions' Ethnic Minority Advisory Group. He chairs Olmec, the Ethnic Strand Advisory Committee to the Household Longitudinal Survey and the Advisory Group to the Centre of the Dynamics of Ethnicity at the University of Manchester. He is also a 2012 Clore Social Leadership Fellow. Omar has also published many articles and reports on race and equality and has spoken widely on these and related topics throughout the UK and Europe. He completed his DPhil in Political Theory from the University of Oxford.

Jill Manthorpe is Professor of Social Work and Director of the Social Care Workforce Research Unit at King's College London where she conducts policy research for the Department of Health and other funders. She has published widely on ethnicity in later life, including studies of older people's strategies, the mental wellbeing of black and minority ethnic older people in rural areas, and the Workings of the Equality Act 2010. She is Emeritus Senior Investigator of the National Institute for Health Research.

Professor Alisoun Milne works at the University of Kent. Her key interests are mental health in later life, older carers, care homes and social work with older people. She has received funding from a range of sources including government departments and research councils. She is widely published in peer-reviewed journals and books. Alisoun is a member of the Standing Commission on Carers, British Society of Gerontology Executive Committee and an academic Special Interest Group on Gerontological Social Work.

Jo Moriarty is a Research Fellow in the Social Care Workforce Research Unit at King's College London. She is an experienced social care researcher who has published widely, and whose research interests span dementia, ethnicity, family carers, the voluntary sector and the social care workforce. She is currently working on a study of recruitment and retention in the social care workforce. She edits the Innovative Practice section of the journal *Dementia.*

Professor Ajit Shah was a consultant in old age psychiatry in West London for many years until his recent retirement from the NHS. He has worked on the epidemiology of mental disorders, suicide, service development and delivery and symptoms in relation to older BME individuals with mental illness. He was the senior author of the Royal College of Psychiatrists' council report on minority ethnic older people and old age psychiatry (2001).

Dr Jan Smith is a Research and Development Fellow at Canterbury Christchurch University, Kent. She has a Phd from the University of Kent focused on the needs, characteristics and experiences of people with learning disabilities and older people from minority ethnic populations living in care homes.

Shemain Wahab is a graduate in Biodiversity Conservation and Environmental Management. She has worked across the public, private and not-for-profit sectors, joining Dementia UK in 2011. Here she coordinated a range of national projects for Uniting Carers, an involvement network for family carers of people with dementia. Additionally, Shemain volunteers with several charities, and is committed to supporting the beyond profit sector in creating positive social impact and outcomes.

Joy Watkins has worked in the voluntary sector for many years, most recently in HIV and AIDS, Crossroads Caring for Carers and Dementia UK. She has experience in project management, training and skills development, with particular interest in carer, service user and volunteer involvement. As the Development Lead at Dementia UK, she led and developed the national network of family carers, Uniting Carers.

Sofia Zarate Escudero undertook her undergraduate medical training at St Bartholomew's and the Royal London School of Medicine and Dentistry, University of London. She obtained an MRCPsych in 2012 and is currently a dual trainee on the St Marys Scheme. Sofia has an interest in research, and has published work focusing on suicides in the elderly population. She was awarded the Daniel Cappon prize in 2012, and is currently a Research Fellow at Imperial College London.

SUBJECT INDEX

AUTHOR INDEX